Greville Philipps Tregarthen

The Story of Australasia

New South Wales, Tasmania, Western Australia, South Australia, Victoria,

Queensland, New Zealand

Greville Philipps Tregarthen

The Story of Australasia
New South Wales, Tasmania, Western Australia, South Australia, Victoria, Queensland, New Zealand

ISBN/EAN: 9783337267247

Printed in Europe, USA, Canada, Australia, Japan

Cover: Foto ©ninafisch / pixelio.de

More available books at **www.hansebooks.com**

AUSTRALASIA

CAPTAIN COOK.

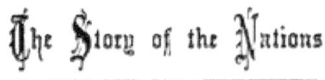

The Story of the Nations

THE STORY OF

AUSTRALASIA

NEW SOUTH WALES, TASMANIA, WESTERN AUSTRALIA, SOUTH AUSTRALIA, VICTORIA QUEENSLAND, NEW ZEALAND

BY

GREVILLE TREGARTHEN

AUTHOR OF "NEW SOUTH WALES : 1860 TO 1866," "A SKETCH OF THE PROGRESS AND RESOURCES OF NEW SOUTH WALES," ETC.

NEW YORK
G. P. PUTNAM'S SONS
LONDON : T. FISHER UNWIN
1893

PREFACE.

THE writer of Australian history is confronted with peculiar difficulties. The clamour of the strife which accompanied the birth of free institutions has scarcely died away and the greater part of the literature dealing with past events is so tainted by the heated feelings of partizans that it is necessary to use it with the greatest caution. Then, again, sufficient time has not elapsed to allow the incidents of former years to disclose their full significance, and matters which are really still producing grave changes in social and political life are apt to appear of little consequence, while others of a less far-reaching character assume an unmerited importance. In the following pages the desire has been to adhere as closely as possible to the story of the seven colonies without entering into questions which are still the subject of contention ; but there are many things in connection with the marvellous progress of these young communities which it has been impossible to mention here. The gradual formation of a new society—a new nation—in a New World cannot fail to be a spectacle of absorbing interest, but to trace each step in the process of its evolution would require far more space than is available. So many books, public documents, and records have been consulted that it is impossible to acknowledge each separately, but the writer is indebted in some degree to most of the accepted authorities on Australasian affairs. This little volume has been written amidst many disadvantages, and under very great pressure of official work; but it is hoped that it may induce some to make a better acquaintance with this Great South Land, which Governor Phillip in 1788 so fitly described as "the most valuable acquisition Great Britain ever made."

SYDNEY.

CONTENTS.

NEW SOUTH WALES.

III.

IV.

CONTENTS.

VICTORIA.

XVI.

XVII.

XVIII.

XIX.

XX.

WESTERN AUSTRALIA.

XXI.

NEW ZEALAND.

LIST OF ILLUSTRATIONS.

AUSTRALIAN COMMONWEALTH.

I.

EARLY DISCOVERERS.

(1503–1772.)

IT is not easy for any one knowing the great
natural wealth of Australia to realise the bitter disappointment which must have been felt by those
venturesome navigators who first sighted the shores
of that continent. The minds of all men were full of
the marvellous discoveries of Marco Polo in the East,
and of Columbus and Cabot across the Atlantic, and
the motive was no longer the discovery of a route
to the Indies by which the treasures of the East might
be carried by sea to Europe, but each explorer was ambitious to rival a Cortes or Pizarro, and hoped in the
Pacific to find countries as rich and as populous as
those annexed by Spain in America. But instead of
wealth and barbaric splendour, an old civilisation and
magnificent cities, such as those of Mexico and Peru,
they discovered the most dreary and uninviting

coasts, with few harbours or rivers and peopled by
a wild and degraded race, showing a bitter hostility
to the visitors.

It is difficult to determine who was really the first
European to discover Australia.   There are several
candidates for the honour, but the validity of the
claims is, in many cases, more than doubtful.   It is
quite possible that long before the more or less systematic exploration of the Australian seaboard the
Malays, or perhaps Europeans bound to or from
Eastern ports, may have sighted parts of the coast ;
but such glimpses did not invite a closer inspection.
The object sought was a rich trading station and not
a land fit for European colonisation, and consequently
Australia, being out of the ordinary track of the merchant ships and offering no harvest of spices, for the
acquisition of which all the world was mad, attracted
but little attention ; indeed, but for the fair prospect
of finding spice-producing lands in these latitudes, the
mysterious slumber which for so many centuries
enveloped Australasia would have continued still
longer.

In 1503 a Frenchman, named De Gonneville, after
rounding the Cape of Good Hope, is said to have
been driven by contrary winds to an unknown shore,
but the evidence goes to support the contention that
Madagascar, and not Australia, was the land visited.
Various claims to the discovery of Australia by the
Portuguese previous to 1606 receive some support, but
there is every reason to suppose that the *Duyfhen*
from Bantam was the first vessel which bore
Europeans over Australian waters.   The voyage of

the Dutch was cut short by want of provisions, and after coasting some little way along the eastern shore of the Gulf of Carpentaria they were compelled to return. The land they described as "for the greatest part desert, but in some places inhabited by wild, cruel, black savages, by whom some of the crew were murdered." For ten years no new explorations were made, but in 1616 Dirk Hartog, another Dutchman, sailed down the west coast, being followed in two years by the *Mauritius* and a little later by the *Leeuwin.* The accounts given by the commanders of these vessels were most unfavourable, but the Dutch East India Company was not yet satisfied, and in 1623 the *Pera* and *Arnhem* were despatched. This expedition was as fruitless as those that preceded it. Not long after making the Australian coast Jan Carstens, captain of the *Arnhem,* and eight of his crew were murdered by the natives, and the *Pera*, although she sailed far round the north coast, carried back a report that " shallow waters and barren coasts were everywhere found, with islands altogether thinly peopled by divers cruel, poor and brutal nations, and of very little use " to the Company. So far exploration had been confined entirely to the west and north coasts, but in 1627 Pieter Nuyts, in the *Gulde Zeepard*, examined the south shore for some hundreds of miles. He was scarcely more favourably impressed than the others. That it was "a foul and barren shore " was all he could say for the country.

The next event of any importance in the story of Australian exploration is full of dramatic interest. The *Batavia*, commanded by Francis Pelsart, meeting with heavy weather, was separated from her companions, and in a storm was driven on the reef called " Houtman's Abrolhos" on the west coast. The ship before long commenced to break up, so it was determined to abandon her and seek refuge on three adjacent islands. The landing was effected safely, but to the consternation of all no fresh water was to be found, and Pelsart at last set out in one of the boats to seek it on the mainland. Here he was also unsuccessful, and therefore determined to steer for Batavia for assistance. Soon after his departure some of the shipwrecked crew mutinied, and, under the leadership of the supercargo, committed the most ghastly atrocities. Another party, however, were able to repulse the attack of the mutineers, and after several conflicts, in one of which the supercargo was captured, the two companies waited for the return of Pelsart. The intention of the murderers appears to have been to seize his ship on its arrival and start on a piratical cruise, and when before long, the *Sardam*, with Pelsart on board, was sighted, the mutineers put off to board her. They had dressed themselves in striking costumes made from the despoiled cargo of the *Batavia*, and their peculiar appearance aroused Pelsart's suspicions and put him on his guard. By threatening to fire on their small boat he compelled them to lay down their arms, and then, having learnt the state of affairs, all but two were summarily hanged. These two underwent, if anything, a worse fate, for they were put on shore on the mainland, and the agony they must have suffered as they watched the ship slowly vanishing from sight, leaving them to their fate amongst those " wild, cruel, black savages" was a just retribution for their crimes.

Another tragedy, similar to that in which Carstens lost his life, was enacted in 1636, when Poole visited New Guinea, and, although the supercargo took charge of the ship and continued the voyage, no new discoveries were made.

From this time the records of Australian exploration are more satisfactory. In 1637 Antony van Dieman, a man imbued with strong ambitions in the field of enterprise and discovery, received from the Dutch the Governorship of Java. He lost but little time in despatching an expedition in search of the Southern Continent, and in 1642 Abel Janz Tasman, with Gerrit Jansen, set sail in the ships *Heemskirk* and *Zeehaan*. Tasman first steered for Mauritius, which was then a Dutch possession, and after a brief stay pursued his travels, sailing in an easterly direction in search of the "Great South Land." On the 24th of November Point Hibbs, a limestone promontory on the West Coast of Tasmania, appeared above the horizon, and before sunset lofty mountains gradually shaped themselves in the distance, and confirmed Tasman's opinion that he had at last touched a portion of the territory of which he was in search. Having doubled the southern extremity of the island, a course was steered close along the shore, and a week after first sighting land the *Heemskirk* and *Zeehaan* dropped anchor in Marion Bay. Boats were lowered and parties sent ashore, but although signs of the presence of natives were found, no human beings were seen. Two days later the carpenter of the *Heemskirk* swam ashore and erected a post on which a compass was carved and the prince's flag hoisted, and the wanderers weighed anchor, and sailing along the east coast again lost sight of land in the unknown seas. On the 8th of the same month the look-out reported land which proved to be the south island of New Zealand. The ships anchored in a little bay, but the natives surrounded them in their canoes and three of Tasman's crew were murdered. On his return to Batavia the voyage was considered to have been so successful that in 1644 the same commander was again despatched with the *Limmen, Zeemew,* and *De Brak,* and on this occasion he explored the west coasts of the Gulf of Carpentaria.

The next explorer of any importance was William Dampier, who, in command of the *Bachelor's Delight* and *Cygnet,* with a crew of buccaneers, examined the west coast from Shark Bay to Dampier's Archipelago. His report of the country on his return to England was not favourable, but, as he was in imminent peril of being marooned on the unknown land by his unruly crew, an unbiassed account could hardly be expected.

In 1696 William de Vlaming while cruising on the west coast discovered and named the Swan River, and three years later Dampier again visited Australia in the *Roebuck,* and made further explorations on the North-west. On his return he wrote an interesting account of his travels, but he had little to say in favour of either the country or its people; the one was sterile and almost devoid of animals, while the other were hideous and filthy. For the next seventy

years little was done in the way of Australian
exploration, although the Dutch sent out one more
expedition in 1705, under Martin van Delft. However,
in 1768 Captain James Cook started on the famous
voyage, with which really began the interest of
Englishmen in the lands of the South Pacific.
Cook's expedition originated with the Royal Society,
which was anxious that some capable person should
observe the transit of Venus over the sun's disc from
the South Seas. A suggestion to this effect was
favourably received by George III., and a small vessel
under the command of Cook, who had already distinguished himself in Canada and in survey work off
the coast of Newfoundland, was fitted out by the
Government. The *Endeavour*, the ship specially
selected by Cook for this service, had been built for
a collier. She was a little barque of 370 tons, of
small draught, but great carrying capacity, and very
strong construction. A scientific staff was appointed
to carry out the observations, Mr. Green acting as
astronomer and Sir Joseph Banks and Dr. Solander
occupying the position of botanists; and on the 26th
of August, 1768, the necessary instruments and provisions having been taken on board, the *Endeavour*
weighed anchor and sailed out of Plymouth Sound.
After a quick passage the wanderers arrived at
Tahiti, where they at once erected a temporary
observatory, guarded by a little fort, and on the 3rd
of June the transit of the planet was most successfully observed. But although the main object of
the expedition had now been accomplished, it was
determined to search for the great Southern Con-

tinent before returning to England. Cook therefore
steered south on leaving Tahiti, and after passing the
Society Islands held his course till land was sighted
from the masthead and a chain of mountains rose on
the misty horizon. On the 8th of October, 1769, the
Endeavour's anchor was dropped in the Bay of
Tauranga, New Zealand, and attempts were at once
made to open communication with the natives, but
without success. Disgusted with the hostility and
distrust of the Maories, Cook sailed along the coast
to the southward, charting carefully as he went, until,
on reaching Mercury Bay, the scientific men again
landed to take observations of the transit of Mercury,
while Cook seized the opportunity of leaving a record
of his visit on a tree. Hoisting the English flag, he
took possession of the country in the name of King
George.   From Mercury Bay he sailed along the
coast passing Tolaga Bay, Hauraki Gulf and the Bay
of Islands, and then, doubling Cape Maria Van
Diemen, shaped his course close to the western shore
of the North Island. At Queen Charlotte's Sound
another stop was made, and more flagstaffs were
erected, then again sail was set and Cook passed
through the straits and, turning South Cape, completed the circumnavigation of the islands.   On
reaching Cape Farewell he steered for the open sea,
and, following a westerly course, after three weeks
came in sight of the Australian coast at Cape Howe.
Turning north-east the coastline was traced, names
being given to Mount Dromedary, the Pigeon House,
Point Upright, and Cape St. George, till Botany Bay
was reached, and here anchor was cast.   As the ship

brought to near the shore a group of natives was perceived apparently cooking by a fire ; but, to the surprise of Cook and his comrades, they paid no attention whatever to the ship, continuing quietly at their occupation. Even the clank and rattle of the cable as it ran out of the hawse-pipe had no effect, and it was not till boats were lowered and turned towards the beach that the natives showed any signs of being aware of the presence of intruders. As soon as the boat headed for the land, however, two men sprang to their feet and, coming down to the rocks, stood brandishing their rude weapons and, with wild gesticulations, warned Cook's party to keep off. A musket was fired between them, which induced one of the natives for a moment to drop his spears, which however he immediately recovered ; and, even when a charge of small shot was fired into the legs of another in return for a stone which he had thrown at the boat, the two warriors ran back into the bush for a moment and then reappeared with bark shields. For some time the *Endeavour* remained in the bay, and her captain, with Banks and Solander, made many excursions into the country, during which the two last obtained such a great variety of flowers and plants that the place was called Botany Bay. Although anxious to have friendly intercourse with the natives, all attempts failed, and, after hoisting the British flag and formally taking possession in the king's name of the country, which he called New South Wales, Cook sailed out between the heads to continue the exploration of the coast. The entrances to Port Jackson and Broken Bay were marked on the chart, but the *Endeavour*

did not again drop anchor until Moreton Bay had
been reached. Only a brief stay was made there
before the voyage northward was resumed, the ship
being kept as close to the shore as was deemed
safe, and the principal features of the coast carefully noted. After about thirteen hundred miles had
been traversed in this way, the first serious mishap
was met with ; about eleven o'clock one night the
water suddenly began to shoal and before soundings
could be taken the ship struck heavily on a sunken
rock, and the water almost immediately rose in the hold
so rapidly that the pumps could hardly keep it under.
The guns and all heavy gear were jettisoned, but still
the *Endeavour* bumped and scraped on the reef. At
last she was floated off, but in such a leaky condition,
that there was every prospect of her foundering. No
land was in sight and the outlook was most gloomy
when, as a last resource, some canvas was passed
under the vessel over the injured spot and the inflow
of water thus greatly reduced. After sailing some
distance in this crippled state land was sighted and
the mouth of a little river entered, where the ship
was careened and examined. The rent in her bottom
was more extensive than had been supposed, and, but
for the fact that the spike of coral which had pierced
her had been broken off and remained plugging the
hole, no possible device could have prevented her
from sinking. In commemoration of the adventure
Cook named the headland he had first sighted Cape
Tribulation, and the river after his little barque.
When two months had been spent in thoroughly
repairing the *Endeavour*, the voyage was continued

and the coast charted as·far as Cape York, whence Cook sailed through Torres Straits to England.

The second and third voyages made by the great explorer were full of interest, but there is not space to follow them in detail here. It will suffice to say that the reports carried to England were so favourable that during the next few years Cook, with the *Resolution*, *Discovery*, and *Adventure*, visited Tasmania and New Zealand; but the determination to occupy Australian territory sprang from the impressions left in the mind of Banks by his short sojourn in Botany Bay. Between the arrival of Phillip's fleet to found a settlement and Cook's departure others sailed in Australian waters, and one of the expeditions was marred by a fatal affray with the natives. In 1772 the French navigator, Marion du Fresne, anchored his ships, the *Mascarin* and the *Castries*, in Marion Bay, Tasmania, and an attempt to communicate with the aborigines led to a fight. Soon afterwards, having sailed to New Zealand, the luckless Frenchman was murdered with twenty-seven of his crew in a quarrel with the Maories at the Bay of Islands. Another Frenchman, De Surville had been cruising in New Zealand waters at the same time as Cook in 1769, though little was added to the knowledge of the Great South Land by either of the French expeditions.

II.

"THE FIRST FLEET," 1788

ALTHOUGH the report carried back by Cook and Banks was in many respects most favourable, a considerable period elapsed before any definite proposals were made to utilise their discoveries. Important and difficult matters nearer home absorbed the attention of the Government and, until a combination of circumstances made it absolutely imperative that some new field for the transportation of criminals should be found, the eyes of statesmen were not seriously turned towards the distant southern land.

The action of Lord North's Government in insisting on the tea duties had produced an insurrection in the American Colonies in 1775, which in the following year developed into the memorable War of Independence and finally severed the bond between the States and the Mother Country. The American plantations were for ever closed as a destination for British criminals, and, as a result, the gaols quickly filled to overflowing, and abuses grew with corresponding rapidity. So serious was the aspect of affairs that an effective method of disposing of convicts became a matter of the first public importance, and numerous proposals, more or less feasible, were continually being put forward.

The deplorable condition of those of the American colonists, who had not taken up arms against England, was also attracting the attention of many, till at last the desire to induce the Government to provide some haven for the people who had lost all in the support of the king's cause across the Atlantic, led James Maria Matra to formulate "a proposal for establishing a settlement in New South Wales."

The proposal was addressed to the Government in August, 1783, the year in which England so reluctantly recognised as Sovereign States what had once been her colonies. Mr. Matra, after mentioning the loss of America, dwelt on the "enticing allurements to European adventurers" held out by some of the newly discovered countries, and more especially New South Wales. He quoted Cook's favourable impressions, and drew a sketch of the capabilities of the new country from a strategical, commercial, and agricultural point of view. Special stress was laid on the character of the soil and climate as especially suitable for the cultivation of spices—that peculiarly tempting bait for the mercantile enterprise of the time—and the New Zealand flax, on specimens of which, brought home by Banks, such encomiums had been passed; "this country," continued Mr. Matra, "may afford an asylum to those unfortunate American loyalists, whom Great Britain is bound by every tie of honour and gratitude to protect and support where

they may repair their broken fortunes and again
enjoy their former domestic felicity."

After further description of the benefits likely to
accrue to the Mother Country from the occupation
of New South Wales, he closed his paper with some
remarks on the policy of emigration. Mr. Matra's
scheme attracted some notice ; but apparently the
Government had not as strong a sense of their obligation to the American loyalists as he had supposed,
and the Ministry went out of office in December
without taking any definite action in the matter.
Lord Sydney, who succeeded at the. Home Office,
saw, however, in Mr. Matra's proposal a solution of
the then most pressing difficulty. Why should not
this distant land be a "very proper region for the
reception of criminals condemned to transportation"?
Mr. Matra jumped at this idea, in which he considered "good policy and humanity are united." The
attempts to form a penal settlement in Africa had
failed. The mortality amongst the convicts was
enormous, and the expense very heavy. Popular
sentiment on the. question of penal treatment was
also undergoing change, and the theory that the
reformation of criminals should be regarded as much
as their punishment was gaining ground. In a
country in which convicts would be some twelve
thousand miles away from their old associations, an
experiment in reformation surely might be tried
without danger and with some chance of success.
Lord Howe, then First Lord of the Admiralty,
threw cold water on Matra's plan ; but Sir John
Young, another naval authority, took the matter up,

and slightly modifying some of Matra's proposals and elaborating others, submitted to the authorities "a rough outline of the many advantages that may result to this nation from a settlement made on the coast of New South Wales." The American loyalists were not forgotten by him ; but perhaps the greatest inducement held out for the establishment of the colony was that "here was an asylum in which felons could be cheaply kept, and from which there would be no possibility of their returning."

A feeling of jealous apprehension existed at this time that the French contemplated forming settlements in the far Pacific, and this doubtless led Lord Sydney to accept more readily the scheme for colonising the distant territory. In August, 1786, the following paper was forwarded to the Lords of the Admiralty, with a request that the necessary arrangements for transport and victualling be made with the utmost despatch :

"Heads of a plan for effectually disposing of convicts, and rendering their transportation reciprocally beneficial, both to themselves and to the State, by the establishment of a colony in New South Wales, a country which, by the fertility and salubrity of the climate, connected with the remoteness of its situation (from whence it is hardly possible for persons to return without permission), seems peculiarly adapted to answer the views of Government with respect to the providing a remedy for the evils likely to result from the late alarming and numerous increase of felons in this country, and more particularly in the metropolis.

"It is proposed that a ship of war of a proper class, with a part of her guns mounted, and a sufficient number of men on board for her navigation, and a tender of about 200 tons burthen, commanded by discreet officers, should be got ready as soon as possible to serve as an escort to the convict ships, and for other purposes hereinafter mentioned.

"That in addition to their crews, they should take on board two companies of marines to form a military establishment on shore (not only for the protection of the settlement, if requisite, against the natives, but for the preservation of good order), together with an assortment of stores, utensils, and implements, necessary for erecting habitations and for agriculture, and such quantities of provisions as may be proper for the use of the crews. As many marines as possible should be artificers, such as carpenters, sawyers, smiths, potters (if possible), and some husbandmen. To have a chaplain on board, with a surgeon, and one mate at least; the former to remain at the settlement.

"That these vessels should touch at the Cape of Good Hope, or any other place that may be convenient, for any seed that may be requisite to be taken thence, and for such live stock as they can possibly contain, which, it is supposed, can be procured there without any difficulty, and at the most reasonable rates, for the use of the settlement at large.

"That Government should immediately provide a certain number of ships of a proper burthen to receive on board at least seven or eight hundred convicts, and that one of them should be properly fitted for the accommodation of the women.

" That these ships should take on board as much
provisions as they can possibly stow, or at least a
sufficient quantity for two years' consumption ; sup-
posing one year to be issued at whole allowance, and
the other year's provisions at half allowance, which
will last two years longer, by which time, it is pre-
sumed the colony, with the live stock and grain
which may be raised by a common industry on the
part of the new settlers, will be fully sufficient for
their maintenance and support.

" That, in addition to the crews of the ships
appointed to contain the convicts, a company of
marines should be divided between them, to be employed as guards for preventing ill consequences that
might arise from dissatisfaction amongst the convicts,
and for the protection of the crew in the navigation
of the ship from insults that might be offered by the
convicts.

" That each ship should have on board at least
two surgeons' mates to attend to the wants of the
sick, and should be supplied with a proper assortment
of medicines and instruments, and that two of them
should remain with the settlement.

" After the arrival of the ships which are intended
to convey the convicts, the ship of war and tender
may be employed in obtaining live stock from the
Cape, or from the Molucca Islands, a sufficient
quantity of which may be brought from either of
those places to the new settlement in two or three
trips ; or the tender, if it should be thought most
advisable, may be employed in conveying to the new
settlement a further number of women from the

Friendly Islands, New Caledonia, &c., which are contiguous thereto, and from whence any number may be procured without difficulty.

"The whole regulation and management of the settlement should be committed to the care of a discreet officer, and provision should be made in all cases, both civil and military, by special instructions under the Great Seal or otherwise, as may be thought proper.

"Upon the whole, it may be observed with great force and truth that the difference of expense (whatever method of carrying the convicts thither may be adopted), and this mode of disposing of them and that of the usual ineffectual one is too trivial to be a consideration with Government, at least in comparison with the great object to be obtained by it especially now the evil is increased to such an alarming degree, from the inadequacy of all other expedients that have hitherto been tried or suggested.

"It may not be amiss to remark in favour of this plan that considerable advantage will arise from the cultivation of the New Zealand hemp or flax-plant in the new intended settlement, the supply of which would be of great consequence to us as a naval power, as our manufacturers are of opinion that canvas made of it would be superior in strength and beauty to any canvas made of the European material, and that a cable of the circumference of ten inches made from the former would be superior in strength to one of eighteen inches made of the latter. The threads or filaments of this New Zealand plant are formed by nature with the most exquisite delicacy, and may be so minutely divided as to be manu-factured into the finest linens.

" Most of the Asiatic productions may also, without doubt, be cultivated in the new settlement, and in a few years may render our recourse to our European neighbours for those productions unnecessary.

" It may also be proper to attend to the possibility of procuring from New Zealand any quantity of masts and ship timber for the use of our fleets in India, as the distance between the two countries is not greater than between Great Britain and America. It grows close to the water's edge, is of size and quality superior to any hitherto known, and may be ob-tained without difficulty."

It is no difficult matter to draft a scheme for a settlement in an unknown country, but the elabora-tion of the details and the inception of the work can only be done by a man of unusual ability. Fortunately for Lord Sydney he knew of a man capable of the extraordinary service required, and had sufficient confidence to appoint him Governor of the new colony, in spite of the scarcely veiled disapproval of the Admiralty. Captain Arthur Phillip, the officer selected, had entered the navy at the age of sixteen, and, after serving in the Seven Years' War as a midshipman, had been made a lieutenant on the capture of Havannah. At the close of hostilities he married and settled down to the life of a country gentleman, until war breaking out between Portugal and Spain, he hastened to seek distinction in the service of the first-named nation. In 1778 he returned to England to take his part in the operations against

ARTHUR PHILLIP,
Captain General and Commander-in-Chief in and over the Territory of New South Wales.

France, and in September of the following year was
made master and commander of the *Basilisk*. Two
years later he was promoted to the rank of post-
captain, being entrusted first with the *Ariadne* and
then with the *Europe*. He must have had opportunities during this period of showing that he possessed exceptional energy and sound judgment;
for, had not Lord Sydney been fully impressed with
his ability, he would hardly have so unhesitatingly
selected him as the most fitting person for a service of
so complicated a nature on which so much depended.

Phillip was no sooner appointed Governor of the
proposed settlement than he began to take a very
active part in the preparations for the expedition.
He soon saw that the arrangements made by the subordinate officials of the Admiralty were in almost every
branch lamentably incomplete and unsatisfactory,
and, had it not been for his watchful care and fore-
thought, and the persistency with which he urged the
necessity of supplying different rations and additional
accommodation both for convicts and guards, it would
have been impossible for the fleet to have reached its
destination without terrible loss of life and indescrib-
able suffering amongst those on board.

Phillip's keen appreciation, even at this early stage,
of all the dangers to be expected on the voyage, and
the administrative difficulties to be provided for and
avoided on arriving at his destination, mark him out
as a man of great capacity as well as the possessor
of genuine humane sympathy. His idea of the proper
mode of procedure is shown in a memorandum written
soon after his appointment. He urged strongly the

advisability of sending some ship with mechanics and others ahead of the transports to make preparations for the convicts : " By arriving at the settlement two or three months before the transports, many and very great advantages would be gained. Huts would be ready to receive the convicts who are sick, and they would find vegetables, of which it may naturally be supposed they will stand in great need, as the scurvy must make a great ravage amongst people naturally indolent and not cleanly. Huts would be ready for the women ; the stores would be properly lodged and defended from the convicts, in such manner as to prevent their making any attempt on them. The cattle and stock would be likewise properly secured, and the ground marked out for the convicts ; for lists of those intended to be sent being given to the commanding officers, mentioning their age, crimes, trades, and character, they might be so divided as to render few changes necessary, and the provisions would be ready for issuing without any waste. But if convicts, provisions, &c., must be landed a few days after the ship's arrival, and consequently nearly at the same time, great inconvenience will arise ; and to keep the convicts more than a few days on board, after they get into a port, considering the length of time which they must inevitably be confined, may be attended with consequences easier to conceive than to point out in a letter. Add to this, fevers of a malignant kind may make it necessary to have a second hospital."

" A ship's company is landed, huts raised, and the sick provided for in a couple of days ; but here the

greater number are convicts, in whom no confidence
can be placed, and against whom both person and
provisions are to be guarded. Everything necessary
for the settlement would be received at the Cape on
board by the commanding officer, and nothing left
for the transports but a certain proportion of live
stock. . . .

"The women in general, I should suppose, possess
neither virtue nor honesty. But there may be some
for theft who still retain some degree of virtue, and
these should be permitted to keep together, and strict
orders to the master of the transport be given that
they are not abused and insulted by the ship's company—which is said to have been the case too often
when they were sent to America. . . .

"I shall think it a great point gained if I can proceed
in this business without having any dispute with the
natives, a few of which I shall endeavour to persuade
to settle near us, whom I mean to furnish with
everything that can tend to civilise them, and to give
them a high opinion of their new guests ; for which
purpose it will be necessary to prevent the transports'
crews from having any intercourse with the natives,
if possible. The convicts must have none, for if they
have, the arms of the natives will be very formidable
in their hands. . . .

"Rewarding and punishing must be left to the
Governor ; he will likely be answerable for his
conduct, and death, I should think, will never be
necessary. In fact, I doubt if the fear of death ever
prevented a man of no principle from committing a
bad action There are two crimes that would merit

death ; for either of these crimes I should wish to confine the criminal till an opportunity offered of delivering him as a prisoner to the natives of New Zealand and let them eat him. The dread of this will operate much stronger than the fear of death. . . .

. . " Women may be brought from the Friendly and other islands, a proper place prepared to receive them, and where they will be supported for a time and lots of land assigned to such as marry with the soldiers of the garrison.

" As I would not wish convicts to lay the foundations of an empire, I think they should ever remain separate from the garrison and other settlers that may come from Europe, and not be allowed to mix with them, even after the seven or fourteen years for which they are transported may be expired.

" The laws of this country will, of course, be introduced in New South Wales, and there is one I would wish to take place from the moment His Majesty's forces take possession of the country—that there be no slavery in a free land, and consequently no slaves."

In addition to the general organisation Phillip had to attend to the most minute details. Numerous communications passed between him and various officials with regard to the quantity and quality of articles provided as rations, the necessity of overseers to look after the convicts, the filthy condition in which the women were sent on board the ships, the insufficient number of scythes and razors supplied, the lack of drugs and surgical instruments, the insecurity of the hatches in the transports, the supply of grog for the soldiers, clothing for the women, and the terrible overcrowding on board some of the vessels. In addition to the innumerable details which required attention, instructions to guide his action in a hundred imaginary emergencies were necessary. .Letter after letter had to be written before abuses were remedied or instructions received, while many matters which Phillip deemed essential to the health and safety of his charges were never attended to at all in spite of his frequent remonstrances. At last Phillip's patience seems to have almost given way, and in March he wrote as follows to Lord Sydney: "As the Navy Board have informed me that no alteration can be made respecting the victualling of the marines during the passage, it is to prevent my character as an officer from being called in question, should the consequences I fear be realised, that I once more trouble your lordship on this subject. . . . I see the critical situation I may be in after losing part of the garrison, that is at present very weak, when the service for which it is intended is considered; but I am prepared to meet difficulties, and I have only one fear. I fear, my lord, that it may be said hereafter, the officer who took charge of the expedition should have known that it was more than probable he lost half the garrison and convicts crowded and victualled in such a manner for so long a voyage. And the public, believing it rested with me, may impute to my ignorance or inattention what I have never been consulted in, and which never coincided with my ideas, to avoid which is the purport of this letter; and I flatter myself your lordship will hereafter point out the situation in which I have stood through the whole of this business, should it ever be necessary." Again, a little later, after a still more emphatic protest to the Under-Secretary, he wrote, "These complaints, my dear sir, do not come unexpected, nor were they unavoidable. I foresaw them from the beginning, and repeatedly pointed them out, when they might have been so easily prevented at a very small expense, and with little trouble to those who have had the conducting of this business. At present the evils complained of may be redressed, and the intentions of Government by this expedition answered. But if now neglected it may be too late hereafter, and we may expect to see the seamen belonging to the transports run from the ships to avoid a jail distemper, and may be refused entrance into a foreign port." At last the arrangements were as complete as they appeared likely ever to be, and on the 11th of May Phillip sat down in his cabin in the H.M.S. *Sirius,* then lying off the Mother-bank, to pen a few last lines to Nepean, the Under-Secretary. To a man of Phillip's temperament the feeling that he was on the eve of a great enterprise was fully present, and in the concluding lines of this letter a glimpse is given of some of his dreams of the future. "Once more," he wrote, " I take my leave of you, fully sensible of the trouble you have had in this business, for which at present I can only thank you ; but at a future period, when this country feels the advantages that are to be drawn from our intended settlement, you will enjoy a satisfaction that will, I am sure, make you ample amends." In these moments of comparative rest when he had done all

that lay in his power to ensure the success of the
expedition, the consciousness that he was destined to
found a great nation and not simply a distant gaol is
again apparent.   On the 13th of May the little fleet
weighed anchor and started down Channel.   It consisted of the vessels contained in the table on p. 28.
These with the *Sirius* and *Supply* made up the fleet.
On the first-named there were a few marines and the
governor belonging to the establishment, in addition
to her own complement.   H.M.S. *Hyæna*, a frigate,
accompanied them some way, returning with a final
despatch from Phillip when they were well clear of the
narrow waters.   All was then going well, but the
Provost-Marshal and the women's clothing had been
left behind, and the *Charlotte* and *Lady Penrhyn*
sailed very badly.   A conspiracy amongst the
convicts on the *Scarborough* had been discovered and
promptly suppressed, and to use Phillip's words, " the
clearing the Channel is one great point gained, and
with which I looked upon all our difficulty as ended."
The ships reached Santa Cruz, Teneriffe, on the 3rd
of June and here Phillip held his first inspection of the
convicts.   " I saw them all yesterday for the first
time," he writes, " they are quiet and contented,
though there are among them some complete villains."
A plentiful supply of fresh provisions was taken in,
and without delay sail made for Rio de Janiero, where
they arrived on the 5th of August.   Phillip must have
suffered some anxiety concerning his reception at
Rio, for fresh provisions were very necessary in order
to preserve the health of his charges, and any
opposition on the part of the Portuguese Viceroy

Name of Vessel	Class	Tonnage	Crew	Convicts Adults M.	F.	Children M.	F.	Marines Officers	Rank and file.	Wives of Marines.	Children of Marines M.	F.	Total number of Persons on board Bond.	Free.	Total.
Alexander	Transport	452	30	198	...	...	...	2	33	1	...	...	198	66	264
Charlotte	"	335	30	86	20	1	1	3	41	6	1	...	108	81	189
Scarborough	"	430	30	205	...	...	...	3	31	...	...	...	205	64	269
Friendship	"	274	25	75	1	3	...	3	41	3	4	1	79	77	156
Prince of Wales	"	350	...	...	19	...	1	2	29	16	2	4	20	53	73
Lady Penrhyn	"	333	30	1	104	2	3	3	3	...	...	...	110	36	146
Fishburn	Store Ship	378	22	...	...	...	...	...	...	...	...	...	...	22	22
Golden Grove	"	375	22	...	...	...	...	...	...	...	...	...	...	22	22
Borrodale	"	275	22	...	...	...	...	...	...	...	...	...	...	22	22
			211	565	144	6	5	16	178	26	7	5	720	443	1163

would have produced serious results. All apprehensions were, however, soon set at rest and the Portuguese showed their visitors every civility, while the Viceroy treated Phillip and his officers with extraordinary attention and honour. A supply of fresh food was obtained and a considerable quantity of spirits purchased ; indeed, rum rose 25 per cent. in price owing to the unusual demand. Here also Phillip seized the opportunity of remedying a remarkable omission in the preparations for the expedition. No ammunition of any sort had been provided for the marines, so that, had a rising among the convicts occurred on the voyage to Rio, the firearms of the guards would have been useless ; "ten thousand musquet balls " were purchased from the king's stores, fruit-trees and plants were obtained, and on the 4th of September the voyage was resumed. Phillip's knowledge of Spanish at once established most friendly relations with the Rio officials, and the success of the visit was mainly due to his tact and courtesy. On the arrival of the fleet at the Cape much trouble was at first experienced in obtaining permission from the Government to purchase what was required, and on this account another month was lost. Eventually all that Phillip asked was granted and the ships took more plants and seeds aboard and some live stock ; but prices were higher than was expected and the space available on the vessels very limited. On the 12th of November sail was set, and about a fortnight later the Governor, leaving the *Sirius,* and embarking on the *Supply,* made every effort to push on in order to select the site for the new settle-

ment and make certain preparations for the reception
of the stores and convicts before the arrival of the
transports. The three fastest of the transports were
directed to follow with all despatch and Captain
Hunter, of the *Sirius*, was left in charge of the remaining ships. On the 3rd of January the coast of
New South Wales was sighted from the *Supply*, but
owing to contrary winds Botany Bay was not reached
till the 18th. The *Alexander*, *Scarborough*, and
Friendship came in next day, and the *Sirius* with the
rest of the ships the day after. Directly he entered
the Bay Phillip looked about for some suitable place
for the settlement, but he " did not see any situation
to which there was not some very strong objection
while the anchorage in the bay was exposed to the
eastward, and the shores were very shallow." So
unfavourable did the surrounding country appear to
be that it was determined to search without delay for
a better site "higher up the coast," but that no time
might be lost if he did not succeed in finding a better
harbour and a proper situation for the settlement,
Phillip instructed the Lieutenant-Governor, Major
Ross, "to at once proceed to clear the land and
prepare for disembarkation." Captain Hunter and
several officers went with Phillip on his exploring
expedition in three boats so that the examination
might be conducted as rapidly as possible. The relief
and joy felt by this little band as they entered Sydney
Heads and saw the peaceful waters of Port Jackson
spreading before them in innumerable bays and coves
with yellow sandy shores and rocky points may be
easily imagined. To Phillip's eye here was a harbour

indeed—" We got into Port Jackson early in the afternoon," he wrote to Lord Sydney, " and had the satisfaction of finding the finest harbour in the world, in
which a thousand sail of the line may ride in the most
perfect security." All the coves were examined in
order to find the spot most suitable for landing, and
one was selected "that had the best spring of water,
and in which the ships can anchor so close to the
shore, that at a very small expense quays may be
made at which the largest ships may unload." On the
third day Phillip returned to Botany Bay to find Ross
disgusted with the country and every one depressed.
Preparations were immediately made to go round to
Sydney Cove, but before the start an incident occurred which created no small amount of excitement.
The account given by Trench, an officer of marines,
so well describes the feelings of astonishment on board
the transports in Botany Bay when two strange sail
suddenly appeared on the horizon, that it is worth
quoting at length. " The thoughts of removal (from
Botany Bay to Port Jackson) banished sleep, so that
I rose at the first dawn of the morning. But judge of
my surprise on hearing from a sergeant, who ran down
almost breathless to the cabin where I was dressing,
that a ship was seen off the harbour's mouth! At
first I only laughed, but knowing the man who spoke
to me to be of great veracity, and hearing him repeat
his information, I flew upon deck, on which I had
barely set my foot, when the cry of ' another sail '
struck on my astonished ear. Confounded by a
thousand ideas which arose in my mind in an instant,
I sprang upon the barricade, and plainly descried two

ships of considerable size standing in for the mouth of the bay." The two sail turned out to be the *Boussole* and *Astrolabe*, under La Perouse, on a voyage of discovery. The officers exchanged civilities, and La Perouse left in charge of the Englishmen, for transmission to Europe, the last letters and despatches which he wrote before his untimely death. Directly some of the transports came round to Sydney Cove, as Phillip called the spot he had chosen, a start was made at clearing the ground. On the 26th of January, 1788, the British flag was unfurled at the head of the bay. Toasts of the King, the Royal Family, and success to the new Colony were honoured, volleys were fired by the marines, and in the evening the remaining ships arrived from Botany.

NEW SOUTH WALES.

III.

BOTANY BAY.

(1788–1792.)

THE erection of stores for the provisions and shelter for the convicts and marines was vigorously pushed on. On the 7th of July all the people had been landed from the ships and the formal inauguration of the colony took place. The whole of the little community assembled on the slope of Point Maskelyne, now known as Dawe's Point, and Phillip's commission and the other documents establishing the Government were read by the Judge-Advocate. The Governor then addressed a few words to the convicts with regard to the future. He assured them that he would do all in his power to render those happy who led orderly lives and showed a disposition to amendment, but he held out no hope of mercy to any who continued in evil courses or transgressed the law or regulations of the colony.

After the ceremony every one turned their atten-

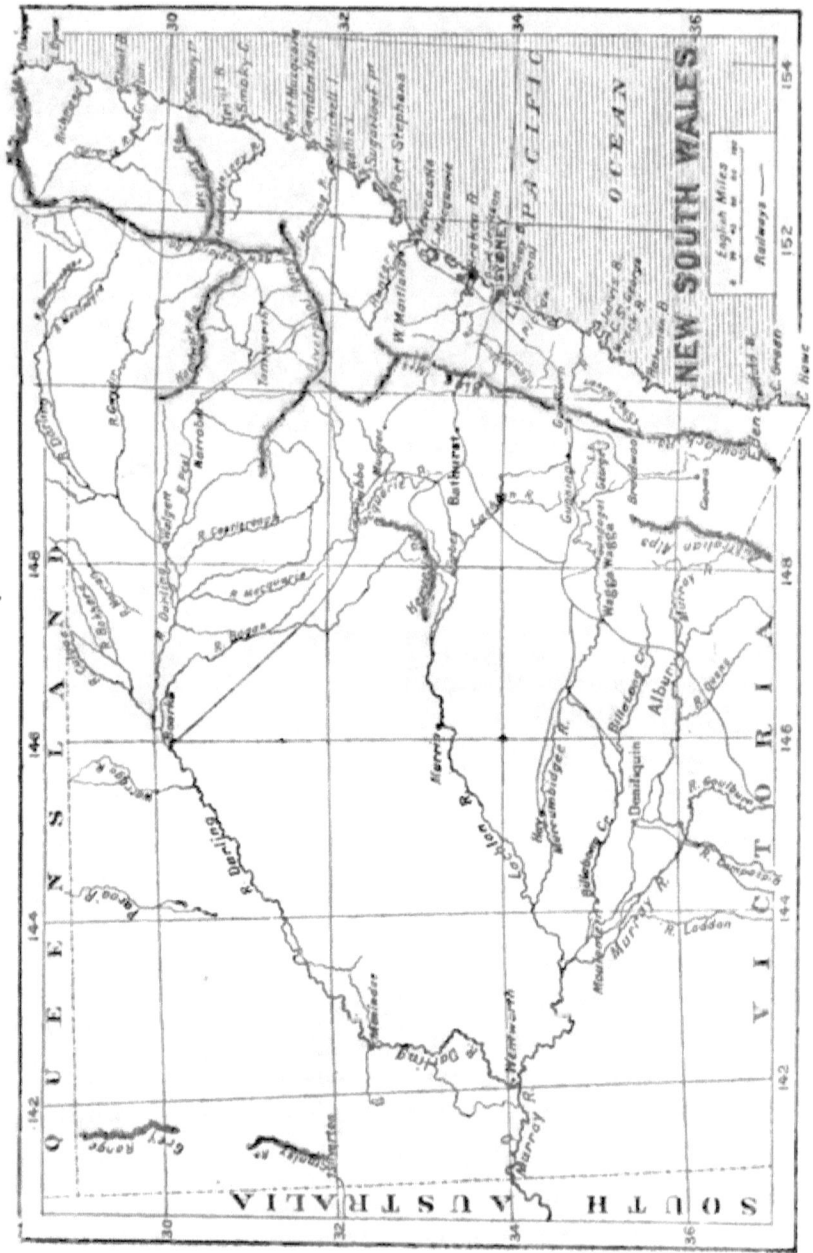

tion to clearing the land and erecting dwellings; but the task proved a difficult one, for the surrounding country was extremely rocky and heavily timbered.

"The scene, to an indifferent spectator at leisure to contemplate it, would have been highly picturesque and amusing," wrote an eye-witness; "in one place, a party cutting down the woods; a second, setting up a blacksmith's forge; a third, dragging along a load of stones or provisions; here an officer pitching his marquee, with a detachment of troops parading on one side of him and a cook's fire blazing up on the other." Phillip had been instructed to immediately occupy Norfolk Island, so a week after the inauguration Lieut. Phillip Gidley King was despatched in the *Supply* with fifteen men, nine of whom were convicts, and six convict women.

It was most necessary that no time should be lost in planting the seeds and shrubs obtained at Rio and the Cape, since, if any misfortune were to overtake one of the store-ships from England, the safety of the colony might before long depend on the local crops. But Phillip, when he tried to cultivate the land, found that there was no one who understood anything of gardening or farming except his own servant, and much of the precious seed was lost in efforts to learn by experience. The agricultural implements supplied were very inadequate, and it soon became clear that, if any good results were to be obtained, it could only be by the arrival of some free settlers skilled in agricultural pursuits. Even before all the stores were out of the ship the Governor wrote: "If fifty farmers were sent out with their families, they would do more in one year in rendering this colony independent of the Mother Country as to provisions than a thousand convicts."

Within a month of landing, attempts to rob the public stores of the very limited stock of provisions which they contained called for prompt and severe treatment, and an execution took place. The ill success met with in farming caused the shadow of famine to hover over the settlement from the commencement, and the stores had to be zealously guarded, for in spite of every effort it seemed impossible to render the colony self-supporting with the materials to hand. A couple of years later Phillip again wrote : " Experience has taught me how difficult it is to make men industrious who have passed their lives in habits of vice and indolence. In some cases it has been found impossible ; neither kindness nor severity have had any effect. There are many who dread punishment less than they fear labour." The discontent of the convicts was increased by a curious omission on the part of the officials in England. Phillip had been supplied with no papers stating the dates of expiration of sentences, so that when men claimed to have served their time he could not release them without referring home. In some cases grants of land were made to be confirmed if the claim proved true, while severe punishment was threatened in any case of imposition. The helplessness of Phillip's position was aggravated by the military, for no assistance was received from Major Ross, the Lieutenant-Governor, who, instead of aiding, used every opportunity of embarrassing Phillip or rendering his efforts at reform and harmony nugatory. Phillip had hoped much from the moral influence of the military on the convicts, but he was bitterly disappointed. He expressed a wish soon after landing "that officers would, when they saw the convicts diligent, say a few words of encouragement to them, and that when they saw them idle or met them straggling in the woods they would threaten them with punishment;" but he was promptly informed that "they declined the least interference with the convicts." During the whole of Phillip's tenure of office the military were a thorn in his side, and, had he not been possessed of enormous self-control, matters must, at an early stage, have reached a crisis which might have been fatal to the prospects of the colony.

As soon as things were fairly in progress at Sydney Cove the Governor commenced a series of expeditions into the surrounding country, chiefly in the hope of finding better arable land than was to be got near the harbour. He first went to Broken Bay and Pittwater, and was much impressed with the fine scenery, but unfortunately, while sleeping on the wet ground, he contracted an illness which proved a continual source of pain and eventually compelled him to return to England.

On his second trip, taken shortly afterwards, he discovered Lake Narabeen, and a week later made his first attempt to reach the Blue Mountains. On the journey some good country suitable for farming operations was found, but the mountains could not be reached owing to lack of provisions. The chief result of these explorations was the establishment of a farm at the head of the harbour, where "the soil was of a stiff clayey nature, free from that rock which everywhere covered the surface of Sydney Cove."

Much of the seed brought in the ships had been heated and otherwise spoilt, and the live stock had also met with serious mishaps. Before long the Governor was filled with apprehensions in regard to the food supply. It was apparent that at the present rate of progress the colony must long be entirely dependent on provisions from England, and Phillip could not but tremble when he thought of the numerous dangers besetting ships sailing in the unexplored waters which surrounded him and the terrible consequences which any misfortune to a store-ship would entail. Ross, in whom Phillip in these difficulties should have found a counsellor and friend, soon developed into an open foe, and displayed a personal animosity which entirely obliterated any sense of duty and responsibility which he may have originally possessed. One of his first acts was to endeavour to persuade the officers of the marines to refuse to sit on the criminal court, a duty imposed on them by a special Act of Parliament. Fortunately the subordinates had more discretion than their commandant, and declined to be made tools of his spleen against the Governor ; but, had this not been the case, the colony for some time would have been left without any means of legally punishing offenders—a situation the gravity of which is obvious in a society threatened with starvation and mainly composed of persons who had already

transgressed the law. Doubtless their refusal to
support the quibbles of Ross strained the relations
existing between him and his subordinates, for before
long he took the remarkable step of placing the
whole of the members of a court-martial under arrest
for declining to alter at his command a sentence
inflicted by them. This action again placed Phillip
in a difficult predicament ; for, unless he took every
officer from his duty, it was impossible to assemble a
court to try the case. The Governor, therefore, offered
a court of inquiry instead of a general court-martial,
but this the officers concerned refused, demanding
either a proper trial or a public apology for their
arrest. The only way out of the dilemma was for
the Governor to order the officers back to their duty
until a court - martial could be assembled, a step
which practically closed the incident ; but the fact
of subalterns demanding an apology from their commanding officer was scarcely an encouraging aspect
of discipline in the regiment. Phillip had been
instructed " by every possible means to open an
intercourse with the natives and to conciliate their
affections," and his policy from the commencement
was characterised by a desire to inspire them with
confidence. On all occasions when he personally
came in contact with them his address, combining
courage and firmness with a fine sense of the natives'
rights, produced the most pleasing effect ; but all the
good done by the Governor was undone by the
convicts and marines, who wantonly destroyed the
canoes and other property which the natives left on
the shore and in many ways provoked acts of re-

taliation which not infrequently ended in loss of life. Ill-treatment of the natives by the colonists, when detected, met with severe punishment, but in spite of every precaution outrages by one class or the other were of frequent occurrence. Phillip, seeing the necessity of an interpreter, if friendly intercourse was to be established, secured a young aboriginal man, named Arabanoo, in December, 1788, and took much pains to instruct him in the language and customs of the white men. This experiment was promising to be successful when Arabanoo died from small-pox. Two other natives, named Bennilong and Colebe, were afterwards captured, and they on many occasions acted as intermediaries between the blacks and the new-comers. Although Phillip was often in positions of very great danger from attacks of the natives, the apparent absence of all fear and the remarkable tact which he displayed saved him, and only once did he meet with any mishap at their hands. On this occasion a native, to whom he had been introduced by Bennilong, misunderstanding his friendly advances and thinking that Phillip intended to seize him as Bennilong had before been seized, threw his spear, which entered above Phillip's collar-bone, the barb passing out at his back. The wound proved not to be so serious as it at first sight appeared, and in ten days the Governor was about again, and made another visit to the tribe of the aggressor, in order to show that he felt no ill-will.

Although the convicts had been landed in better health than the most sanguine could have hoped, sickness broke out soon after they were on shore, and scurvy and dysentery greatly weakened the effective strength of the settlement. The number of unproductive consumers was day by day growing more out of proportion to the producers, and the food question assumed a very serious aspect. Rations were reduced, and the *Sirius*, leaving behind guns and everything she could dispense with, in order to make more room, was despatched to the Cape, the *Supply* being sent at the same time to Batavia for provisions. After a lengthy voyage the *Sirius* returned, "every officer's department and all the store-rooms being completely filled ;" but even then the food she brought could not postpone the impending disaster for more than a few weeks. Numerous attempts were made by convicts to escape from the settlement: some started to walk to China, which they imagined to be only 150 miles distant ; others wandered away into the bush and were never heard of again ; while a few seized boats and put to sea.

The most successful of these latter was a man named Bryant, who, in a fishing-boat, sailed, with his wife and two children—one of whom was an infant— and seven convicts, and arrived safely at Timor. Owing to want of discretion on the part of some of the convicts, their identity was discovered, and the Dutch Governor handed them over to the captain of H.M.S. *Pandora*, who was at that time in port. Crime—more especially robberies of food, both by the soldiers and convicts—increased with the decrease of the food allowance, and executions and other punishments occurred with appalling frequency. The absolute necessity of protecting the public stores and the little vegetable gardens of the settlers was apparent to every one but Ross, who seized the opportunity afforded by the arrest of a soldier by the night watch for robbing a garden to make one more attempt to embarrass the Governor. Ross even went so far as to advise his men to use their bayonets to protect themselves when molested in their predatory expeditions.

At last resources became so low, that it was determined to send a further detachment to Norfolk Island, under Major Ross, who was appointed Lieutenant-Governor in succession to King, to relieve the main settlement of some of the mouths to be filled, employing the services of King as a special envoy to England to lay before the Government more forcibly than could be done in any despatches the desperate straits to which the settlement had been reduced, in the matter of food as well as the various reforms in the Government and military which were so urgently needed. The *Sirius* and *Supply* sailed with Ross and a large body of marines and convicts, provided as well with stores. Norfolk Island was reached safely, and the passengers landed; but while discharging the cargo, the *Sirius* drifted on a reef and became a total wreck.

The intention had been to proceed to China for provisions, taking King, who was to have made his way thence to England; after the wreck, however, King at once returned to Sydney in the *Supply*.

At headquarters matters were gradually going from bad to worse. The fleet had left England with two years' supply of provisions, and although next to nothing had been obtained from the land, three years had already passed without any additional support or news from home. The rations had been so reduced, that it was found necessary to serve them " daily to every person in the settlement, without distinction," so that it might not be possible for any one to devour a week's rations at one meal and then starve. All Government work had to be stopped, owing to the extreme weakness of the convicts, and every one was occupied in procuring food by fishing or shooting, and for this purpose all private boats were pressed into the public service. The only hope of saving the people from starvation was to send the little brig *Supply* to Batavia ; this was therefore done, the commander having instructions to there charter a large ship, at any price, and send her to Sydney with provisions. Trench, an officer of marines, draws a graphic picture of the terrible straits to which the colony was reduced : "Three or four instances of persons who have perished from want have been related to me. One only, however, fell within my own observation. I was passing the provision store, when a man, with a wild, haggard countenance, who had just received his daily pittance to carry home, came out. His faltering gait, and eager, devouring eye led me to watch him ; and he had not proceeded ten steps before he fell. I ordered him to be carried to the hospital, where, when he arrived, he was found dead."

The one bright spot in this scene of misery was the demeanour of Phillip. With a patient endurance, he bore the privations in common with his meanest subject. Famished and in ill health, he none the less gave every thought to the welfare of those under his charge ; while the grievances which called forth bitter lamentations from his subordinates, he wrote about as " The little difficulties we have met with, which time and proper people for cultivating the land will remove." In the colony's darkest hour he never swerved from the opinion " that this country will prove the most valuable acquisition Great Britain ever made." His example was not confined to words. " The Governor, from a motive that did him immortal honour," wrote Collins, "gave up three hundred weight of flour, which was his Excellency's private property, declaring that he wished not to see anything more at his table than the ration which was received in common from the public store, without any distinction of persons ; and to this resolution he rigidly adhered, wishing that, if a convict complained, he might see that want was not unfelt even at Government House." Actions such as these were not uncommon during his rule, and they lost none of their virtue from the fact that he always forgot to mention them when writing officially or privately to England.

A flagstaff was erected on the South Head, so that the appearance of any approaching sail could be at once made known to the starving inhabitants ; and the following extract from a letter to England of one of the men stationed on the look-out brings home the aching anxiety with which the glittering horizon was watched for relief: " Early and late do I look with anxious eyes towards the sea ; and at times, when the day was fast setting and the shadows of the evening stretched out, I have been deceived with some fantastic little cloud, which, as it condensed or expanded by such a light, for a short time has amused impatient imagination into a momentary idea that it was a vessel altering her sail and position while steering in for the haven ; when, in an instant, it has assumed a form so unlike what the mind was intent upon, or has become so greatly extended, as fully to certify me of its flimsy texture and fleeting existence."

At last a sail appeared ; and on the evening of June 3, 1790, the joyful cry of "The flag's up !" resounded in every direction. "I was sitting in my hut," wrote Trench, "musing on our fate, when a confused clamour in the street drew my attention. I opened my door, and saw several women, with children in their arms, running to and fro with distracted looks, congratulating each other, and kissing their infants with the most passionate and extravagant marks of fondness. I needed no more, but instantly started out and ran to a hill, where, by the assistance of my pocket-glass, my hopes were realised. My next-door neighbour, a brother officer, was with me ; but we could not speak ; we wrung each other by the hand, with eyes and hearts overflowing."

The vessel turned out to be the *Juliana*, with 222 female convicts, for whom Philip had asked in more prosperous times, in order to render the proportion of sexes in the colony more equal. She also brought some provisions and part of the cargo of the storeship *Guardian*, which had been wrecked off the Cape of Good Hope by collision with an iceberg, and the loss of which had been the cause of the long delay in arrival of help for the colony. A few weeks after the *Juliana*, the *Justinian* storeship made the port, followed, a little later, by the *Supply* and the vessel chartered in China ; so that the full ration was restored. But before long three more transports arrived full of prisoners, amongst whom sickness and pestilence were raging. No less than 261 deaths of male convicts had occurred on the passage, while 488 persons were under medical treatment on landing, and the resources of the little colony were taxed to the utmost.

Philip lost no time in sending aid to the people at Norfolk Island, where the sufferings from want of food had been almost as severe as at Sydney. The settlement was saved by the discovery of what the sailors called mutton birds—a species of petrel— which alighted in thousands on the highest peak in the island. From two to three thousand of these birds were captured nightly, and for some time they formed the principal support of the inhabitants.

The first detachment of the newly-formed New South Wales Corps arrived in the transports, to relieve the marines who had come out with the first fleet. This corps had been raised by Major Grose, for special service in the settlement, and it was hoped by the English Government that the change would remove all the friction which had so long existed between the civil and military powers. Ross was recalled with the marines, for his erratic behaviour had not met with approbation.

A few of the men of the marines, under Captain-Lieutenant Johnston, joined the new corps, which

was to play a very prominent part in the later history
of the colony. The very large increase in the population, and the inability of the greater proportion of
the new-comers to do any productive work, brought
the community once more to a state of famine. A
vessel was sent to India to obtain supplies; but while
waiting for her return, rations were cut down to the
smallest amount which would keep body and soul
together. The extremities to which the colony was
reduced may be gathered from a letter written by
Phillip to King, in which he says that, " When the
Atlantic arrived, we had only thirteen days' flour and
forty-five days of maize in store, at $1\frac{1}{2}$ lb. flour and
$4\frac{1}{2}$ lb. maize per man for seven days."

King had returned towards the close of 1791 from
his mission to England, where he had been most
successful, receiving promotion and being especially
appointed Lieutenant-Governor of Norfolk Island.

Phillip's health gave way under his arduous duties,
and shortly after King's departure to resume his
command at Norfolk Island, the Governor asked to
be permitted to return to England. Very reluctantly
leave was granted, but the English Government
delayed appointing his successor, in the hopes of
persuading him to again take up the duties which he
had performed with such signal success and discretion.
On the 11th of December, 1792, Phillip left the
colony, and Major Francis Grose, the Commandant
of the New South Wales Corps, assumed the reins of
government, in virtue of his commission as Lieutenant-
Governor.

IV.

THE CONVICTS AND THEIR GUARDS.

(1792-1806.)

WERE any demonstration of the wisdom and beneficial influence of Phillip's rule needed, it is abundantly provided by the errors and incompetence of his immediate successors. One of the first actions of Grose was to supersede the civil magistracy and place the government entirely in the hands of the military. In a society such as then existed in the colony the change might have had no very bad effect had the New South Wales Corps been composed of respectable and reliable men. But the knowledge that they possessed practically uncontrolled power rapidly produced an impatience of every kind of restraint. No sooner was Phillip's back turned than all the elements for evil, both in guards and convicts, were given full play, and lust, profanity, and crime reigned unchecked.

Instructions had been received shortly after the Governor's departure authorising him to make grants of land, and to assign convict servants within pre-

scribed limits to officers of the New South Wales
Corps. Grose therefore lost no time in availing himself of this permission, but he entirely disregarded
the specified limitations. The baneful influence of
the military did not confine itself to example, and
those whose most obvious and solemn duty it was to
try and improve the moral condition of the convicts
had no hesitation in encouraging vice and debauchery
amongst them for their own material gain. Phillip,
although he had never tolerated any special indulgence to the soldiers in the way of an undue allowance from the public stores, had nevertheless been
mindful of their comfort, and had recommended the
English Government to send out certain luxuries,
such as wine, spirits, and tobacco, to be sold at cost
price to those of the officers who might wish to
purchase them for their own consumption. When
the military became the largest farmers and employers
of labour, they did not take long to discover to what
very profitable account this concession could be
turned. The craving for spirits amongst the convict
population had always been very great ; possibly a
desire to forget their misery in intoxication may have
strengthened it, at the same time, owing to the small
quantity which Phillip had permitted to be landed in
the colony, prices were exceedingly high. Men who
would not work for wages would readily engage for
rum ; the lucrative nature of the traffic open to the
officers is apparent. Before Grose had been in command many months spirits became the common and
recognised medium of exchange, the military pur-
chasing at from 4s. to 5s. per gallon and retailing at

prices ranging up to £8 per gallon. There can be no doubt that the officers by this means got far more work done than otherwise would have been possible, but the effect on the community needs no description. Religious observances became a farce, murders and robberies multiplied, and attacks of terrible brutality upon the natives called forth reprisals of equal violence, and laid the foundation of the inhuman cruelty which is a dark blot on the page of Australia's history.

At Norfolk Island King continued to rule his little colony with justice and wisdom ; but the great dissimilarity between the methods pursued by Grose and his subordinate must inevitably have sooner or later produced a collision. The crisis, when it came, strikingly exemplified the characters of the two men. Even at Norfolk Island the military had become infected with the arrogance and licentiousness of the corps in Sydney, and the relations between free or freed settlers and the soldiers were by no means cordial. One day a settler found that a soldier had very grievously wronged him, and in the heat of his passion shot and wounded the offender. King, himself a pure and honourable man, sympathised with the settler, and only inflicted a small penalty on him, whereupon other soldiers took up their friend's cause, and shamefully maltreated the man who had shot their comrade, taking the occasion of a theatrical performance at which King was present, to behave in a riotous and insubordinate way. After the entertainment they demanded from Lieutenant Abbot, their commanding officer, that the settler should be more severely punished, and swearing that they would not permit any soldier to suffer for an offence against a convict, displayed such a mutinous temper, that King and Abbot in consultation decided that the company had better be promptly disarmed and a militia enrolled from the free settlers to act in its stead. This course was followed, and the ringleaders of the mutiny were sent to Sydney for trial. That King should presume to interfere with the New South Wales Corps so angered Grose that he completely lost his head, and censured King's action in a despatch which is a truly remarkable specimen of official correspondence. Another cause of friction was in connection with two New Zealand chiefs who had been kidnapped in order that they might instruct the colonists at Norfolk Island in the preparation of the native flax. King, fearful that, after they had imparted all the knowledge they possessed, they would not reach their own country in safety, himself accompanied them to New Zealand being absent from his government ten days. Grose took this opportunity to severely reprimand him. The most serious trouble, however, was the dishonouring by Grose of the bills drawn by King to pay settlers in Norfolk Island for crops purchased on Government account. These bills had been drawn in strict accordance with Phillip's instructions, and the refusal of Grose to meet them so disheartened the farmers that an irremediable blow was struck at agricultural development in the island.

All these matters were referred to the English authorities ; Grose, it is true, was censured, while King's action was commended, but the effect of this

breach of faith could not be removed by the tardy
payment of the money.

Surrounded by disaffection among his own corps,
in spite of all he had done for them, and conscious of
the disapprobation of his conduct in England, Grose
felt no desire to remain, so in December, 1794, he
left the country, resigning the command to Captain
Paterson, as senior military officer. Captain Hunter,
who had charge of the *Sirius* up to her wreck, had
been appointed to succeed Phillip before Paterson
began to rule, so that that officer can scarcely be
blamed for permitting things to continue as Grose
left them and troubling himself very little with affairs
of government. Hunter arrived in September, 1795,
carrying with him imperative instructions to reinstate
the civil magistracy and suppress the liquor traffic.
The first he did, but he was unequal to the latter
task. In less troublous times he might have governed
successfully, but he was not strong enough to battle
with the great abuses which permeated every grade
of society, and his official reports are one long lamen-
tation that the task was too hard. In his efforts at
reform, he received no help from the corps, which he
described as containing "characters who have been
considered disgraceful to every other regiment in his
Majesty's service, who were often superior in every
species of infamy to the most expert in wickedness
among the convicts"; but he feared to provoke them
to open hostility. If he could only have done what
he wished to do all would have been well, for his
successor gave a fitting epitaph to his government
when he wrote: "His public conduct has been guided

CAPTAIN JOHN HUNTER.

by the most upright intentions, but he has been most shamefully deceived by those upon whom he had every reason to depend for assistance and advice."

King had been so successful at Norfolk Island that he appeared the most fit person to cope with the difficulties which had overwhelmed Hunter. He was, moreover, still in England on leave, and by his personal experience of the present state of affairs in New South Wales, was of considerable assistance to the Secretary of State in the consultations which took place with Phillip and Banks as to the best means to be pursued for the reformation of the colony.

It was acknowledged that Hunter had acted to the best of his ability, and it was recognised that his recall would be a bitter disappointment to him ; so the Duke of Portland determined to send out King as Lieutenant-Governor, with a dormant commission appointing him Governor in case of Hunter's absence or death. King was made the bearer of very stringent instructions with regard to the liquor traffic, monopoly and military traders, and he was directed to lose no time in promulgating them and enforcing obedience.

In April, 1800, he arrived in the colony, but, although the hint conveyed by the dormant commission was clear, Hunter, unwilling to confess himself beaten, clung to office. King's position was anomalous ; until Hunter left New South Wales he had practically no power or authority, and Hunter himself was disinclined to carry out the instructions of which he had been made the bearer. For some months

King assisted in the general administration of public business, but Hunter discouraged any attempt to deal with the principal abuses, so that all that could be done in this direction was to pave the way for future reforms by cutting off the supply of spirits at its source. With this end in view King communicated with the Governor-General of India and the British Consuls in America, requesting either that the shipment of spirits to New South Wales should be stopped, or, where this was impossible, that shipowners and masters should be warned that the landing of spirits in the colony had been prohibited. At last in September the Governor reluctantly yielded to King's entreaties, and consented to the promulgation of the orders respecting military traders, and the barter of spirits. As the New South Wales Corps were so deeply concerned, Colonel Paterson was first informed, and desired to make the substance of the new regulations known to the officers under his command ; shortly afterwards the instructions from the British Government dealing with these matters were published, and created a profound sensation among all classes of people. The immediate enforcement of the new order of things would have entailed great loss, and possibly even ruin on many persons ; so King made some slight temporary concessions, though the command that no military officer should partake in any form of trade caused acute irritation amongst the military. Captain Macarthur, who had already by his energy and ability taken a prominent position as farmer, trader, and soldier, with characteristic impetuousity, determined to shake the dust of New

South Wales from his feet, and with this object offered the whole of his valuable collection of sheep and cattle to the Government at a low price. King, who on several occasions obtained his end by meeting extravagant conduct of this sort with imperturbability, gravely recommended the purchase to the Secretary of State, but, as he had doubtless anticipated, before an answer was received Macarthur had plunged afresh with undiminished enthusiasm into his schemes for fine wool growing.

Hunter now perceived that his return to England was advisable, so left King with a free hand. The new Governor at once set about reform. Certificates for landing were refused for most of the spirits, which arrived in large quantities from India, America, the Cape, and Brazil. In the first fourteen months of his rule no less than 32,000 gallons of spirits and 22,000 gallons of wine were sent out of the harbour, and the small quantity, which was permitted to be landed, had to be sold at a fixed price of from 4s. to 10s. a gallon. As much as £8 per gallon had, just previously to Hunter's departure, been recovered in the Court, the judgment having been sustained by Hunter on appeal; so the violent reaction which King's proceedings must have produced is evident. Steps were also taken to prevent smuggling; regulations were framed to govern the landing of spirits, very heavy penalties being attached to the infringement of them.

The population at King's departure was only 7,519 persons, 3,295 of whom were women and children, but, during the six years which he governed the colony, shippers were refused permission to land cargoes to the amount of no less than 100,777 gallons of spirits and wine. Having taken effective steps to control the importation of liquor, the next thing to be done was to regulate the trade within the colony, and King determined to limit the power to sell spirits to persons specially licensed on the recommendation of the magistrates. In this way all retailers of liquor were brought under the notice of the Government, and any irregularities perpetrated by them could be easily punished. It was not to be expected that abuses of such deep growth could be removed without much difficulty, and King's energetic measures called forth " much animadversion, secret threats and officious advice," from those with whom the reform interfered. The Governor was no respecter of persons, and all classes, from officers to convicts, were given to clearly understand that obedience to orders was necessary, and that disregard of the regulations carried severe and inevitable punishment.

The spirit traffic was not the only trade which received attention, and a general order was issued in October, 1800, by which an attempt was made to deal with monopoly and extortion. The price at which private retailers might sell articles was fixed by the Governor at 20 per cent. on the price paid to the shippers, which was estimated at from 80 to 100 per cent. on the value of the articles in Europe or India. In order to prevent evasion of this regulation, it was also ordered that no cognisance should be taken by the Courts of any promissory note or bill, unless the consideration for which it had been

given was clearly set forth thereon, and printed promissory note forms were supplied by the Government. Butchers and bakers were licensed, and the
quality and price of meat and bread regulated, and
various other traders were treated in a similar way.
The following notice promulgated by King in March,
1806, is an example of the prevailing method of
dealing with commercial matters :—

" NOTICE.

" March 23, 1806.
" The following ordinance of the 8th of May, 1801, and general
order of the 17th of May, 1802, are repeated, and required to be
duly observed and enforced, viz. :—

"It is hereby ordered, that no other than one quality of wheat-
bread is to be made throughout the colony, viz., such bread to
be composed of meal, from which only twenty-four pounds of
bran are to be taken from one hundred pounds. As this regulation is necessary to prevent a distressing scarcity, any inhabi-
tant or person resident in the colony disobeying this ordinance
will be punished according to their respective situations, exclusive of the penalty of five pounds for each offence. Bakers of
any description disobeying any part of this ordinance will, on
conviction, have their ovens taken down, and be fined in the
penalty of ten pounds for each offence."

The Female Orphan Institution was the most permanent and, probably, the most beneficial of King's
early reforms. One of the first things which he
noticed on arriving in the colony was the terrible
temptation to a life of degradation and infamy which
surrounded the children, and even before Hunter's
departure he decided to found an institution, in which
the girls at any rate could be received and rescued
from the fate which otherwise awaited them. A house

in Parramatta was purchased by bills drawn on the British Treasury, and a committee formed to manage the home.

Long after King had retired the Female Orphan Institution continued to do good work, and the full benefit derived by the country from this humane effort to keep the rising generation uncontaminated by the terrible vice which ran riot through the land was reaped in later years. But King had other matters of equally serious character to occupy him. The Irish rebellion of 1798 had supplied large numbers of convicts for transportation, and these political prisoners brought with them a restless energy, which was a constant cause of anxiety to their guards. The French wars at this time also tended to excite the bond population, amongst whom vague and unfounded reports of the intention of the French to seize the settlement and set them at liberty were continually circulating. Sometimes these hopes were stimulated by the arrival of privateers with their prizes in the harbour, and in 1804 an engagement between two ships took place off the Heads, within sight of the inhabitants. Rumours of intended insurrection had reached the Government before Hunter's departure; therefore it became necessary, in the first months of King's rule, to take extra precautions against surprise, and an " Armed Association," composed of loyal free settlers, was enrolled. From this time forward there were continual conspiracies and outbreaks among the convicts. The widespread feeling of suspicion and expectation seriously interfered with progress in peaceful development. The Governor's time was so fully occupied in preparing for or dealing with revolts of one sort or another that little chance was left for the encouragement of agriculture or other industries. In 1802, so grave were the apprehensions that a proclamation ordering a general search for arms was promulgated, accompanied by very stringent regulations with regard to seditious meetings or utterances. During the early months of 1803 there were several acts of lawless violence reported on the part of the convicts, and at the end of that year the "Loyal Associations" had been again embodied on receipt of the news of the renewal of hostilities with France. At the commencement of March, 1804, curious rumours reached the authorities. Captain Abbot at Parramatta, and Mr. Arndell, at the Hawkesbury, both heard "several mysterious informations about an intended insurrection." On the 4th of March Marsden learnt that that date had been determined on for a general rising, and that the password was "St. Peter." By midnight King, who was in Sydney, had been informed ; he started immediately for Parramatta, and before 1.30 a.m. on the 5th Major Johnston, with a small force, was on his way to the disturbed districts. The further particulars received by King on his arrival at Parramatta had convinced him that this movement was much more serious than anything that had yet taken place, and that strong and immediate action was necessary.

Not a moment was lost. By noon, on the 5th, the country had been scoured for arms lest they should fall into the hands of the rebels, and martial law had been proclaimed throughout the disaffected districts.

Johnston with his little band arrived at Parramatta at dawn, and, after a halt of twenty minutes to refresh the men, set off in pursuit of a body of rebels who were said to be marching towards the Hawkesbury. As the direction they had taken was uncertain, the detachment of soldiers were divided in half, one party under Lieutenant Davis following the Castle Hill road, while Johnston and the remainder hastened towards Toongabbee. On catching sight of the insurgents, Major Johnston rode forward, attended by a trooper and Mr. Dixon, the Roman Catholic priest, and called to them to halt, saying that he wished to speak to them. "They desired that I would come into the middle of them," writes Johnson in his official report, "as their captains were there ; which I refused, observing to them that I was within pistol shot, and that it was in their power to kill me, and that their captains must have very little spirit if they would not come forward to speak to me ; upon which two persons (Cunningham and Johnston) advanced towards me as their leaders, to whom I represented the impropriety of their conduct, and advised them to surrender, and that I would mention them in as favourable terms as possible to the Governor. Cunningham replied that they would have death or liberty." At this moment the rest of the detachment came up and Major Johnston gave the command to charge. The order was obeyed with such irresistible ferocity, that the rebel line broke after but slight resistance, and the convicts fled in all directions. Twelve were killed, six wounded, and twenty-six, a number equal to the whole attacking force, taken

prisoners. Cunningham, one of the rebel leaders,
was at once hung ; and on the 8th, after trial by
court martial at Parramatta, several others suffered
the same fate. The prompt action of King and
Johnston had a good effect, and with the first
reverse the insurgent cause was ruined. On the
10th of March, martial law was cancelled and civil
authority restored, but the Governor took every
precaution to prevent a recurrence of such a revolt.
No man free or bond was in future to be permitted
to leave the place he resided in without a pass from
a magistrate, and other stringent regulations governing the general management and control of convicts
were rigorously enforced. Doubtless these restrictions were necessary in the existing conditions of
society, but it is impossible to read the chronicles of
this date without feeling that an effort on the part
of the bond to regain their freedom was justified
by the brutality of the treatment they received in
bondage. The blood-curdling cruelty and outrage,
to which convicts were often compelled to submit
on the voyage out, was equalled only by the un-
mentionable horrors of the road gangs after arrival ;
while the vexatious bullying, which was a frequent
characteristic of assignment, in spite of King's efforts
to render justice alike to bond and free and to prevent cruelty by masters to their servants, frequently
made the lot of those transported unalloyed misery.

Reference has already been made to the singular
restrictions placed upon trade ; but the peculiarity of
the Governor's connection with commercial undertakings was not confined to the licensing of traders

and the regulations of prices. In 1801 the settlers
at the Hawkesbury sought his aid to extricate
themselves from the state of hopeless insolvency,
to which their dissolute and drunken habits had
reduced them. The particular means which they
suggested for their relief was "one year's suspension
of the Civil Courts of Judicature," so that it should
be impossible for creditors to obtain judgments, and
effect executions on their property. King met this
questionable proposal with a severe rebuke, but
expressed the hope that their creditors would not
be very harsh, as he feared the effects on the development of agriculture. There was perhaps more excuse
for the Hawkesbury settlers' demand than would at
first sight appear, for the improvidence and reckless
dissipation of the people had bred a class of equally
disreputable usurers, who lost no opportunity of
battening on the follies of their fellow colonists.
In 1804 the abuses of usury had reached such
dimensions, that King fixed the rate of interest
at 8 per cent., and ordered that all persons
attempting to extort more were to forfeit "treble
the value, to be appropriated to such fund as the
Governor may direct." King at this period was
very much inconvenienced by the want of a qualified
legal adviser, a want which repeated requests to the
Secretary of State failed to remove. The Judge-
Advocate was an illiterate and dissipated retired
officer, and King in 1803 complained that from the
judgments of the Court there "has scarce been a
cause without an appeal, which takes up too much
of the Governor's time," as he had himself to decide

in all such cases.   The military officers, composing the jury no doubt gave decisions to the satisfaction of their own consciences, but many were
of such an extraordinary character that law and
justice fell into contempt.

As with all his predecessors from the foundation of
the colony, the military were a source of continual
trouble.   They had always regarded the civil power
with no friendly eyes, and King's activity in connection with the suppression of the liquor traffic still
further estranged them.   In 1802 certain officers of
the New South Wales Corps made unfounded charges
against the officers of the French discovery ships
under Baudin, then in port, and were compelled by
the Governor to apologise; by this unfortunate occurrence things were brought to a head, and Paterson,
the Colonel of the corps, endeavoured to bring King
to his knees by means of the very instructions which
the Governor had been so zealous in enforcing.   The
words of the Commander-in-chief with regard to
military traders were that no officer was to be
"permitted on any account whatever to engage
in the cultivation of farms or any other occupation to detach them from their military duty";
Paterson, therefore, objected to the employment by
the Governor of any officers in any other way than
that specified.   The naval officer, or collecter of
customs, and a gentleman who acted as military
and civil engineer were affected, so King at once
dispensed with their services, thanking them for the
efficient manner in which they had always performed
their duties.   But he did not stop here.   Paterson

was informed that the guard which had usually attended the Governor was no longer required, and a paymaster who had been a magistrate was removed from the commission of the peace, while the Governor himself, as Commander-in-chief of New South Wales, directed "that no officer or soldier in the territory be employed on any other than their military duty." The places of the guard were filled by convicts pardoned for the purpose, and the position of artillery instructor and engineer was conferred on an officer who had been transported from India for killing his antagonist in a duel. Phillip had managed the military by patience and tact, and Hunter had succumbed to them; but King gained his end by showing them that he was quite indifferent as to whether he received their support or not. At the same time King pointed out to the Secretary of State that it was by no means desirable that the Governor should be so utterly dependent on one regiment, and suggested that a small force of artillery should be despatched to the colony. It is only fair to the New South Wales Corps to add, that when real need of their services presently occurred on account of insurrection of the convicts, they displayed a loyalty and devotion to duty beyond all praise.

The position of Governor was in these days certainly no sinecure, and few of those who fearlessly performed what they considered to be right were able to long withstand the hostility which their action could not fail to excite, and the terrible strain which the responsibility and isolation of their office entailed. King's health gave way, and the craving for peace and the opportunity to disprove the numberless, malicious, and groundless charges against him which his enemies showered upon their friends in England, induced him to resign. The effects of the good work done were lost sight of in the turbulent times which followed, but the noble fight he made against the difficulties and dangers which had proved insuperable to Hunter was crowned with a large measure of success, and the lofty ideal of duty, which was the load-star of his whole career, made him a fitting successor to his friend and mentor Phillip.

V.

THE DEPOSITION OF GOVERNOR BLIGH.

(1806–1810.)

CAPTAIN WILLIAM BLIGH was appointed to fill King's place, and entered on his short but eventful government in August, 1806. He was unfortunate in the time of his arrival, for the colony after a period of prosperity was suffering severely from a terrible flood, which in March of that year had swept down the Hawkesbury valley, carrying flocks, herds, crops, and homesteads before it. The Hawkesbury settlers, who had always been the most prosperous in the settlement, were ruined and hopeless, and about fifteen hundred persons out of a total population of the colony of 7,500, were for the time reduced to the verge of starvation, and had to be supported by the Government, or the charity of their fellows. The loss of the grain crops made it expedient to reduce the ration from the Government store, and the irritation caused by King's measures to suppress the liquor traffic and monopoly was increased by the apprehension and depression consequent upon the flood.

CAPTAIN BLIGH.

The community was still disturbed by rumours of insurrection, and in February, 1807, a serious plot was discovered. The *Sydney Gazette*, the semi-official paper, thus describes the conspiracy: "We are happy to announce to the public that by extreme vigilance the most atrocious and wicked plan of insurrection has been averted. It was planned in a most secret manner by some designing Irish prisoners, who had artfully instilled into the minds of their countrymen a certainty of taking the country and gaining their liberty. But their means to accomplish those ends were most horrid ; they were to have destroyed the Governor. . . . The New South Wales Corps were to have been surprised ; the leading gentlemen of the colony were to have been killed at the same time ; the *Porpoise* and shipping were to have been seized ; and a general massacre was to have taken place, so far as to have secured their intended purposes. Such was the nature of this diabolical plot, when the ringleaders were taken at the same moment by a party of the New South Wales Corps, whose soldier-like conduct, loyalty, and regard for their king and country, deserves the highest praise that can be bestowed upon them. This rising of the croppies, as it is called, has been more or less in agitation for a long time, they having forgot the calamitous consequences of their insurrection in 1804 ; and we have further to lament the infatuation of these men, when at the present moment they are, particularly, living under greater comforts than fall to the lot of the labouring poor of any part of the world."

The history of Bligh's rule is little but a record of the events which led up to his arrest ; before reviewing these it may be well to glance at the new governor's previous experience. Bligh had early in his career won distinction. After the bombardment of Copenhagen he had been publicly thanked by Nelson on the quarter-deck of the flag-ship, and on several other occasions he had shown himself able and gallant. The achievement which gained him most notoriety was the wonderful voyage of over 3,500 miles, which he made in an open boat after he had been deserted by the mutineers on his ship the *Bounty.* The perils of the voyage and the extraordinary skill with which he navigated his frail craft seemed to have diverted public attention from the events which had led, not only crew, but officers to seek by violence a release from his rule. The glamour of romance which surrounded his great voyage made him the hero of the hour, and when Sir Joseph Banks was consulted as to a fitting successor to King, Bligh's name at once occurred to him. Banks's letter to Bligh is of special interest, for it shows the inducements held out to the latter, and also the great influence the former had in the direction of matters affecting the colony. On March 15, 1805, the great botanist wrote :—

"MY DEAR SIR,—An opportunity has occurred this day which seems to me to lay open an opportunity of being of service to you, and, as I hope I never omit any chance of being useful to a friend whom I esteem as I do you, I lose not a moment of apprising you of it.

SIR JOSEPH BANKS, BART., K.B., P.R.S.

"I have always since the first institution of the new colony at New South Wales taken a deep interest in its success, and have been constantly consulted by his Majesty's ministers, through all the changes there have been in the department which directs it, relative to the more important concerns of the colonists.

"At present King the Governor is tired of his station, and well he may be so : he has carried into effect a reform of great extent which militated much with the interest of the soldiers and settlers there ; he is consequently disliked and much opposed, and has asked leave to return.

"In conversation I was this day asked if I knew a man proper to be sent out in his stead, one who has integrity unimpeached, a mind capable of providing its own resources in difficulties without leaning on others for advice, firm in discipline, civil in deportment, and not subject to whimper and whine when severity of discipline is wanted to meet (emergencies). I immediately answered, 'As this man must be chosen from among the post-captains I know of no one but Captain Bligh who will suit, but whether it will meet his views is another question.'

"I can, therefore, if you choose it, place you in the government of the new colony with an income of £2,000 a year, and with the whole of the Government power and stores at your disposal, so that I do not see how it is possible for you to spend £1,000 ; in truth, King, who is now there, receives only £1,000 with some deductions, and yet lives like a prince, and I believe saves some money ; but I could not undertake to recommend any one unless £2,000 clear was given, as I think that a man who undertakes so great a trust as the management of an important colony, should be certain of living well and laying up a provision for his family.

" I apprehend that you are about fifty-five years old, if so you have by the tables an expectation of fifteen years' life and in a climate like that, which is the best I know, a still better expectation, but in fifteen years £1,000 a year will at compound interest of 5 per cent have produced more than £30,000, and in case you should not like to spend your life there you will have a fair claim on your return to a pension of £1,000 a year. . . .

" Tell me, my dear sir, when you have consulted your pillow what you think of this. To me I confess it appears a promising place for a man who has entered late into the status of post-captain, and the more so as your rank will go on ; for Phillip the Governor is now an admiral, holding a pension for his services in the country."

The troubles which culminated in the disastrous termination of Bligh's government were almost entirely attributable to the lack of those very qualifications in the Governor which Banks enumerates in his letter as essential to the successful tenure of the post. Had Bligh been a little more " civil in deportment," had he depended a little less on the advice of others, and had all his actions been such as to preserve his integrity from assault by his enemies, he probably would have had no difficulty in compelling the respect of his subjects while faithfully performing the duties of his office. Unfortunately, when he had only been a few days in the colony he disclosed the flaw in his character. The stories of his sayings and doings indicate boorishness and violence of temper which might easily, in a less difficult position, have been his undoing. In a private letter from a gentleman occupying the responsible position of naval officer it is stated that Bligh, going " to church in full uniform, conjectured that the soldiers laughed at him. . . . . He abused the soldiers in the church and had a whole bench of them confined for some days, but thought proper to liberate them without trial." At the end of the first year of Bligh's rule the same person wrote that—"It is completely the reign of Robespierre or that of terror. . . . He destroys and makes away with all private property, saying everything is his ; . . . in short, everybody is in a state of dread. . . . Such, then, is the land we exist in (not live) ; how long it can remain in such a state I know not, but I think not long." Other evidence to the same effect is not wanting in the correspondence of the time, but what has been quoted is sufficient to show that within twelve months of the assumption of government Bligh had earned a reputation for coarse and passionate abuse of power. The immediate occasion of his overthrow was John Macarthur, who had some time previously resigned his commission and thrown himself heart and soul into his fine wool enterprise. Before Bligh had been a week in the colony, he had insulted Macarthur by asserting in a particularly offensive way that the land which had been granted him had been obtained by fraud, and from that time

forward relations between the two men were by no
means friendly. Bligh would seem to have done all
in his power to harass Macarthur, and Macarthur
showed no inclination to submit tamely to what he
considered injustice. Amongst other speculations of
the latter was a schooner which traded to and from
the islands, and it so happened that a convict, unknown to Macarthur, escaped in his vessel. Macarthur
was summoned before the Judge-Advocate, under an
old general order to prevent the escape of convicts,
and fined, but he declined to pay the fine on the
grounds that he was unintentionally and unwittingly
an offender. The schooner was promptly seized to
satisfy the judgment, and Macarthur determined to
abandon her to the officers of the court. When the
Government took possession of his schooner Macarthur
ceased supplying provisions for the crew, and, as the
Government gave them nothing, they were compelled
to come ashore. But a port order forbade the crew
of a vessel to land without special permission, under
which they were arrested and tried for the offence.
They pleaded that the exigencies of their position
necessitated their landing, and that, had Macarthur
provided them with food, they would not have left their
ship. Atkins, the Judge-Advocate, immediately issued
a warrant for Macarthur's arrest for causing them to
commit an illegal act, and he was seized by a body of
armed police and committed to take his trial before
the criminal court by a bench of magistrates, over
whom Atkins presided. On the 5th of January, 1808,
Macarthur appeared before the court, which consisted
of a jury of six officers of the New South Wales Corps

and the Judge-Advocate as president.   After the jury
had been sworn, and as Atkins was about to take the
oath, Macarthur objected.   He stated that he had
vainly tried to obtain a copy of the indictment against
him, and that he had appealed to the Governor to
appoint a disinterested person to preside at the trial
in the place of Atkins, but that he had been refused.
He besought the court to protect him, and grant him
at least a fair trial.   He gave numerous reasons why
Atkins should not preside, and closed a passionate
appeal with the assertion that Atkins and an emancipated attorney named Crossley had conspired to ruin
and destroy him—" I have the proof in my hands in
the writing of Crossley (here it is, gentlemen ; it was
dropped from the pocket of Crossley and brought to
me)."   Atkins failing to prevent the reading of the
protest, adjourned the court, and hurriedly left ; Macarthur, however, went on to assert that he was in fear
of his life, and, refusing to give bail, asked for a guard
to protect his person, a request which was granted by
the court.   During the rest of the day the officers
forming the court were in constant communication
with the Governor.   They supported Macarthur's
claim for a disinterested president, but Bligh refused
to listen to them.   Again they requested that some
one should be appointed to act instead of Atkins, but
the only reply was a demand for the papers relating
to the trial, so that they could be delivered to Atkins.
The officers declined to give up the papers except to
a new president.   Bligh responded by demanding,
" finally in writing, whether you will deliver up these
papers or not."   The officers expressed their willing-

ness to give attested copies, but refused to part with the originals until the trial was completed. Bligh then sent a message to Major Johnston, who commanded the New South Wales Corps, desiring to see him at once ; Johnston returned an answer that he was too ill to leave his house or write. Early on the morning of the 26th Macarthur was arrested on a warrant and lodged in gaol, and the court again appealed for an impartial president, asking for Macarthur's release to the bail which they had granted. Bligh returned no answer, but issued the following summons to each of the officers composing the court :—

> "The Judge-Advocate having presented a memorial to me in which you are charged with certain crimes, you are therefore hereby required to appear before me at Government House at nine o'clock to-morrow morning to answer in the premises. Given under my hand and seal at Government House, Sydney, this 26th day of January, 1808."

A letter was also sent to Johnston informing him that six of his officers had been summoned for " treasonable practices." The position seemed too serious for delay, so Johnston, in spite of his indisposition, hastened to Sydney. " On my arrival," he stated during his trial in England, " as I passed through the streets everything denoted terror and consternation ; I saw in every direction groups of people with soldiers amongst them, apparently in deep and earnest conversation. I immediately repaired to the barracks, and in order to separate the military from the people, made the drum beat to orders." The excitement was intense. A clamorous crowd surged round Johnston in the barrack-square and urged him to at once release Macarthur and depose the Governor, and an order directing the release of the former was despatched. Macarthur, as he walked, attended by his friends, from the gaol to the barracks, was plainly visible from the windows of Government House, and Bligh, possibly warned by previous experience, realised that he had gone too far, and at once prepared for flight. Meanwhile in the barrack-square a petition was drawn up praying Johnston to take command of the colony. It ran as follows :—

" SIR,—The present alarming state of this colony, in which every man's property, liberty, and life are endangered, induces us most earnestly to implore you instantly to place Governor Bligh under arrest, and to assume command of the colony. We pledge ourselves at a moment of less agitation to come forward to support the measure with our fortunes and our lives."

Johnston yielded to their importunities and at once acted. A few officers were sent to request the Governor to resign, and Johnston followed at the head of the corps to Government House. At first Bligh was not to be found ; the house was therefore searched from kitchen to garret, and eventually he was discovered in an upper bedroom under circumstances which have been the subject of much controversy, some asserting that he showed cowardice, and others that he was not himself hiding under a bed, but was attempting to conceal certain papers. To both theories there is objection. It is indeed hard to believe that a man of unsullied honour and a reputation for exceptional bravery should have proved a coward on this occasion ; but, on the other hand, no papers which there could be any particular object in concealing were ever found or again alluded to. Possibly the man with courage to do great deeds in honourable warfare may have quailed before the wrath of those who had at last been goaded beyond endurance by his injustice and tyranny. How far Bligh was the dupe of his friends it is hard to say. Crossley, who was "the principal adviser to the Governor," was convicted at various times of forgery, perjury, and other offences. Atkins, who was also an adviser, was described by Bligh himself, in a despatch to the Secretary of State, as a man "accustomed to inebriety, the ridicule of the community, pronouncing sentence of death in moments of intoxication, of weak determination, and floating and infirm opinions." Grose, another friend, was also of bad repute ; in fact, the only two respectable advisers he seems to have had were Campbell and Palmer, and of the former it will be remembered that he had fallen foul of King on account of his attempts to import spirits.

After his capture Bligh was placed under arrest, and Johnston assumed the reigns of government. He dismissed all those who had served under Bligh, and appointed his friends in their places ; but, beyond this, few changes were made in the general administration of affairs. No illegal indulgence of the military, similar to that permitted by Grose, was sanctioned, and Johnston seems to have honestly and fearlessly obeyed the instructions he found in the despatches from the Secretary of State, and to have done his utmost to prevent the importation of spirits and smuggling. On the 28th of July Lieutenant-Governor Colonel Foveaux arrived in the colony. He was on his way to assume command of Norfolk Island, and was ignorant of the events that had passed at Sydney. He now undertook the government of New South Wales, in the room of Colonel Johnston, but made no changes.

Governor Bligh was confined in his house, with the permission of only sometimes walking in the garden attended by a military guard. The *Porpoise* was despatched to Van Dieman's Land for Paterson, who superseded Foveaux as senior military officer, and continued to suppress the liquor traffic and illicit distillation. Bligh was still under arrest, although he was treated with respect and his comfort was consulted as much as possible, but he lost no opportunity of endeavouring to stir up his friends to reinstate him in the government. At the commencement of 1809 Paterson determined to send Bligh, Johnston, and Macarthur to England to answer for their conduct ; and consented, at Bligh's earnest solicitation, to permit him to sail in H.M.S. *Porpoise*, on condition that he signed a declaration that he would " neither touch at nor return to this territory until he shall have received his Majesty's instructions or those of his ministers." Bligh readily

signed, but as readily broke his covenant.   No sooner
had he set foot on the deck of the *Porpoise*, and was
out of Paterson's reach, than he levelled proclamation
after proclamation at the heads of the persons who
had participated in his deposition.   A little incident
which occurred when Bligh went on board is recorded
in the evidence given by Lieutenant Kent, who commanded the *Porpoise*, and throws a strong light on the
manner of man the deposed Governor was.   "He told
me with extreme violence," says Kent, "if I knew
my duty, the moment the guns were on board the
Porpoise that I should begin and batter the town of
Sydney until such time as they delivered him up the
government.   I replied I did not conceive my duty
led me to sacrifice so many innocent lives.   He then
flew into a most violent rage, and told me that one
day or other he would make me repent not knowing
my duty."   Bligh, to use Paterson's words, "in direct
violation of his word of honour as an officer and a
gentleman solemnly pledged thereto" did not steer
for England, but remained about the coast endeavouring to create disorder.   The danger of serious trouble
being caused by his presence was a real one, for there
were many persons who had benefited by his humane
exertions to relieve the distress caused by the Hawkesbury flood, as well as some influential and honourable
settlers who deemed no abuse of power a justification
for an insurrectionary movement such as that adopted
by Johnston and his friends, and were willing and
ready to aid Bligh in an attempt to reassert his government.   One gentleman let his loyalty so far outweigh
his discretion as to write a letter to Foveaux express-

7

ing contempt for the existing *régime.* " On Thursday
morning at ten," says the *Sydney Gazette,* " the court
assembled, when Mr. George Suttor, of Baulkham Hills,
settler, was placed at the bar and indicted for having
directed to his Honour the Lieutenant-Governor a
letter, containing certain contumelious expressions,
with intent to bring into contempt his Honour's
authority in this territory, &c. The indictment being
gone through and Mr. Suttor being called upon to
plead, he replied, ' Gentleman, I deny the legality of
this court ; you may do with myself as you please ;
my unfortunate wife and family I leave to the mercy
of God, until peace shall be restored in the colony : I
have nothing more to say.'

" The Judge-Advocate then addressed the prisoner
as follows : ' Mr. Suttor, you are called upon to
plead to your indictment ; and whatever you may
have to offer in your defence will be attentively considered. I again ask : are you guilty or not guilty ? '

" *Prisoner.* Sir, all that I have to say I have
already said. I deny the legality of this court. My
allegiance is due to Governor Bligh, and Governor
Bligh alone ; and every drop of blood within my veins
prevents me from ever acknowledging the legality of
this court. You may do with me as you think proper.'

" *Judge-Advocate.* Mr. Suttor, it is my duty to
acquaint you that it is provided by Act of Parliament
that in case a prisoner shall refuse to plead to his
indictment, the effect will be the same as if he pleaded
guilty. Once more I call upon you—are you guilty
or not guilty ? '

" *Prisoner.* I stand as before ; I have said all I

have to say ; you are to do with me as you think proper.'

" The court was ordered to be cleared, and in about twenty minutes re-opened, when the Judge-Advocate addressed the prisoner as follows : Prisoner at the bar, in consequence of your refusal to plead to your indictment, the court, in conformity to Act of Parliament, have found you guilty, and sentence you to be imprisoned six calendar months, and to pay a fine of one shilling.' "

Nothing of any very great importance occurred during the rule of Paterson, who continued to direct affairs until the arrival of Governor Macquarie. Kent and Johnston were after much delay tried in England for the share they had taken in the arrest and deposition of Bligh, and the former was honourably acquitted. The court martial on Johnston after a lengthy investigation " were of opinion that Lieut.-Col. Johnston is guilty of the act of mutiny described in the charge, and do therefore sentence him to be cashiered." Macarthur was not brought to trial, but suffered a severe punishment, the Government refusing to give their consent to his return to New South Wales. For eight long years he strove to obtain permission to return to his home and family, but indignantly refused to accept any concession based on an acknowledgment of guilt. He maintained that he possessed irrefutable proof of Bligh's peculations, and only asked for an opportunity to produce them ; unfortunately such opportunity never arose. At the beginning of 1817 his importunity prevailed, and he was granted the permission to go back, for which he had so long and earnestly craved.

VI.

THE EMANCIPISTS.

(1810-1822.)

THE deposition of Bligh had been an extremely popular move, but the enthusiasm which had overcome Johnston's scruples cooled rapidly when the cause of irritation disappeared. Men began to realise the serious character of the action they had taken, and to speculate about the probable reception of the news in England. Bligh's misdeeds lost colour by the lapse of time, whilst, on the other hand, besides the usual causes of estrangement attendant on the office of governor in a society in which the domestic details of the inhabitants' lives were matters of state concern, surrounded, as they were, by their supporters in the late stirring events, all of whom considered that they had a just claim to particular recognition, the military administrators of necessity gave offence in many quarters.

It was, then, with a feeling of relief, that the greater part of the population welcomed Macquarie. By his

arrival the suspense at any rate was ended, and there
was good reason to hope that Bligh's mishaps would
have warned those in authority in England to be
more careful in future in their selection of governors.
The military officers and others hastened to worship
the rising sun with an alacrity which augured well
for the peace of the settlement, and, if feeling about
the past still ran high, there appeared to be on all
sides a desire to avoid a repetition of unhappy disturbances. Macquarie had been instructed to reinstate Bligh for twenty-four hours, to express His
Majesty's unqualified disapproval of Johnston's behaviour, to send that officer home under close arrest,
and to immediately relieve the 102nd Regiment,
formerly the New South Wales Corps. In the
absence of Bligh, who was still hovering about the
coast of Tasmania in H.M.S. *Porpoise*, the first part
of these instructions could not be carried out, but
Macquarie's own regiment, the 73rd, under Col.
O'Connell, had accompanied the new governor, and
at once took over the military duties with the assistance of an auxiliary force specially enrolled in the
colony under the title of the Royal Veteran Company.
All the appointments made since Bligh's deposition
were annulled, and the persons who had occupied the
positions previous to that event were reinstated.
Bligh was sent for, and on his return was received
with honour, and to all appearances general amity
prevailed until his departure for England. Nevertheless the signal failure of two public meetings,
which were called by the late governor's friends in the
hope of strengthening his hands in the anticipated

THE OLD TANK STREAM, SYDNEY.

investigation into the causes of the mutiny, show that his offences were bitterly remembered.

Macquarie immediately set about reform, whilst his energy in exploration, and the construction of public works, did much to awaken a lasting spirit of enterprise in the community. Unfortunately his extreme personal vanity made it almost impossible for him to benefit by the experience of others, or accept advice even from the most trustworthy sources. Thus the very fact of Marsden, the chaplain, urging the necessity of building barracks for female convicts at Parramatta, so that the women might be under some sort of control, was quite sufficient to prevent Macquarie from doing it. Neither money nor labourers were forthcoming to stem the horrible immorality and degradation at Parramatta, although the Governor did not scruple to spend a considerable sum on the erection of stables for his horses. Another instance of the grave errors which Macquarie occasionally made is found in the contract for erecting a hospital which he conceived to be immediately required. An agreement was signed by which three men, one of whom, D'Arcy Wentworth, was a prominent official, undertook to build it in consideration of a monopoly being granted them of the sale of spirits in the colony. As the Governor had just promulgated an order forbidding all government or military officials from trading and all persons from bartering spirits for produce, his action would in any case appear anomalous, but in the face of those very evils which had resulted from the liquor traffic, which it had required such stupendous exertions to conquer, it is truly incomprehensible. The "spirit contract" called forth severe censure from England, but nevertheless the building was actually erected by this means, and an already depraved society was still further degraded by the widespread influence of the nefarious transaction.

The colony about this time was beset with numerous dangers, both social and commercial. The assignment system, which had answered well enough when properly administered, had of late fallen into grave abuses. No discrimination had been shown in the allotment of servants, and many masters practically leased to the convicts assigned to them the liberty of which the law had expressly deprived them. This evil was somewhat modified by the recall of large numbers of the bond from private employers, so that they might be put on the public works and buildings which, under Macquarie's direction, were being pushed forward on all sides; at the same time the cost of the establishment was considerably increased, and the sudden withdrawal of labour from the country occasioned much loss.

Both internal and external trade had been growing more quickly than the population, and the more complicated and extended transactions were much hampered by the scarcity of a satisfactory medium of exchange. Some curious remedies were resorted to. In order to increase the metallic circulation, the centre of the Spanish dollar, the principal coin in use, was struck out, and thus two coins of a combined nominal value were more than equivalent to the unmutilated piece. Stringent regulations were also promulgated to enforce the acceptance of promissory notes and bills, which were issued in profusion by all manner of persons and were usually subject to a discount of about 50 per cent. Commercial transactions must have indeed been reduced to chaos by the combination of a debased metallic currency and the forced circulation of worthless paper.

The want of coin was augmented by the withdrawal of convict servants from private to government employ, and by the cessation in a great measure of the use of liquor for barter, brought about by the energy of Governor King. The "spirit contract" already alluded to directed the attention of the authorities in England to the whole question of allowances and concessions, the result being that in 1814 Lord Bathurst, who was then in charge of colonial affairs, took steps to put a stop to the practice of granting supplies from the public stores and assigning servants, victualled and clothed at the public expense, to officers of the Civil Government. In the following year the indulgences to the military, by which they had been permitted to purchase certain luxuries from the stores at prime cost, were discontinued, and the practice of issuing spirits to all officials and licensed publicans at a rate below the current market value was prohibited. The great growth of trade caused the establishment of the Bank of New South Wales in 1816, and three years later Macquarie instituted a savings bank, in the hope of encouraging thrift amongst the large class of small farmers and traders. Soon after the Governor's arrival the whole aspect of affairs had been changed by the achievements of Messrs. W. C. Wentworth, Lawson, and George Blaxland. The first was a son of D'Arcy Wentworth, whose name has already figured in these pages, and all three were interested in pastoral pursuits. When, in 1813, a severe drought visited the colony, and much loss and inconvenience was felt owing to the limited area of the pasture lands available to the rapidly increasing flocks and herds, these three men determined to make yet another attempt to pierce the mountain barrier, which had hitherto confined the settlers to a narrow strip of country by the coast. After a journey, during which they had to contend with almost insurmountable difficulties, they reached a point from which the promising country just beyond the range could be seen; on their return the value of the discovery was fully recognised. Macquarie, ever ready to encourage exploration, at once sent Surveyor Evans to complete the investigations commenced by Wentworth and his friends. Evans successfully crossed the watershed and found the first Australian inland river which he named the Macquarie, but, his immediate object being attained and provisions running short, he turned back. So favourable was his report of the country beyond the barrier that a road was commenced, and in 1815 the Governor and a large suite crossed the mountains to inspect the new territory, which had been called Bathurst Plains.

A settlement was formed, and Evans, making this the base of operations, started again on his travels. When another river flowing west was discovered, the belief gained favour that the two streams emptied themselves into a great mediterranean sea. A party was formed under Surveyor-General Oxley to test the hypothesis, but, after following the course of first one and then the other river, it was found that they only led into uninviting swamps. The spirit of exploration had been aroused by Wentworth's success, and in 1814 a lad named Hamilton Hume and his brother, attended by a native, traversed the country around Berrima, reaching the tablelands more to the south. Three years later Hume and Meehan found Lakes George and Bathurst and the Goulburn Plains, so that the area of lands suitable for both pastoral and agricultural expansion appeared practically unlimited. The knowledge of the coastline was also being perfected by Captain Phillip P. King, a son of the Governor of that name, and Allan Cunningham, a botanist, who between 1817 and 1820 were constantly at work in the cutter *Mermaid*. It was supposed that Lake Bathurst had some outlet leading to the sea, and an effort to decide the point led to one of those catastrophes from which fortunately the explorers of this period were exceptionally free. Captain Stewart set out in a boat with a few followers to seek along the coast the expected opening, but in Twofold Bay the boat was lost, and the whole party, while trying to reach Sydney overland, was cut off and murdered by the natives. The colonists lost no time in turning the discoveries to practical account, sheep and cattle being driven out on the new pastures in all directions. With the extension of settlement their troubles with the natives increased, though in most instances the Europeans were the aggressors. Far from control, the worst passions of a degraded class had full play, and brutal outrages on natives were of common occurrence, provoking terrible acts of retaliation from the tribe of those wronged. The natives, finding the animals on which they subsisted becoming scarce in the country invaded by the settlers, committed thefts of corn, vegetables, and stock from the farms, and, in order to punish them, raids were organised by the colonists, in which every native they met was indiscriminately butchered. Men, women, and children, quite innocent of the offence, were ruthlessly shot down, if not at the instigation, at any rate with the tacit consent, of the Government. It is true that Macquarie made some half-hearted attempts to civilise the blacks by establishing a school for native children at Parramatta and holding annual conferences with the chiefs ; but woebetide all those who neglected to obey his invitation or commands, for an order went forth that they should be captured or "destroyed" as soon as found. At intervals a small military force was despatched to "disperse" a more than usually turbulent tribe, and the race, who had for so long dwelt in the land, rapidly vanished before the hand of the white man.

The events which caused Macquarie's rule to be one of the most important periods in the history of Australia are connected with the change which was taking place in the composition of the community, for both Bligh and Macquarie owed their downfall in a great degree to their inability to cope with a social problem which had not presented itself with anything approaching the same force to the other governors. As the numbers of those who had become free by pardon or servitude increased, they became a new and important factor in society, and the question arose as to what position this new class was to occupy. Did a pardon or the expiration of a sentence completely wipe out all former disgrace, or was every man who had been convicted to be regarded by the law and by society as tainted for all time?

Bligh does not seem to have had any very strong opinions on these points, although by his actions he favoured the emancipists; but Macquarie's whole conduct was guided by the determination to, if possible, raise those, who had expiated their misdeeds, to the position which they had originally occupied in life. The colony, as he pointed out, had been established in a large measure in the hope of reforming as well as punishing the criminal, and the value of reformation would be incomplete were not restitution the reward of repentance. On the other hand, those opposed to this principle urged that, were ex-convicts permitted to occupy posts of honour and reward, transportation would lose half its value as a deterrent from crime; that as a matter of fact the emancipist class was mainly composed of those who showed no spirit of repentance for past sins and often led openly shameless and debauched lives; that it was impossible for those who had never been stained with crime to associate or permit their children to associate with men who had suffered the

degradation of conviction.   Do what you would, they
asserted, those who had felt the clutch of the law
could never be *free*, there was always that one
little letter, which called up all the past, and
the free firmly refused to accept the *freed* as their
peers.

In the case of Bligh the field was clear, and it
is not probable that, had he used discrimination in
the selection of the emancipists whom he wished to
employ or favour, his efforts to rehabilitate the de-
serving would have excited any serious opposition.
Unfortunately his choice was guided not so much
by personal merit as by utility.   Macquarie, however,
was encumbered from the outset by the disreputable
protégés of his predecessor.   First espousing their
cause under the direct influence of Bligh, he was
unwilling to admit that he had been duped, and
clung with stubborn persistence to those whose
actions, he himself was compelled to admit, marked
them as the most despicable of mankind.   By this
means he placed a weapon in the hands of his
opponents ; they were enabled to disregard the just
aspirations of the emancipated as a class, when the
reputations of those selected by the Governor as
representatives of that class stank in the not too
sensitive nostrils of the community.   Macquarie's
methods were unfortunate.   He hurled commands
and threats broadcast about matters which should
have been approached with delicacy and tact.   His
efforts to force his emancipist friends into the society
of free men first provoked the military to insult
them, and then led him into serious quarrels with

Marsden, who refused to sit with them on the bench or as co-trustee, and Ellis Bent, who declined to allow them to practice in his court. The first-named should have been a valuable councillor, and the second, as judge of the newly-created Supreme Court, which had superseded the old military tribunal in 1814, was the most important official in the colony next to the Governor himself. The emancipists, by fulsome flattery and ostentatious gratitude played upon a character naturally vain, until Macquarie, in the heat of the strife, disappointed by his failure to reform those who had fallen beyond the reach of help, was led into extravagances which it is hard to believe he would have committed, had not his judgment been greatly warped. Tales of strange doings in the colony had been finding their way to England for some time, but the crisis came when the Governor ordered some persons who had never been bond to be flogged by the public castigator without trial, for trespassing in the grounds of Government House. The punishment was carried out, but both in the colony and in England it was seen that the time had come when a stop must be put to the vagaries of the Governor.

In 1818 a special commissioner, Mr. Bigge, was despatched to make a searching inquiry into the condition of the colony and the general administration of the Government, and on receipt of his report in 1821 Macquarie was recalled. Although he had failed to re-organise society, and crime and vice were still appallingly prevalent at his departure, the colony had grown enormously in wealth, population, and importance. The settlement, on which he so reluctantly turned his back in February, 1822, was a very different place from that which he had approached with such benevolent intentions twelve years before.

VII.

THE RULE OF BRISBANE AND DARLING.

(1822–1831.)

THE reports of Mr. Commissioner Bigge had
attracted a good deal of attention in England, and
the Government determined to reform the administration of New South Wales in accordance with his
recommendations. As Bigge had been compelled to
condemn in a great measure the policy of Macquarie,
it was clearly impossible to use that gentleman as the
instrument with which to carry out the changes ; Sir
Thomas Brisbane, a man of less pronounced views,
was therefore selected for the duty. Brisbane arrived
in November, 1821, but, pending the determination of
the new constitution, then under consideration, he
attempted no important reforms but contented himself with gradually weeding the public offices of the
most undesirable of the emancipists who had been
appointed by his predecessor. In the unsettled state
of affairs he was particularly anxious to avoid being
drawn into the class quarrels which so deeply troubled
the community, and for a time he escaped, by retiring
to Parramatta, where an observatory was built and he

was able to devote himself with but little interruption to his favourite science, astronomy. The changes which were made in the constitution, however, compelled him before long to return to Sydney and take his part in the turmoil of political life.

The New South Wales Judicature Act received the Royal Assent in July, 1823, and embodied most of Bigge's suggestions. A Supreme Court and Court of Record was established and the jury principle was introduced, the qualification being fixed at 50 acres or a dwelling worth £300. A Legislative Council of not more than seven nor less than five members, nominated by the Crown, was created, but the actions of the Governor were left untrammelled and he could do whatever seemed to him best irrespective of the advice of the Council. Should it disapprove the course followed, its objections were to be recorded and transmitted to England where a final decision would be made. It was provided that no tax should be imposed for other than local purposes, the power of the Governor to levy duties was confirmed, and sundry other matters were dealt with connected with details of administration.

The Chief Justice under the new Act was Mr. Francis Forbes, who had served on the Bench in Newfoundland, and Mr. Saxe-Bannister was appointed first Attorney-General. Both gentlemen arrived early in 1824, and a court was opened without delay. The advent of Forbes, who was a man of strong feelings, soon caused the Governor to become involved in one of the disputes which so frequently took place between the more prominent members of the community. Marsden alleged that a Dr. Douglas had committed very serious irregularities in his capacity of magistrate, and Douglas responded by charging Marsden with cruelty and excessive severity on the Bench.

Brisbane, under the influence of Forbes, took an active part in the strife, which waxed fiercer and fiercer until the air was full of recriminations. The Attorney-General recommended and Marsden demanded that the whole question should be investigated, but the Chief Justice, who had more friendship for than faith in Douglas, did not desire an inquiry. He therefore persuaded the Governor to introduce a Bill to indemnify magistrates for actions committed "in the execution of their office." Saxe-Bannister was instructed to draft the Bill, but declined to have any hand in a measure to indemnify so horrible a practice as torture to extort confession, and Brisbane was compelled to seek assistance elsewhere. The Bill eventually became law, but the successful attempt to burke inquiry into charges of such gravity created a profound impression and excited on all sides expressions of strong disapprobation. One of the chief parts of Bigge's scheme was the introduction of free immigrants who could be settled on the soil, to whom convicts could be safely entrusted, thereby removing the necessity for the employment of large gangs of criminals in the towns. Grants of land and servants were offered to persons willing to come to Australia, and during Brisbane's administration large numbers of young men arrived, for the most part possessed of capital, who at once engaged in pastoral pursuits. Great progress was made and the country rapidly became covered with the increasing flocks and herds of the colonists. The distribution of the population over such a large area, however, bred some evils. Convicts frequently escaped, and two or three, banding themselves together, committed horrible crimes and lived by plundering the farms of the settlers. At length the robbers became such a serious scourge that it was necessary to enrol a special force to protect the sparsely populated districts, and the mounted police were formed from the regiments in the colony. By their perfect discipline and great courage they did yeoman service, and for some time successfully held the bushrangers in check.

The immigration of free settlers soon produced an effect upon society, and New South Wales became less and less like an overgrown gaol. The relative importance of the emancipated class was reduced, and the introduction of an instalment of free institutions rendered the administration of justice less capricious and the rights of the inhabitants more secure. But Brisbane and his Council, in their eagerness to welcome the salutary change, took a step which the Governor within twelve months regretted, and which created inextricable difficulties for his successor. The only newspaper in the colonies when Brisbane arrived was the *Sydney Gazette*, a semi-official organ and the medium of all Government announcements, all contributions being carefully scrutinised by the authorities previous to publication. In October, 1824, Brisbane came to the conclusion that the censorship of the press could be safely abolished, and issued a general order to that effect. Almost immediately other prints sprang into life, the most prominent being the *Monitor* and the *Australasian,* in the columns of which William Charles Wentworth, who had recently returned from England after being called to the Bar, and another barrister, Dr. Wardell, warmly espoused the emancipist cause, and gave voice, often in immoderate tones, to the demand for still further concessions in the direction of popular government.   So violent were the writings in these papers and so dangerous their influence upon the minds of the convicts that Brisbane, in January, 1825, less than four months after the concession of freedom, felt it necessary to obtain the consent of the Secretary of State to the enactment of some measure which would bring the press again under the control of the Government; but before Lord Bathurst's answer was received Brisbane had resigned office, and Sir Ralph Darling had been appointed in his stead.

The new Governor arrived in December, 1825, and his first act of importance was an attempt to deal with the newspaper question.   He was instructed to legislate at the earliest opportunity for the control of the press, making an annual license a preliminary to publication.   By the constitution of 1823 it had been provided that no Bill could become law until the certificate of the Chief Justice had been obtained to the effect that the proposed measure was not repugnant to the laws of England.   But Forbes, whose sympathies were with the cause advocated by the *Australasian,* hesitated to certify to a Bill directly aimed at that paper. At last, when it became plain that the necessary certificate could not be obtained for the Bill as sketched by the Secretary of State, Darling laid before his council two measures with the same object, to which however he hoped Forbes would have no objection. The first prescribed certain penalties for the publication of seditious or blasphemous matter, and the second imposed a duty on newspapers sufficient to raise its price to a figure beyond the reach of the greater part of the convict population. Both Acts were passed by the Council and promulgated, but in each instance Forbes refused to certify, and they had to be suspended. This action of the Chief Justice was severely criticised by the council and free settlers, and the newspapers which had so narrowly escaped burst forth with new vigour and violence. "You can have no idea," wrote Macarthur to his son in England, "of the operation of these firebrand papers upon the common people, and every one not connected with the convict interest admits that the most dangerous consequences are to be dreaded." The Governor, realising the impotence of his position as far as new legislation went, resolved to make an effort to curb the unbridled licence of the press by means already in existence, and instituted prosecutions for libel or slander whenever an opportunity occurred. But this only called forth more revilings from the papers, and the Government was drawn into an unseemly and violent wrangle, discreditable alike to Darling and the journalists. The ultimate results of these disputes will be dealt with presently, but it is necessary first to refer to some events of no small importance which occurred at this time.

In 1828 an amending Constitution Act was passed, the principal provisions of which were the abolition of the grand jury and the enactment that all offenders should be "prosecuted by information in the name of His Majesty's Attorney-General." The small council formed in 1823 was enlarged to fifteen members, and the scope of its legislative powers extended, while the necessity of obtaining the Chief Justice's certificate, which had caused so much trouble in the case of the Newspaper Acts, was removed. Darling at once introduced a Bill differing but little from the Act of 1827. The measure was certainly calculated to prevent seditious publications, but the provisions were ridiculously harsh and were modified a few years later at the instance of the Home Government.

The jury question was early dealt with by this new council, and a law passed excluding emancipists from serving in criminal trials, thus settling for the time the much vexed point of their eligibility to act as jurymen. By a rule of Court in the same year the professions of barrister and attorney were formally divided, and regulations governing admission to them first drawn up. Perhaps the best index of the growing wants of the community at this period of social development is afforded by the constant changes effected in the methods of administering justice; as the free population increased the machinery of the law was correspondingly elaborated.

The punishment of a murderer named Worrell was brought about in 1826 by such a curious sequence of events that it is worthy of special mention. Frederick Fisher, a freed convict, who lived at Campbell Town with Worrell, and was reputed to be possessed of considerable property, suddenly disappeared, and Worrell caused it to be supposed that he had gone to England. Worrell sold off Fisher's property and no one seems to have suspected foul play till one, Farley, declared that he had seen Fisher's ghost sitting on a rail not far from his old home. Oddly enough this story obtained listeners, and a police constable with two natives were set searching in the neighbourhood of the spot at which the vision was said to have appeared. Blood was found on the rail picked out by Farley as the ghost's seat, and one of the native blacks following the direction in which the ghost was said to have pointed went into a pool and, to quote the words of the constable's evidence, " took a cornstalk which he passed over the surface of the water, and put it to his nose," and said he "smelt the fat of a white man." The blacks then followed the creek leading from the pool till they came to a branch creek up which they went some little way when one of them put a rod into the ground and said, "There's something wrong here." Sure enough at this spot the body of Fisher was found. Worrell was tried and convicted, confessed to the murder, and was hanged ; but no satisfactory explanation of the apparition and the other strange circumstances attending the case has ever been supplied.

The flow of free immigration which commenced in 1822, continued unabated for the first few years of Darling's administration, and as a consequence the question of land grants called for attention. In 1826, regulations were framed with the object of rendering the support of assigned servants equivalent to payments for land; and in 1828, a Board was appointed to assist the Governor in dealing with the numerous applications which poured in. These reforms, combined with the discoveries of new and fertile territory, gave even greater impetus to pastoral settlement. The demand by the colonists became heavier than the supply, and one after another of the Government farms, which only a few years before had been all that stood between the population and famine, were broken up. The distribution of the bond over so large an area did much to check the horrible criminality which characterised the large gangs employed by Macquarie on the roads and public buildings.

In 1827, the mania for speculation in land and stock had become excessive, and cattle were sold for utterly fictitious prices. Unfortunately 1828 and the two following years were exceptionally dry. Grass and crops failed, stock died, and prices came tumbling down even lower than circumstances warranted. Free emigration abruptly ceased. The convicts' rations had to be reduced, and the colony passed through a severe commercial crisis. When rain came in 1830 the recovery was almost as violent as the disease, and farmers were unable to reap their crops owing to their inability to obtain sufficient labourers. But the days of scarcity left a legacy of crime, and bushranging assumed such serious dimensions that special legislation was necessary. Donohue and his gang infested the districts round Sydney, and in other parts of the country bands of robbers terrorised the settlers. On the 21st of April, 1830, the situation seemed so grave that the Council passed a Bushrangers Act through all its stages in one day, conferring extraordinary power on magistrates, and making other provisions which practically placed the country for the time almost under martial law.

According to Macarthur the effects of the Act were magical; but another enactment, the Newspaper Act already mentioned, passed in the same year, did not meet with equal approval ; and it was in a large measure the hostility created by it against the Governor that eventually brought about his recall. Although this was the cause, the particular event which was made the occasion of complaint was the alteration by the Governor of a sentence passed upon two soldiers named Sudds and Thompson. Soon after Darling's arrival he discovered that the prosperity of the emancipated convicts had filled their guards with envy, and that self-mutilations and the perpetration of crimes were common among the soldiery, who hoped thereby to escape further service and enter the happy ranks of the convicted. Two men who had mutilated themselves were sent by Darling's order to an out-station instead of being discharged, and a little later when two other soldiers, Sudds and Thompson, committed an offence with the avowed intention of escaping by transportation from the regiment and joining the convicts in Tasmania, Darling thought it high time to put a stop to such practices. The penalty of transportation was altered to labour on the roads in chains, a

sentence which did not relieve the men from further
military service on its completion, and they were
drummed out of the regiment in irons and the convict
garb.   Darling was unfortunate in the persons he
selected as examples.   Sudds, overcome by mortifica-
tion at his failure and the ignominy of his punishment,
appears to have deliberately moped and starved himself to death.   Sudds's fate was after several years
seized upon by Darling's enemies as grounds for
impeachment, and Wentworth in 1829, wrote a letter
to the Secretary of State with that object.   Meanwhile the local opposition press denounced the
Governor's brutality and barbarous cruelty, and
made assertions as to the weight of the irons and
other particulars which were certainly not in accordance with fact.   After numerous inquiries, in all of
which Darling was acquitted absolutely of any im-
proper conduct, the farce reached a climax in the
appointment of a select committee of the House of
Commons to investigate the charges.   On this occasion also, although every one who had ever had a
grievance against Darling hastened to bring charges,
the conduct of the Governor was pronounced to have
been "entirely free from blame."   But before these
events Darling had been recalled, and had left the
colony without much regret.   His departure was
made the occasion for a display of rejoicing by his
enemies which was much more discreditable to themselves than to the object of their spleen.

During the rule of Brisbane and Darling the work
of exploration went on steadily.   The Goulburn
river was discovered in 1822 during an attempt to

reach the Liverpool plains; and in the following years Captain Currie and Major Ovens struck the Murrumbidgee, and by following its course found the fertile district of Monaroo, while the indefatigable Allan Cunningham discovered the much-desired stock route to the Liverpool plains.

Although the coast to the southward of Sydney had been explored and charted by Flinders and others, the country inland remained quite unknown. In 1824, Sir Thomas Brisbane, in order to induce exploration, suggested that a party of convicts should be put ashore at Wilson's Promontory, and that a free pardon should be offered to those who successfully travelled to Sydney overland, Hamilton Hume, a young man born in the colony, being offered command of the expedition. This he declined, but at the same time consented to start from Sydney and journey overland to the south. His services were accepted, and a sailor named Hovell having volunteered to go with him, the two explorers set out from Lake George with six convicts and a large supply of provisions which they carried in two carts drawn by teams of bullocks. Until the Murrumbidgee was reached all went well, but the river was broader and the current stronger than they had expected to meet; crossing with difficulty by covering the bottoms of the carts with the tarpaulins, they converted them in this way into punts in which the stores were safely ferried. The men and oxen had to swim, but all reached the opposite bank without mishap and once more pushed forward. Soon the country on their line of march became so rough and thickly

timbered that the waggons were abandoned and the
oxen loaded instead. For days their way led
through forest so dense that little of the surrounding
country could be seen, but occasionally they caught
a glimpse of the snowy peaks of mountains on their
left. Perseveringly they journeyed on and at length
came to the banks of another river which is now
known as the Murray. Again boats were improvised,
this time of wickerwork, covered with the tarpaulins
and the obstacles successfully overcome. The
country was now more open, and holding their course
south-west they struck first the Ovens and then the
Goulburn rivers. They had now travelled far and
expected each day to come to the open sea, but time
slipped by and there was no change in the view of
eucalyptus-clad hills which stretched around them on
all sides as far as the eye could see. At last the
two leaders espying a more than usually lofty peak,
not far off, left the remainder of the party to rest a
few days in camp, and after encountering enormous
difficulties reached the summit of the mountain from
which they hoped to sight the waters of the Southern
Ocean. Their hearts failed them when looking to the
south nothing met their gaze but endless gum trees
stretching away into the distance ; and, naming the
place Mount Disappointment, they turned back and
rejoined their comrades at the camp. It was decided
to still push on, although in a slightly different
direction, and the weary travellers were in a few days
rewarded by the sight of what appeared to be a great
lake lying beyond beautifully grassy and park-like
country. Hovell declared that they had arrived at

Western Port, but Hume persisted that the bay was Port Phillip, and, as the two leaders both adhered to their opinion, a serious quarrel arose which still raged when the return journey to Sydney had been accomplished, and the leaders had been rewarded with grants of land and the rest of their party with freedom.

When between 1826 and 1828 a long stretch of exceptional drought had been experienced, it occurred to Darling that the marshes, which had so baffled Oxley when he had attempted to explore the country round the river Macquarie, would now probably be dried up, and an expedition would be able to penetrate the interior. He therefore appointed a party comprising Captain Stuart, Hume, two soldiers, and eight convicts to undertake the work. They were provided with portable boats with which it was expected they would be able to navigate the river, but on reaching the point at which Oxley had turned back, they found nothing but nauseous mud flats, and parched cracking ground from which the rushes grew so thickly that even with the greatest exertion it was almost impossible to make any headway. They therefore turned to the west, and after travelling through a level and uninteresting country in which there were evidences of frequent floods, they at length reached a river which they named the Darling, in honour of the Governor. For about ninety miles they followed its course, and then turning towards Sydney retraced their steps.

In the following year, Stuart again set forth, and this time took his portable boats to the Murrumbidgee,

where he, with Macleay as naturalist and eight convicts, embarked, and rowed steadily down the river.
After an eventful voyage, during which they were in
constant danger of being wrecked on snags, or cap-
sized by the rapid current, they shot forth on to a
broad river, the clear waters of which flowed gently
over a sandy bottom ; they drifted down-stream
during the day, and at sunset moored their boats
to the bank, and formed a camp on shore. They
had frequent intercourse with the natives at almost
every point where they touched, but with the
exception of some petty thefts no hostility was
shown towards them, and they always left the
black fellows on the most friendly terms. After
following the course of the Murray for about two
hundred miles below the point at which they had
emerged from the branch stream, they came to the
junction of another large river flowing from the north ;
this was not explored, as a short distance up they
found a fence erected across the river, apparently to
catch fish, and as Stuart was anxious not to displease
the natives he turned down stream again, and allowed
himself to drift further with the current. Eventually
the boat floated out on to a broad lagoon, which they
called Lake Alexandria, but on crossing it they discovered that the entrance from the ocean was blocked
by an impassable bar. Drifting down-stream was one
thing, but pulling back against the current quite
another, and, when day after day had to be spent
wearily at the heavy oars under a broiling sun, the
crew got thinner and thinner and more despondent,
until at last one man went mad, and it was only by

the greatest exertion that Stuart could prevent the
rest of his companions from throwing down their
oars and giving themselves up to despair. At last,
after a journey which seemed a life-time, they arrived
in occupied country once more, and rested at some
of the homesteads on the banks of the Murrumbidgee
until they were so far recovered as to be able to return
to Sydney. Two years later Major Mitchell suggested
that he should lead an expedition to the far north-
west, but an unfortunate affray with the natives
resulted in the death of two of his men and the loss
of his stores, so that a hasty retreat had to be made
to the point of departure. In 1835 another attempt
was made to pierce the interior, but on this occasion
again it had to be abandoned, owing to the murder
of Cunningham, the botanist of the party, and the
determined hostility of the natives who barred further
progress. .Having failed in a north-westerly direction,
in 1836 Major Mitchell started to the south. Following the Lachlan to its junction with the Murrumbidgee,
he formed a depôt, from which excursions were made
into the surrounding country, but here again his
operations were seriously impeded by attacks from
large bodies of natives. At length Mitchell crossed
the Murray and entered a country so fertile and
beautiful that he was unable to adequately express
his praise of it. Passing along the Grampians he
came to the river Glenelg, and here launching the
portable boats which they had brought with them
the party drifted down-stream. The scenery on either
side was exquisite, and the vegetation most luxuriant ;
but they were stopped eventually, as Stuart had been,

by a sandy bar which blocked the mouth of the river, and, having landed, they went a little way to the east along the shore, and then turning back traversed the country towards Portland Bay. Here, to Mitchell's astonishment, he suddenly came upon a house with all the signs of prosperity and occupation about it, while a small vessel rode at anchor in the bay. This turned out to be the settlement of the brothers Henty, who were the first colonists who crossed to the Port Phillip district from Van Diemen's Land. Mitchell, after having rested, ascended Mount Macedon from which he was able to view the park-like expanse which induced him to name the district " Australia Felix."

VIII.

CHANGES IN THE CONSTITUTION.

(1831–1846.)

ON the 3rd of December, 1831, Sir Richard Bourke landed and was presented with numerous addresses more or less extravagant in tone. The unpopularity of Darling with a section of the community caused the welcome to his successor to be exceptionally cordial. The new governor was, however, a man of ability; fulsome flattery combined with abuse of his predecessor failed to make him commit himself to either the "emancipist" or the "exclusive" parties. There were several matters of considerable importance to be dealt with foremost amongst which was the question of finance.

Bourke at once endeavoured to fall in with the views of Wentworth and his party on this point, and when he met his council for the first time in January, 1832, he expressed the intention of in future submitting estimates of expenditure. A further concession to Wentworth was made by an extension of the jury law; but, when in the following year Bourke wished to permit juries in criminal trials, his measure was only carried by the Governor's casting vote, the old question of the admission and exclusion of the emancipated being revived with all its accompaniments of party feeling.

Bushranging, although checked by the extraordinary powers conferred on the police and magistrates, was still not uncommon, and violent outrages were occasionally committed close to the centres of population. The Bushranging Act, which had been passed during the rule of Darling, was about to expire in 1832, and the Governor recoiled from what appeared to him the unnecessarily severe provisions which it contained ; but the opinion was unanimously expressed by the magistrates that it should be renewed, while a select committee of the council went further, and recommended that some of the provisions should be made even more stringent.

But measures of harsh suppression were repugnant to Bourke's nature, and although in this instance he yielded to those in whose memory the deeds which produced the Act were still fresh, he attempted to improve the condition of the bond population by passing a law to regulate and lessen the severity of the punishments which could be inflicted by magistrates on assigned servants, and encouraged thrift among those of the convicts who were earning money, by permitting them to make deposits in the Savings Bank, on the condition that nothing could be withdrawn without the Governor's written authority.

Wentworth and his friends recognised the humanity

which inspired Bourke's measures, and consequently gave him their support; but in the concession with regard to estimates of expenditure a fresh opening was afforded for agitation in favour of responsible government.   In 1833 a public meeting was convened at which Wentworth held forth on the subject of taxation only by representative assembly.   He urged his audience on this occasion to "demand the right the common law gives you, but which an iniquitous parliament, an unreformed parliament, has for forty-five years withheld from you."   It is needless to say that his eloquence was greeted with applause, and if to any one the ludicrous picture of Phillip presiding over the deliberation of his ironed subjects presented itself, he refrained from calling attention to the absurdity of Wentworth's assertion.   The greatest enthusiasm prevailed, and a petition to King and Commons was carried, while at a subsequent meeting the Governor and his council were also addressed.   In the following year Wentworth convened another meeting, and the House of Commons was again petitioned, but meanwhile the Patriotic Association, of which Wentworth was the mouthpiece, had been active in its efforts to influence the British Parliament in favour of the autonomy of the colony.   A few years later the criticisms of finance took more concrete shape, and the attack was directed to pensions of imperial officers paid out of colonial funds and the annual charge for police and gaols.   Wentworth contended that as the persons who needed supervision and punishment were British convicts, Great Britain should pay the greater part of the expense.   Up to

1834 the charge had been borne by the military chest, but in that year the Governor was directed by the Secretary of State to make the necessary provision out of the colonial revenues. The moment chosen for the change was inopportune, for the cost of police and gaols had increased rapidly in recent years, and the movement in favour of the criticism of finance was at its height. All through the remainder of Bourke's administration the police and gaol question continued to be a popular cry with reformers.

As the population became larger, governors ceased to take such a personal interest in the social and moral condition of their subjects individually, but Bourke's attention was drawn to the urgent necessity of doing something to improve the morality of the community. One of the judges of the Supreme Court, Burton, addressed the jury at the termination of the sittings of the Criminal Court in 1835 on the great prevalence of crime, producing statistics to show how serious was the condition of the settlement from a moral point of view. The picture drawn was indeed a terrible one, and the Governor sought a remedy in the moral police, education and religion. An attempt was made to inaugurate a policy of state aid to undenominational schools on the lines of the Irish National School system ; but this was not what the various religious bodies wanted, and such violent opposition was aroused that Bourke abandoned the idea. Although a system of unsectarian education was for the present unattainable, it was still possible to establish religious equality. Up to this time the Church of England had, as in the mother country, received special consideration, although other bodies had been helped from the public funds; but Bourke distributed aid both for stipends and buildings to all denominations impartially. A marked revival both in religion and education was the result, and, although in later years the ecclesiastical expenditure became a serious burthen on the country's treasury, the improvement produced was worth the money spent. In spite of Bourke's tact and care he at last became entangled in the old feud between the emancipists and free inhabitants. The assigned servants of a Mr. Mudie, a magistrate, seized arms, committed a few violent acts, and left their employ. They were captured and convicted, but denounced the cruelty of the treatment to which they alleged that they had been subjected. The case called forth much comment, and a pamphlet signed "Humanitas" attacked magistrates and all masters of assigned convicts in no measured terms. Possibly the fact that there was some foundation in many instances for the charges preferred by "Humanitas" caused all the greater display of anger and resentment by the class aspersed. At any rate, when it at last became known that a convict named Watt, who occupied an editorial position on the *Sydney Gazette*, a newspaper which usually warmly supported Bourke, was the author, he was vigorously denounced, and, as Watt led a notoriously immoral life, the magistrates saw an opening for retaliation. Complaints regarding Watt were made to the Governor; but Bourke declined to interfere, till charges having been brought against the offender in the magistrates' court, and his case being referred to the Governor, he was compelled to take some action. Throughout the case, Mr. Roger Therry had taken a prominent part in support both of Mudie's servants and Watt, and had consequently made himself obnoxious to the magistracy. It so happened that the position of chairman of Quarter Sessions fell vacant about this time, and some one had to be elected by the magistrates to fill the place. Bourke nominated Therry, but the magistrates supported Mr. C. D. Riddell, treasurer and a member of the Executive Council. Bourke warned Riddell that he could not hold the positions together, but Riddell still remained a candidate, and was duly elected. Bourke at once suspended him from the Council, and in reporting the matter to the Secretary of State expressed a desire to resign if his action was not supported. The suspension was disallowed, and Riddell again took his seat in the Council, but Bourke, although urged to retain his office, persisted in his resignation and was relieved.

The enormous growth of pastoral occupation, which had taken place in consequence of Bigge's report, and a fuller knowledge and appreciation of the country's resources had caused a demand for labour, which even the constant inflow of convicts was insufficient to satisfy; at the same time the increase of the free and freed population, which had for long been steadily going on, threatened shortly an undesirable competition between the forced labour of the bond and free-wage earners. This last aspect of the question caused those who so earnestly desired to see transportation altogether abolished to support the proposal to assist free labourers to come to Australia; for in the introduction of immigrants, whose interests would be diametrically opposed to any increase in the number of assigned servants, they saw a weapon ready to their hands. Various impracticable schemes for raising funds with which to encourage emigration from Great Britain to the colony were put forward, and shortly before Bourke's arrival commissioners had been appointed to deal with the whole question. As a result of their labours it was determined to use the money obtained by the sale of Crown lands as an immigration fund, and to pay half the cost of a passage to Australia to all suitable persons who might desire to settle in New South Wales.

In 1831, during the administration of Bourke, free grants of land were discontinued, and all the unoccupied portions of the colony were in future only to be parted with at five shillings per acre. Under this new arrangement the land revenue grew rapidly, and during the five years between 1832 and 1836 increased from £13,684 to £132,607. Unfortunately the funds were not expended with discretion at the commencement. Females were most urgently required in the colony, so the first step taken in the new departure was the creation of a Female Emigration Board in London, to which the selection and despatch of the emigrants, from whom so much was hoped, was exclusively entrusted. But either from carelessness or inefficiency on the part of those to whom the selection was delegated, the persons sent out were, for the most part, of a character which not only made them quite worthless as reformatory examples, but greatly increased the difficulties of future purification. New South Wales was, in fact, made the dumping ground for all the unconvicted as well as the convicted criminals of the United Kingdom. Nor had the importation of such labour as was really required been attended to, and consequently employers were compelled to bring coolies, Chinese, and South Sea islanders to New South Wales at their own expense; while the public moneys of the colony were being expended on the passages of undesirable women. In 1837, however, this maladministration was rectified by the then Secretary of State for the Colonies; and several ships full of respectable free labourers and farmers were despatched at the expense of the land fund which had now accumulated to a considerable sum. The new arrivals were greedily looked for and warmly welcomed by the settlers, and all industrial pursuits revived amazingly. With the increase of enterprise, wages rose, and the standard of living was greatly improved. The thrifty and industrious found that, with the expenditure of the same amount of energy which was required at home to keep the wolf from the door, they could earn sufficient to live in comparative comfort and luxury. Glowing accounts went to England of the magnificent prospects of the colony, while the demands of the increased and more industrious population caused a rapid expansion of trade and commerce. The eyes of European capitalists were attracted to Australia as a possible field for the profitable investment of their money, and capital soon began to flow into the country with a stream relatively greater than even the stream of immigration.

There were already two large banks in existence— the Bank of New South Wales and the Bank of Australia ; now four new banks were established, to say nothing of other loan and trust companies. With increased facilities for borrowing came an increased desire to borrow, and enormous transactions in land and live stock took place all over the country, payment usually being made by long-dated bills on one or other of the banks. The prospects of the colony seemed excellent and fascinating, dreams of rapidly-acquired fortunes began to float before the eyes of farmer, pastoralist, and merchant alike. It is true that the harvests of 1838 and 1839 were poor, and the colony had been suffering from one of the periodical droughts, while the great staple, wool, had experienced a heavy fall in price in London ; but the abundance of the following years only added to the rage for speculation. The Government, apparently not apprehending the unsound condition of business, would seem to have done everything in its power to heighten the fever and precipitate the crisis.

For instance, the area of Crown lands offered for sale was very much restricted, so that the supply was in no way equal to the demand, even for genuine settlement, a course of action which unduly inflated prices and stimulated competition to an unhealthy extent. Then, again, the rate of interest demanded for Government deposits in the Banks was raised from 4 to 7 per cent., entailing a corresponding increase in the charges of these institutions to their customers, as well as a tendency to accept any security, provided an investment for their funds could be obtained. In this way advances were made in many cases far in excess of the value of the property mortgaged. An instance is quoted by a contemporaneous writer of an estate on which £10,000 had been lent by one of the companies, but which only brought in £100 per annum to the mortgagees, after they had been compelled to take it over. Still, while the mania lasted, there was a great appearance of prosperity. Wages continued to rise, and every one, from the highest to the most humble, conducted their domestic affairs on much the same extravagant scale as the prevailing business transactions. For those who had no money, or very little, it was the simplest thing in the world to borrow it, of course with the assurance that the enormous prospective profits of the speculation entered upon, whatever it might be, would justify an immediate expenditure of a great deal more than the borrower then possessed. This sort of thing could not go on for long. The huge paper circulation had to be redeemed sooner or later, and although the confiding British capitalist might for some time be gulled into lending his money with no security, and only promises for interest, he was sure to awaken after a little while to the unsatisfactory character of his debtors.

The signs of the coming storm were not long delayed. The Crown land sales fell off and ugly rumours were whispered from one corner of the colony to the other. At first the failures came one by one, but presently, in the year 1843, the whole unsubstantial fabric went with a crash and credit was completely destroyed.   The men who had been living luxuriously on other people's money found themselves brought up with a round turn, and at once tried to realise what they could.   Property upon property was forced into a market in which all were sellers and none buyers, and prices fell to ridiculous figures.   The rebound was even more unreasonable than the inflation.   Sheep were sold by the sheriff's officer for sixpence per head, and large stations near Yass and on the Hunter River sold, land and all, at the price of about three shillings per head for the sheep which were on them ; the same authority referred to above, quotes instances in which cattle bought at six guineas each were parted with for three and sixpence per head.   Houses and personal property all went the same way.   Carriages, which in the prosperous days had cost £140, sold for £3, and were run as cabs by the servants of the late owners.

The Auction Duty returns throw a strong light on the extent of the general ruin.   In 1837, at a time of inflated prices, sales amounting to £321,346 are recorded ; three years later, in spite of the enormous shrinkage in values, the figures stand at £1,246,742, and it is asserted that, had the goods sold in 1840 realised anything like their value in 1837, the sales by auction would have amounted to fully six millions sterling.   The Bank of Australia was unable to withstand the storm and by its fall involved a very large number of persons, both shareholders and depositors; at one time starvation was so near a section of the population that the Governor issued rations from the public stores at less than cost price.

The effects of the failure of the Bank of Australia threatened to be very serious, for its ramifications were great, and, in order to prevent "a panic which would annihilate the value of property," if the shareholders were called upon to meet the liabilities of the Bank, Wentworth introduced a Bill into the Council authorising the disposal of the property of the Bank by a lottery. The Bill was passed, and although the Royal assent was refused, the lottery was nevertheless held before the law officers could intervene to prevent it. Relief for the pastoral interest was found by Mr. O'Brien, who occupied a run in the Yass district. Sheep had practically ceased to have any market value; but Mr. O'Brien discovered that a uniform price of about six shillings per head could be obtained by boiling them down for tallow, and this experiment was the commencement of a large and well-sustained trade.

The treatment of the native races had become more and more brutal with the extension of occupation, until Sir George Gipps, who succeeded Bourke in February, 1838, determined to mete out equal and indiscriminate justice to all, whether white or black. The aboriginals were looked upon by the great bulk of settlers as little, if at all, better than wild beasts, and the shepherds and servants on the distant runs were in the habit of murdering black men, women, and children, without the smallest provocation. The

Government had for so long disregarded these proceedings that a profound sensation was created by
the arrest and arraignment of eleven white men on a
charge of murder in connection with the massacre at
Myall Creek of between thirty and forty natives, more
than half of whom were women and children.   Seven
of the offenders were hanged, and no stronger con-
demnation of the existing state of affairs could be
uttered than that pronounced by them when they
sought to excuse themselves because "They were
not aware that in killing blacks they were violating
the law, as it had been so frequently done in the
colony before."   The Myall Creek massacre was
only one of many similar barbarities which took
place about this period, but it was the first event
of the description which was dealt with in the
Criminal Courts, and both Gipps and the judge
who presided were abused in no measured terms
by an indignant public for their share in the proceedings.   The state of public feeling is shown by
the fact that the Governor's efforts to protect his
black subjects were described by a leading newspaper as "drawling philanthropy and mawkish
sentimentality."   Great changes were made in the
land laws in 1842.   An Act was passed by the
House of Commons directing that all lands should
in future be sold by auction, and fixing the upset
price at a minimum of £1 per acre.   Survey and
charting were made necessary preliminaries to sale,
except in the case of special blocks of 20,000 acres,
and certificates were to be issued to persons paying
money into the British Treasury entitling them to

any unsold surveyed land they might select on arrival in New South Wales. The point in the Act which caused the greatest trouble was the authority conferred on the Governor to grant annual licenses for the occupation of Crown lands, fixing the rent himself and being able to raise it to any figure which might appear to him proper. In the same year, 1842, the long-anticipated measure reconstructing the constitution of the colony and granting the elective principle was passed almost unanimously by both Houses of the English Parliament. The existing Legislative Council was empowered to arrange electoral districts and other details for a new legislative body consisting of thirty-six members, twelve to be nominated by the Crown and twenty-four to be elected by all persons possessed of a low property qualification. The Act went on to make certain provisions for the establishment of District Councils, whose principal duty it would be to collect funds for the maintenance of police and the construction of local works. The first district councillors were to be appointed by the Governor, and subsequent vacancies were to be filled by election, but failing an election the Government had power to fill the positions by his nominees. These arrangements shortly caused friction between Gipps and his new Legislature.

On the 1st of August, 1843, the new Council met after an election which was characterised by rioting and loss of life. There were many matters requiring urgent and careful attention, the foremost being the extreme prostration which had followed the financial crisis and now appeared to threaten the very existence of the community. Wentworth considered the only hope of infusing new spirit into commerce and industry was to make by some means the vast herds and flocks of the pastoralists negotiable ; with this end in view he introduced a Bill, which was passed, legalising liens on growing wool and the mortgage of live stock. Although the Secretary of State for a long time demurred to this Act, the Royal assent was eventually obtained, and all the benefits anticipated by Wentworth were fully realised. By a resolution of the house a parliamentary agent in London was appointed to attend to the affairs of the colony in England, and a corresponding committee was nominated to instruct him, but the principal part of the session was taken up with disputes as to expenditure and the application of certain funds, and objections to the District Council clauses of the Constitution Act. During the next session the Council continued to squabble with the Governor over questions of finance, and matters were brought to a crisis in 1845 when Gipps sent down bills to continue the " unauthorised occupation of Crown Lands Act," and to make provision for the maintenance of border police. Here was the opportunity for which Wentworth and his supporters had been waiting. The bills they declared could never pass through the Council, first, because the legislature "was not disposed to continue summary powers which had been used to support a claim to tax by prerogative alone ; " secondly, because the Governor had repeatedly

asserted that the Crown was the absolute owne rof
waste lands, and that the prerogative was sufficient
for their management, so that the interference of the
Council would be unnecessary ; thirdly, because the
legislature would be disinclined to tax the squatters
so long as the Governor had the power to tax them
as much as he chose by the raising of rent and by
the rates levied by the nominee District Councils ;
and fourthly, because they entirely disagreed with
the regulations framed by Gipps for the management
of the Crown lands of the colony. These resolutions
were conveyed to the Governor by deputation, and
the Council adjourned to a date later than that on
which it was supposed that Gipps would be relieved
by his successor ; the continued strain of government had wrecked his health and he had been compelled to resign his office. Gipps was equal to the
occasion, and, in order to prevent the new Governor
from being confronted by difficult questions before
he had had time to make himself acquainted with
the circumstances of the country, promptly prorogued
Parliament to a date which would afford his successor
ample leisure to learn the true state of affairs. At
the same time he reissued the regulations which had
given so much umbrage.

In spite of the turbulent ending to his reign,
Gipps left the colony amidst expressions of genuine
regret, for none were insensible of his ability and
the purity of his motives, even in those matters
which had aroused most popular resentment. It
had been his misfortune to quarrel with Wentworth and Lowe, the leading spirits of the Council,

and it is impossible to believe that many of the actions of that body which tended to strain the relations between the Governor and the Legislature were not prompted as much by personal as by public motives.

IX.

THE STRUGGLE FOR FREE INSTITUTIONS.

(1846-1851.)

Sir Charles Fitzroy arrived in H.M.S. *Carysfort* on the 3rd of August, 1846, and entered on what was the most memorable term of office of any Australian governor. One of his first acts was to submit estimates, in which were included the details of the schedules, and the Council, led by Wentworth, affirmed that they had no intention in asserting the right to deal with the sums named therein, "to propose alterations in any of the salaries to which the faith of Her Majesty's Government had already been pledged." Thus the strained relations which had so long existed between Gipps and his council were soon removed by mutual concessions and a spirit of mutual confidence, and difficulties, which at one time threatened to cause a serious rupture, were by a few civil words made the occasion of expressions of amity and friendship. The question of quit rents, which had been another stumbling-block, was also satisfactorily settled by permitting all debtors to commute them at twenty years' purchase, the excess of that sum being refunded to persons who had already paid more. By an order in Council transportation to New South Wales had been abolished in 1840, but in the years following the great commercial crisis of 1843 its revival was seriously contemplated both within the colony and in England. Lord Stanley had proposed the formation of a new settlement as a receptacle for British criminals in 1845; two years later Colonel Barney, an officer of Engineers, was appointed superintendent, and actually sailed for Port Curtis, but he was unsuccessful in his search for a suitable site for the new colony, and before anything had been done, orders were received from England directing the abandonment of the project. In 1848 the attractions of the Californian gold-fields drew large numbers of the more adventurous spirits from New South Wales, and again complaints as to the dearth of labour began to be heard. The Secretary of State for the Colonies saw his opportunity, and lost no time in making use of it. The order in Council which terminated transportation was at once revoked; but popular sentiment had been misjudged, for, although a few persons considered that the only hope of averting the ruin which the depreciation in station and farm properties threatened was to resort again to assigned service, the great bulk of the population viewed the reintroduction of criminals as a thing to be prevented at all hazards. In February, 1849, there was a public meeting in Sydney to protest against Earl Grey's action, but meanwhile Mr. Gladstone, undeterred by the ex-

perience of his predecessor at the Colonial Office, had
suggested that the time had come when convicts
should be again received, asserting " that the practical
mischief of exciting jealousies by controverting the
alleged promise of the discontinuance of transportation would be greater than any that can arise
from acquiescence in the assumption of its correct-
ness." This curious method of circumventing an
acknowledged compact only intensified the opposition of the colonists, and popular expressions on the
question became ominously violent. Matters were
brought to a head by the arrival of the *Hashemy*
in Port Jackson with convicts on board. A public
meeting, hurriedly held at Circular Quay, was largely
attended, and speeches in no moderate language were
received with acclamation by the excited crowd. A
deputation was appointed to immediately wait upon
the Governor to inform him of the determination
of the populace to resist the debarcation of the
convicts ; but as it was clearly out of the power of
Fitzroy to send the *Hashemy* back with her cargo
of criminals, and it was equally impossible to keep
the wretched prisoners cooped up in the ship for
any extended period, a compromise was at length
arrived at ; the Governor permitted most of the
convicts to be hired on board by settlers, on condition
that they should not be employed in Cumberland,
the metropolitan county, and the rest were promptly
despatched to Moreton Bay, whither those who
arrived subsequently were also sent. The incident
of the *Hashemy* called forth more deliberate and
unmistakable protests from the inhabitants, and in

1850 forty-eight petitions, eight with five hundred and twenty-five signatures in favour of the continuance of transportation and forty with no less than 36,589 names attached against it were forwarded to the English Government, while the Legislative Council resolved " that no more convicts ought, under any conditions, to be sent to any part of this colony." But although the people of New South Wales would not receive the outpourings of the British gaols, free immigrants were eagerly sought and gladly welcomed. Large numbers of assisted immigrants arrived each year, and usually met with a ready demand for their services, but occasionally some hardship was experienced owing to the inability of the settlers far inland to make their requirements known, and the tendency of the new arrivals to cling to the city or its neighbourhood. Mrs. Caroline Chisholm did much to alleviate these evils by travelling through the country with batches of immigrants to the localities in which they would be most likely wanted, and after leaving the colony the same lady formed a Family Colonisation Society in London, which did good work in despatching suitable settlers to Australia.

Previous to 1848 the system of primary education had been purely denominational, and, although various suggestions had been made for a scheme of public instruction, for one reason or another no definite action had been taken. In the year named, however, a committee of the Council reported in favour of the adoption of the Irish National School system, and an Act was passed appointing a Board of National Education, and also a Denominational School Board. The two bodies did not work in harmony, and the national schools were vehemently opposed by the ministers of most religious bodies. The same year saw the birth of the first Australian university. The hopes of colonists now soared high, and aimed at equality with the mother country, not only in material, but also in intellectual advantages. "I believe," said Wentworth, when speaking on the Bill authorising the foundation of the Sydney University, "that from the pregnant womb of this institution will arise a long line of illustrious names—of statesmen, of patriots, of philanthropists, of philosophers, of poets, of heroes, and of sages, who will shed a death-less halo not only on their country, but on that university we are now about to call into being."

But if these brilliant anticipations were to be fulfilled, the colonist must first obtain full political rights, and in the struggle for political freedom Wentworth again appeared as the champion of the better aspirations of the people. Earl Grey's des-patch, authorising the separation of Port Phillip, had arrived at the end of 1847, and in the same document was sketched an amended constitution, which it was proposed to introduce into New South Wales as soon as practicable. Two houses were to be established, one nominated by the Crown and the other repre-sentative, but the people were to elect Municipal Councils who, in their turn, were to be the con-stituents of the Legislature.

It was hinted that there should be some method

SYDNEY UNIVERSITY.

"for enabling the various legislatures of the several
Australian colonies to co-operate with each other in
the enactment of such laws as may be necessary for
regulating the interests common to those possessions
collectively; such, for example, are the imposition
of duties of import and export, the conveyance of
letters, and the formation of roads, railway, or other
internal communications traversing any two or more
of such colonies," and the creation of such a central
legislative authority was foreshadowed, although no
details were stated. This despatch was published by
Fitzroy, and was not unfavourably received. In
January, 1848, a huge public meeting was held in
Sydney, at which all the leaders of the people for
once united in vigorous opposition to the proposed
alteration in the constitution. It was asserted that
such a measure would have the effect of depriving
the colonists of the elective franchise, which had
only been obtained after a severe fight, and was declared by Mr. Stuart Donaldson, one of the speakers,
to be "our unalienable right as British subjects."
Earl Grey bowed to the storm and consented to
withdraw his proposals, simply introducing a
measure enabling the colonies to create two
chambers, should they so desire. But the emphatic
protest which this scheme had called forth awoke
the authorities in England to the importance of the
subject and the earnestness of the desires of the
settlers, and the whole question of the Australian
constitutions seemed so serious that the Committee of the Privy Council on Trade and Plantations was requested to report. After a few months'

deliberation they advised that as free scope as possible for public opinion in Australia should be permitted, and that an enabling measure, giving the colonies power to devise their own constitutions within certain broad limits, should be passed. Although they deemed municipal institutions an essential to effective government, and "the only practicable security against the danger of undue centralisation," it would be impolitic in the present temper of the colonies to "force unwelcome duties" on them "under the name of franchises."

Instead of direct taxation through District Councils, it was suggested that any balance of the land revenue received from each district, remaining over after charges for immigration had been met, should be handed to the local councils for expenditure on the construction of public works. They strongly urged "that there should be one tariff common to all" the settlements, "so that goods might be carried from one into the other with the same absolute freedom as between any two adjacent counties in England." All common questions were to be settled by "a general assembly of Australia," presided over by the Governor of New South Wales in his capacity of Governor-General. The necessary revenue for this central authority was to be obtained by "an equal percentage from the revenue received in all the colonies."

The English Government expressed the intention of immediately introducing a Bill based on the report, but troubles nearer home delayed the matter till early in 1850.

When the Australian Colonies Government Bill was read the second time in the House of Commons the debate was a keen one. Various amendments were proposed, and the franchise was lowered. All the colonies were expressly disabled from interfering with the Crown lands and the revenue derived therefrom. The existing council was convened in March, in order to pass the measures required to give effect to the new arrangements, but Wentworth condemned the proposed constitution because by it "all material powers exercised for centuries by the House of Commons were still withheld." A select committee of the existing council was obtained, which in its report protested against the proposals on the grounds that all revenue and taxation should be entirely in the hands of the Colonial Legislature ; that all offices of trust and emolument should be filled by the Governor and Executive Council, unfettered by instructions from the Minister for the Colonies ; that plenary powers of legislation should be conferred on the Colonial Legislature ; it concluded by "solemnly protesting against these wrongs, and declaring and insisting on these our undoubted rights ; we leave the redress of the one and the assertion of the other to the people whom we represent and the legislature which shall follow us."

An electoral Bill was passed providing thirty-six representative and eighteen nominee members for the new Council of New South Wales, and twenty elected and ten nominee members for Victoria, which, on their election, was to become a separate colony. The lowering of the franchise produced a strange alteration in public feeling, and at the election of 1851 Wentworth's name stood last instead of first of the three members for Sydney; John Dunmore Lang leading the poll. The new council met on the 16th of October and reaffirmed the protest of the defunct body. In their report they stated that they were "prepared upon the surrender to the Colonial Legislature of the entire management of all our revenues, territorial as well as general, in which we include mines of every description, and upon the establishment of a constitution similar in its outline to that of Canada, to assume and provide for the whole cost of our internal government, whether civil or military." The petition was carried and transmitted by Sir Charles Fitzroy to the Secretary of State as expressing "the general and deliberate opinion of the most loyal, respectable, and influential members of the community." Sir John Pakington was at this time Secretary of State, and he at once fell in with the views so unmistakably expressed. In his despatch to the Governor he stated that the English Government were "ready to accede to the wishes of the Council and of the colony in a spirit of entire confidence." The Council was invited to frame a constitution for itself, and the whole of the revenues demanded would be surrendered by the Crown as soon as the contemplated changes in the constitution had been effected. Transportation to Australia was to be finally abolished, and the despatch closed with the expression of the hope that the proposed enactment "will not only tend to promote the welfare and prosperity of the great colony . . . but also to cement and perpetuate the ties of kindred affection and mutual confidence which connect its people with that of the United Kingdom."

Some time elapsed before the details of the new constitution could be finally settled, but Sir John Pakington's despatch irrevocably conceded the principle that the Australian Colonies, on showing their ability to do so, had the right to demand the control and management of their own affairs. In the foregoing pages it has been shown how, step by step, the power of the people advanced, how the taint of crime rapidly, though almost imperceptibly, disappeared from the popular assemblies. The old divisions of society had gone, and instead of "emancipated" and "free" a united people is to be seen vehemently contending for those same rights and privileges in this distant possession which they would have been enjoying had they remained or been born in the mother country. To the early political life of this settlement at the antipodes was given peculiar interest by the strong individuality and remarkable ability of the leading characters. Wentworth fired with love of his native country, and embittered by the feeling that the land of his birth was tainted by foreign crime, first made his appearance as the champion of the "freed" whom he longed to make free, but, as the colony grew, he perceived that the future was too grand to be bound up with the personal hopes of a section of the inhabitants. As the struggle for the elective principle progressed he became aware that, if Australia was to be a mighty nation, higher ideals than those of the mob must lead her. Although extremely violent in his language he ever professed to keep within the bounds of parliamentary usage ; and his love of England and her liberties was only eclipsed by the love he bore the land of his birth. But when the fighting days were over, and, the victory being won, it was necessary to order affairs of state with caution and moderation, he lost the marvellous hold he had previously exercised over the lower classes of the community, and, although always a power in the council, he ceased to be a popular idol.

Perhaps the next most prominent figure at this time was John Dunmore Lang, a Presbyterian minister and polemical politician. An advocate of the severance of the British connection, violent and coarse in language though undeniably able and eloquent, he took the place which Wentworth lost in the affection of a section of the masses. Always mixed up in transactions which his opponents called by very ugly names, he occupied a unique position on the political stage and a volume could be filled with an account of his extraordinary vicissitudes and curious dealings.

Robert Lowe, afterwards Lord Sherbrooke, was another participator in the stirring events attending the birth of responsible government. A man of great gifts he had many admirers but few friends. First entering the Council as a personal friend and nominee of Gipps, he soon became that governor's most dangerous opponent, and Wentworth aptly described him, when at the elections of 1848 he said—" Long ago I felt the deep conviction that, having had to bear his praises, I must soon be doomed to bear his bitterest and most envenomed censure. The principle of the man's life is change."

But not the least noticeable figure in the group of leaders was that of Deas Thompson, the Colonial Secretary. With wonderful tact at a most difficult period he successfully conducted the Government business in a sensitive and hostile council, and in the measures framed under his hand, a broadness of view and a keen appreciation of the people he had to deal with is everywhere visible. His *rôle* was not as brilliant as that of the champions of popular rights, but his influence as a high-minded and honourable gentleman was extensive.

X.

THE DISCOVERY OF GOLD.

(1851.)

THE extraordinary activity displayed in the social and political development of New South Wales at this period is the more remarkable as the commercial and financial prospects were not encouraging. The colony had never really recovered from the crisis of 1843. Confidence had then been destroyed, and the credit, so essential to business transactions of any magnitude, had received a shock from which it could only be restored by years of patient and steady industry. Then the sudden cessation of assigned labour combined with the emigration to California, had been a severe ordeal, and many persons prophesied the speedy collapse of the whole settlement. Looking back through the records of these troublous times, it seems strange that some people were not tempted to seek for gold during the years of depression. It was known by many that the precious metal had been found in the Bathurst district, and from time to time since the very early days of occupation, reports had been made to the authorities concerning the discovery of gold in various places. As far back as 1823 there is an entry in the field-book of a surveyor named James McBrian, under date of February the 16th, which runs: "At eight chains, fifty links to river, and marked gum-tree—at this place I found numerous particles of gold in the sand and in the hills adjacent to the river," the river referred to being the Fish River, about fifteen miles from Bathurst, and not far from the discoveries of Hargraves.

Again, in 1839, Count Strzlecki found gold, and informed the Governor, Sir George Gipps; and, although he was requested by the authorities to suppress, as far as he was able, the knowledge of his discovery, for fear of gold fever rendering the convicts unmanageable and disturbing the settled industries of the country, there can be little doubt that the fact was disclosed to a large number of people.

In 1841 the Rev. W. B. Clarke found gold in the Macquarie Valley and the Vale of Clwydd, and stated that he was convinced that the metal would be met with in large quantities in various localities throughout New South Wales, and, for some time previous to 1851, a shepherd named McGregor had, while tending his flocks, collected particles of gold, while other persons had not unfrequently come across small deposits.

But, in spite of all these incidents, it would seem that the possibility of Australia being possessed of this kind of wealth never seriously occupied men's minds. It was not for some seven years after the acute stage of the commercial crisis that any general interest in the gold discoveries was shown, and then attention was drawn to the matter, not by the prophecies of geologists, but by the conviction of a man named Hargraves, that the country, so like in character the great gold-bearing places in California, would, in all probability, be also auriferous. The story is a curious one. Hargraves was one of the numerous adventurers who left the colony in 1848 for California, but the first thing which impressed him on his arrival was the great resemblance between the gold country and some of the places which were well known to him in Australia. The more he pondered upon the likeness, the stronger grew the conviction that there must be gold too, near his old home. Each day he felt more forcibly impelled to return to Australia and test the accuracy of his surmises. At last he could resist the inclination no longer, and on the 12th of February, 1851, his enterprise was rewarded, and he succeeded in finding gold in the Lewis Ponds and Summerhill Creeks, the very spots which had been in his mind during his sojourn in California.

Having fully assured himself of the payable character of the field, Hargraves approached the Government. He at first asked for a reward, on receipt of which he expressed his willingness to point out the places at which he had experimented, but Deas Thompson declined to entertain any other proposal than that the localities should be shown and proved to Mr. Stuchbury, the geological surveyor, and that Hargraves should trust to the honour of the Government for an adequate reward after his discoveries had been confirmed and their value ascertained. This

offer was accepted, and on the 6th of May it was
announced in Sydney that a gold-field had been
found. Three weeks later Mr. Stuchbury wrote to
the Colonial Secretary that "the number of people at
the diggings on the Summerhill Creek is daily increasing upon an extent of about a mile. I estimate
the number to be not less than 1,000, and, with few
exceptions, they appear to be doing well, many of
them getting large quantities of gold." The rush to
the gold-fields before long seriously affected other
industries, and the apprehensions of collapse from
stagnation were converted into fears of ruin from too
great speculation. Indeed, it was urged upon the
Governor by some of those engaged in pastoral and
agricultural pursuits, that martial law should be
proclaimed, and all gold-diggings peremptorily prohibited, in order that the inducement, which seemed
so irresistible, for persons to quit their ordinary occupations might be removed. It is needless to say that
such an absurd request was not entertained, Fitzroy
expressing his opinion that to try to stop the rush to
the diggings would be as futile "as to attempt to
stop the influx of the tide." Nevertheless, there can
be no doubt that in some quarters the exodus of
labourers from the more settled industries of the
country was very keenly felt. Stations in some cases
were left without hands, and farmers saw their crops
spoiling because they could not obtain sufficient men
to harvest them.

When the rush first commenced, the Council was
not in session, so the new conditions had to be provided for by the executive. Deas Thompson, the

Colonial Secretary, drew up rules for the regulation of
the gold-fields, imposing a license fee of thirty shillings
per month on all persons digging gold. The revenue
arising from this source was promptly placed at the
disposal of the Colonial Government to meet the
extraordinary expenditure consequent on the changed
circumstances of the colony, and, when the Council
met, it was considered that Deas Thompson's regulations had worked so satisfactorily that there was no
need to make any alterations. Only one serious
disorder threatened. At the Turon field four hundred
armed diggers prepared to resist payment of the
license fee; but the Government at once despatched
half a company of the 11th Regiment with reinforcements of police to Sofala, and showed such
a firm determination to maintain the law that the
turbulent spirits quailed, and the rioters melted away
without causing further trouble. It is not surprising
that ordinary methods of gaining a living became
unattractive in the face of some of the early finds of
gold. He would indeed be a cold-blooded philosopher
whose mind would not be inflamed by such a discovery
as that made by a Dr. Kerr on the Turon. This
gentleman, or rather a native employed on his station,
discovered, accidently, a lump of gold weighing about
one hundred and six pounds, and worth, approximately, £4,500 ; another mass of gold was unearthed,
in November, 1858, at Burrandong, near Orange,
which, after melting at the mint, yielded £4,389
worth of the metal ; and the " Brennan " nugget, which
was sold in Sydney, in 1851, realised £1,156 ; while
numerous other finds of a similar character were quite

sufficient to tempt even the most cautious to go and try their fortunes at the diggings. In the early days, moreover, apart from the extraordinary discoveries of huge lumps, good results were obtained by the greater number of the miners on the alluvial workings. In the "Quarterly Review" for September, 1852, a writer asserted that in New South Wales "the average monthly earnings of gold-diggers amounted to £31 3s.," and supported this estimate by the evidence of the commissioners on the various fields who commonly spoke of £1 per day as the average result of the miner's labour. The general excitement and unsettled state of the colony caused very great discomfort and loss to those who had, from one reason or another, to remain at their ordinary avocations, for the enhanced value of the principal articles of common consumption made serious inroads on the pockets of all who reaped no direct advantage from the mines. A special "gold allowance" was paid to public servants, to enable them to meet the changed circumstances, and the dearth of labour caused a somewhat similar advance in remuneration to persons in private employ. Wheat rose between 1850 and 1855 from 4s. to 16s. 5d. per bushel, tea from 1s. 10d. to 2s. 5d. per lb., potatoes from 7s. to 21s. 4d. per cwt., and beer from 2s. 9d. to 4s. 7d. per gallon. On the gold-fields prices of the commonest things reached prodigious figures, and as the roads became cut up the cost of carriage rose from £2 10s. to £30 per ton. The condition of things sketched above did not continue for very long; what has been fitly described as the "allure or dazzle of the gold-seeker's life" gradually laid he,

dimmed by the privation, discomfort, and disappointment which, as the numbers of miners increased, and
the alluvial beds became exhausted in the majority
of instances, were all that was experienced on the
gold-fields; in consequence people returned to their
former occupations in less fascinating but more safe
and permanent paths of industry. But the work of
the great discovery had been accomplished in the
first few years following 1851. Not only had new
life and fresh impetus been given to enterprise in
New South Wales, but an entirely new class of
labour had been attracted to the province, bringing
with it a far higher standard of living than that
previously obtaining, and thus permanently im-
proving the condition of workers for the future.
The thirst for gold and feverish excitement which
accompanied the birth of the mining industry in
Australia, was probably all the more acute owing
to the extreme depression which immediately preceded it, for it is a somewhat remarkable fact that,
although only a small portion of the auriferous area
of the continent of Australia has been explored, and a
still smaller portion properly developed, so that the
chances of marvellous finds are as great as ever, there
has never since the rush between 1851 and 1857 been
anything resembling the overmastering fascination
which the search for the precious metal at first exercised. Of course, every now and then there is what
is called commonly a " boom " in mining circles, but
no considerable number of persons have been attracted
from other pursuits.

XI.

RESPONSIBLE GOVERNMENT.

(1853–1885.)

IN 1853, on the receipt of Sir John Pakington's despatch, a committee of the Council, of which Wentworth was the guiding spirit, was appointed to draft a Constitution Bill. It was not long in bringing up its report, which, however, met with considerable opposition both in the Council and from the people outside. Wentworth desired to make the Upper Chamber hereditary, after the example of the House of Lords, and provided for a species of colonial peerage, the the only point which raised much comment; but public meetings vigorously protested against the introduction of the hereditary principle, and eventually, after a hard fight, Wentworth consented to withdraw this particular arrangement, and substitute a nominated chamber. He gave in with reluctance, and only because he feared the wreck of the whole scheme, were he to adhere to his opinion. His contention had been that some special inducement must be offered to successful persons to remain in the colonies; "For who would stay here if he could avoid it?" said he,

" who with ample means would ever return, if ever he
left these shores, or identify himself with the colony,
so long as selfishness and ignorant democracy held
sway? Yet what a great country would those have
to live in if higher and nobler principles prevailed!
Blessed by the bounteous gifts of Providence, it affords
in its illimitable tracts happy homes for millions yet
unborn." Wentworth's forecast has been singularly
verified, and one of the greatest misfortunes of the
colonies at the present day is that no sooner do
Australians accumulate wealth, than they fly to
Europe to dissipate it. Whether his remedy would
have been effective or not, it is impossible to say, but
few will deny that there is something lacking in
colonial society, which is essential to retain those from
whom it should receive its greatest advancement and
support.

On December 21st a Constitution Bill was passed,
and forwarded to the Secretary of State for the sanction of the Imperial Parliament, and, after a somewhat
stormy passage through the House of Commons, the
measure became law. In 1856 the old council was
dissolved, having first made the necessary arrangements for the election of the new assembly, and on
May 22nd the first Parliament under responsible
government was opened by Sir William Denison.
There were two chambers, the Upper House, called
the Legislative Council, consisting of members nominated by the Crown, and the Legislative Assembly,
which contained fifty-four elected members. The
first Ministry included Sir Stuart Alexander Donaldson, as Colonial Secretary and Premier ; Mr. Thomas

Holt, Treasurer ; Sir William Manning, Attorney-General ; Mr. J. B. Darvall, Solicitor-General ; and Mr. W. C. Mayne as Representative of the Government in the Legislative Council. The principles of the Constitution, as originally laid down, have never been altered, but there have been some changes in minor details. In New South Wales, as in the other Australian colonies, the democratic element was increasing, and before long the Electoral Act was amended and the franchise reduced to practically manhood suffrage. At the same time, the old system of voting was abolished, and all elections have since been conducted by means of the ballot-box. Various other amendments of the Electoral Act have taken place from time to time, and the few restrictions of political privilege which remained have been removed. The Legislative Council now contains sixty-seven members—though there is no fixed limit of numbers— and there are one hundred and forty-one members of the Assembly. The tenure of a seat in the Council is for life, and the only qualification required of members is that they shall be twenty-one years of age, and naturalised or natural born subjects of the Queen, while the qualification of the Lower House is practically the same. The representatives of the people now receive £300 per annum each, in return for the services which they are supposed to render to the country, but members of the Council are unpaid with the exception of the privilege of travelling free on the State Railways, which is enjoyed by members of both Houses. The duration of the Assembly is limited to three years, and the only condition at present necessary to obtain elective rights is six months' residence before the rolls are compiled.

Within the first five years of responsible government, under the guidance of Sir John Robertson elaborate regulations were framed for the alienation and occupation of Crown lands. The circumstances of the colony had been greatly altered by the discovery of gold, and the question of land settlement had to be dealt with in an entirely new spirit to meet the wants of a class of a different type to that contemplated by the framers of former enactments. The new scheme excited great public interest, and a monster torchlight meeting was held in Wynyard Square to discuss the land question generally, but more particularly to condemn the proposals which had been made. A ministerial crisis followed, and the Government were beaten by a large majority on the question of "free selection before survey." The Governor was urged to dissolve Parliament, but this he declined to do, and before long public sentiment underwent a complete change ; the cry of "free selection before survey" was made the watchword of the democratic party ; and the measure on its re-introduction consequently became law. The Act of 1861 was intended to facilitate the settlement of an industrial agricultural population, side by side with the pastoral tenants, by means of free selection in limited areas. To this privilege was attached the condition of *bonâ-fide* residence, and the land was to be sold at a fixed price, payable by instalments, or partly remaining at interest. All public lands, with the reservation of existing rights, were to be thrown open to conditional purchase before or after survey, to all comers, in lots ranging in area from 40 to 320 acres. At the same time leases of stations for pastoral purposes were granted on appraised rents, the tenancy being for a period of five years, on the condition that such lease had no power to bar purchase, either conditional or by auction, should any one desire to become possessed of the property. The effect of this law was an apparent increase in agricultural settlement; but, although it induced a large amount of *bonâ-fide* occupation, the power to select allotments within the boundaries of runs, caused serious friction between selectors and the Crown tenants, and without doubt led to extortion and fraud on an extensive scale. Another result of the fears of indiscriminate selection on their leasehold areas was that the Crown tenants, in order to protect their properties from the inroads of free selectors, plunged into debt, money being recklessly borrowed for the purchase of the freehold of the land which they were then holding under lease.

The new Parliament did not confine its liberalism to the administration of the Crown lands. Before it had been many years in existence an Act was passed abolishing all grants from the State Treasury in aid of religious denominations, while a further levelling measure found its place on the statute book in an Act providing for the abolition of the law of primogeniture. A peculiar political crisis occurred at the close of the rule of Sir William Denison, over a matter of trivial importance in itself, but one which—involving the question of the Royal prerogative—is interesting as exemplifying the temper of the colonial legislature

in its infancy. A grant of land to a certain person
had been recommended to the Governor by the
Secretary of State, but such grant was distasteful to
the Governor's ministers, who advised him that he
had no power to make the concession, and several
successive ministers declined to give effect to it. The
Governor thus found himself in a difficult position, as
either he must disregard the advice of his responsible
ministers or disobey the imperative commands of the
Secretary of State. Shortly before his departure,
therefore, he applied for the seal of the colony, for
the purpose of completing the deed without ministerial sanction; it was eventually yielded to him
by Mr. Cowper and his colleagues under protest,
the members of the Government at the same time
tendering their resignations. Denison used the seal
and returned it to its former custody, and also exercised his privilege of refusing to accept the resignations
of his ministers; there the matter ended, for he
very shortly relinquished his office.

The material progress of the colony had meanwhile
been great. For the first twenty-three years of the
settlement's existence there had been no postal
facilities whatever, and it was not till 1810 that the
first post-office was established, and even then the
arrangements were of a most primitive character. In
1825 an attempt was made to improve the organisation, and tenders were called for the conveyance of
mails between the principal centres of population;
but the charges for transmission and delivery were
extremely high, and varied according to the distance
the letter or packet was carried, and the difficulty of

access to the recipient. Twelve years afterwards pre-payment of postage by means of stamped covers was instituted, and in 1849 the whole of the postal arrangements were remodelled, the rates greatly reduced, and an agitation in favour of more regular communication with Great Britain commenced. Three years later a contract was let for a monthly steam mail service between Sydney and England, the time for the passage being limited to fifty-eight days. This was a great advance but the steamers were very irregular and scarcely ever up to time.

Macquarie's energy in road-making had provided access to many districts; but the wants of the community had so greatly increased that in 1846 a movement in favour of railway communication received strong support. A meeting was held in Sydney to promote the construction of a line to connect the metropolis by rail with the city of Goulburn, and two years later a company was formed with a capital of £100,000 having for its object the construction of lines to Parramatta and Liverpool, with a possible extension in course of time to Bathurst and Goulburn. The first sod of the first railway in the Australasian colonies was turned in 1850 by the Hon. Mrs. Keith Stewart, the daughter of the Governor, but the company which was constructing the line did not prosper, and its property was taken over by the Government. Another company, in 1853, commenced a railway from Newcastle to Maitland, but it fared no better, and its interest also was before long transferred to the State. The works thenceforward were pushed on with vigour, and in September, 1855, a line from Sydney to Parra-

matta was declared open for public traffic. Fourteen
years later the extension to Goulburn was completed,
and additions to the railways have since been made
nearly every year, although until 1875 the progress
was not very rapid. An unnatural impetus was given
to all other pursuits by the discoveries of gold, and
agricultural and pastoral enterprises, as well as manufacturing industries, made great strides. But in 1857
there were signs of a reaction, and by 1860 the fictitious
prosperity had entirely disappeared; work became
scarce, and there was great distress amongst the labouring classes, who attended in large numbers before
Parliament House and clamorously demanded the
assistance of the Government. At the same time the
trades commenced an agitation for a reduction of the
hours of labour, mainly on the plea that by this means
work would be available for a greater number of hands,
and from these beginnings arose the " eight-hour movement" which has since gained such a firm hold on
Australian wage-earners. As the local labour market
appeared to be overstocked, the amount voted by
Parliament to assist immigration to the colony was
reduced from £60,000 to £30,000, and gradually
things improved. But the gold-rush had introduced
many unruly spirits, and the hard times which followed
led to outbreaks of lawlessness, with which the Government found it difficult to contend.

The whole country was terrorised for many years
following 1860 by the exploits of bushrangers, and
for a time the executive appeared to be incapable of
dealing with these offenders. Some of the bushrangers seized very large amounts in gold and specie

on the roads to and from the diggings. In June, 1862, for instance, a daring raid was made on the gold escort on its way from the Lachlan, and upwards of £14,000 worth of gold carried off. The mail coach was constantly waylaid and robbed in all parts of the colony. Sometimes passengers offered a vigorous resistance, and defeated their assailants, but more often they quietly submitted to the depredations of the ruffians. The country settlers became alarmed. Public meetings were held, and the Government were petitioned to take more active steps to suppress highway robbery, for it was alleged that life and property on the main roads in the interior were at present in continual jeopardy. As the months slipped by and the success of some of the marauders excited the fancy of other criminals, lawless acts became more and more frequent and impudent. If a bush-ranger was caught he usually suffered the last penalty, and when a magistrate, near Mudgee, shot dead a bush-ranger known as Heather, the jury at the coroner's inquiry brought in a verdict of "justifiable homicide." But this severity had no effect, and during the month following Heather's death the mail from Cassilis to Mudgee was "stuck up" and robbed under arms, and in September of the same year a police camp near Wombat was surprised by a gang of bushrangers, and after a small resistance the whole of the trooper's horses were appropriated by the outlaws.

So prevalent had this particular class of crime become, that lengthy debates on the state of lawless-ness in the country districts took place in Parliament, and, as a result, high rewards were offered for the apprehension or conviction of offenders. Outlawry only seemed to make the bushrangers more bold, and in September, 1863, a notorious thief named Gilbert, and his gang, robbed a jeweller's shop in the heart of Bathurst, and a few days later held the township of Canowindra for three days, and levied toll on all arrivals. During 1864 mail and other robberies by Hall, Gilbert, Morgan, and Dunleavy were of daily occurrence, and, if the slightest opposition was offered by their victims, they received scant consideration at the hands of the plunderers. Morgan was especially reckless, and in June fired on three men one of whom died from his wounds, and within a week shot a serjeant of police dead. During a successful attack on the Gundagai mail, which was travelling under police escort, a severe encounter took place which resulted in the death of a sub-inspector, the capture of a serjeant, and the flight of a constable. But it is useless to multiply instances of the crimes which were being perpetrated, for a record of all the outrages which occurred at this period would fill a large volume. It is sufficient to say that no man's life or property was safe. Fortunately the wretched state of the country was relieved by numerous instances of the bravery and heroism of many of the settlers, both men and women, who displayed a courage and determination to resist the attacks of the bushrangers which more than counterbalanced the reckless daredevilry of the murderers. Eventually the law prevailed, and bushranging and its accompanying evils were completely stamped out.

The year 1861 was marked by a disgraceful outbreak amongst the miners at Golden Point, Lambing Flat. A considerable number of Chinese had assembled at these diggings shortly after the first discovery of gold, and a hostile feeling against them had arisen amongst the other miners. A monster meeting was held, ostensibly for the purpose of deciding "whether Burrangong is in European or Chinese territory," and resolutions were passed to the effect that the Chinese must go, peaceably if possible, but, in case they should offer any resistance, steps were taken to organise an armed force to expel them. When news of these disorderly proceedings reached Sydney, a detachment of the military was despatched to Lambing Flat to maintain order, and Mr. Cowper, who was Premier, himself proceeded to the diggings, where he was received with enthusiasm by the miners. But in spite of his presence another and large anti-Chinese meeting was held, at which a miner's "Protective League" was formed, with the avowed intention of ousting the Chinamen. Further reinforcements of the military were sent up, and this so reduced the number of soldiers in Sydney that the services of the volunteers had to be obtained to mount the necessary guards at Government House, and elsewhere. But after peaceful assurances had been made to Cowper, it was thought unnecessary to maintain the same military strength in the vicinity of the diggings, and a large number of Chinese, who had previously been driven from the mines, recommenced work.

Suddenly an attack was made by the miners on the Chinese quarters. Three thousand men made

an onslaught, disfigured by every imaginable act of
violence and barbarity. Every Chinaman met
with was maimed or terribly maltreated, their
tents were burned, their goods looted, and for some
time the diggings were in a state of anarchy. In hot
haste a mounted patrol was despatched from Sydney,
under the charge of the Inspector-General of police,
and on its arrival an engagement took place, in
which several of the police were wounded, one rider
killed, and about a hundred others injured. Troops
were sent to support the police, and order was
eventually restored. There was no room for doubt
as to the atrocious characteristics of the attack
upon the Chinamen, but strangely enough the
action of the mining population received considerable popular support. Anti-Chinese petitions were
poured in upon the Governor, and deputations
besieged his doors. Meanwhile the ringleaders of
the outbreak had been apprehended, and lodged in
Goulburn gaol, and the Governor, though importuned
to intervene in their behalf, or to hold a special inquiry, declined absolutely to take any action in the
matter, asserting that the ordinary course of justice
would thresh out the rights and wrongs of the
question much better than any informal inquiry.
This proved, however, to be a mistake, for the same
failure of justice occurred on this occasion in New
South Wales, as had taken place at the trial of
Ballarat insurgents in Melbourne; when ten of
the rioters were placed in the dock at Goulburn
circuit court, the jury declined to convict.

Measures of a liberal character continued to occupy

the attention of Parliament, and the change which has taken place and is still going on in popular sentiment is clearly discernible in the early fate of some of the Bills which have now become law. Thus the idea of payment of members of parliament for their services was in the sixties rejected by large majorities ; a proposal for triennial parliaments met at first with the same fate, but the opposition to it melted away more rapidly than did the objection to the remuneration of the people's representatives.

Early in 1868 the Duke of Edinburgh visited the colony, and met with an unfortunate mishap which cause a violent outbreak of sectarian and class ill-feeling. On March the 12th, while the Duke was attending a picnic at Clontarf, a man named O'Farrell attempted to assassinate him. This naturally caused a great commotion and the offender was nearly lynched on the spot, being rescued with difficulty from the violence of the crowd. Great indignation was felt throughout the colony at the outrage, and public meetings were held to express sympathy with the sufferer, and abhorrence of the crime. The legislature was affected with the wave of emotion, and a Treason Felony Act was passed through the Assembly in one day for the purpose of providing legally for the execution of O'Farrell. The wildest reports as to the significance of the crime were current, and, while some held that the deed was the outcome of a far-reaching Fenian conspiracy, others as strongly took the opposite view, and contended that the prisoner was nothing but a lunatic, and that the crime was devoid of real motive. Anyhow, the

Treason Felony Act became law, and O'Farrell
was promptly hanged, leaving, as a legacy to the
country, the seeds of sectarian strife. The Duke of
Edinburgh was not very seriously wounded, and
soon recovered, and when the Treason Felony
Act reached England it was pronounced repugnant
to British law. Meanwhile in the colony it was the
occasion for much mutual abuse by the leaders of
the people, and Orange and Roman Catholic guilds
increased and multiplied with an amazing rapidity.

Previous to 1848, the system of primary education
in force was purely denominational. Assistance from
the Public Treasury was given to the heads of the
principal religious bodies, in proportion to the amount
which they themselves collected and expended upon
instruction ; but there were no schools entirely under
State control. As early as 1834, dissatisfaction was
expressed at the prevailing system, and five years'
later a sum was voted by the Council with the object
of securing undenominational education for the
children of those who preferred it ; the innovation,
however, met with some opposition, and little was
done until 1844, when a Committee of the Legislature reported in favour of the adoption of the Irish
National School system, and an Act was passed
constituting two boards, to one of which was
entrusted the management of denominational, and
to the other undenominational education. This
arrangement was in force until the passing of the
Public Schools Act of 1866, which provided for two
distinct classes of schools, though all schools receiving aid from the State were placed by it nominally

under a Council of Education. The public schools were entirely under the control of this board, but the denominational schools were still managed to some extent by the various religious bodies to which they had hitherto belonged. Good work was done under this system, although in many respects it was defective; but the principle of granting State aid to religious schools became more and more unpopular, and in 1880, State aid to denominational education was finally abolished.

By the new Act, which is still in force, the entire educational system of the colony was remodelled; the Council of Education was dissolved, and a Minister of Public Instruction created in its place. Public schools to afford primary instruction to all children without sectarian or class distinction were established, as well as superior public schools, in which a more advanced course might be followed. Evening public schools were formed for the benefit of those who need education but cannot attend the day schools; and high schools for boys and girls, in which a course of instruction is provided to complete the public school curriculum and prepare students for the university. In all State schools the teaching is strictly non-sectarian; but "secular instruction" is supposed to include "general religious teaching, as distinguished from dogmatic or polemical theology." The history of England and of Australia form part of the course of secular instruction; and it is further provided that four hours during each school day shall be devoted to secular instruction exclusively, but one hour each day may be set apart

FREE PUBLIC LIBRARY.

for religious instruction, to be given in a separate class-room by the clergyman or religious teacher of any persuasion to those children of the same denomination, provided the parents offer no objection.

Attendance at school is compulsory for children between the ages of six and fourteen years, for at least seventy days in each half year (unless reasonable cause for exemption can be shown); parents are required to pay a weekly fee of threepence per child, but not exceeding one shilling in all for the children of one family. The fees, however, may be remitted where it is shown that the parents are unable to pay. Children attending schools are allowed to travel free by rail. Arrangements have been made for the establishment of provisional schools, the appointment of itinerant teachers in remote and thinly-populated districts, as well as the establishment of training schools for teachers. Parents are not compelled to send their children to the public schools, but have free choice in the matter, the State only insisting that instruction shall be given.

The events which culminated in the death of General Gordon and the capture of Khartoum in 1885 were watched with the keenest interest by the people of the Australian colonies, and the widespread sympathy which was felt for the mother country, as the troubles multiplied and the prospect became more threatening, found expression in the offer of Mr. William Bede Dalley, the Attorney-General and acting Premier of New South Wales, to send within a month to the aid of the British arms

in the Soudan a fully-equipped force, eight hundred
strong. The proposal created much surprise in
England and in Australia, and many in the colony
vehemently opposed the idea. But Mr. Dalley's
action won generally popular approval. After some
hesitation, the English Government accepted what
it called the "splendid offer," and for a time the
voices of the malcontents were drowned in the busy
hum of preparation for the despatch of the contingent.
Two large steamers were chartered as transports, and
all arrangements were made, with a lavish profusion
which clearly indicated the excitement which had
taken possession of the people. Private citizens vied
with one another in making presents of stores and
other requisites, and a patriotic fund started for the
relief of the widows and orphans of those who might
fall, soon mounted up to a prodigious figure. Men
from all quarters hastened to volunteer their services,
and had it been desired, a force twice or three times
as large could easily have been enrolled. Within
three weeks of the acceptance of Mr. Dalley's offer,
all arrangements had been completed, and on the
3rd of March, amidst the greatest enthusiasm, the
soldiers embarked before a crowd of close upon a
quarter of a million people. The significance of
this event was unquestionably very great. The
other colonies would gladly have joined New South
Wales in its enterprise, at the same time it showed
the nations of Europe that Great Britain had a latent
power which had hitherto never been suspected or
admitted into their calculations. The whole business
—offer, acceptance, and despatch of the soldiers—was

so hurried, and carried through on such a remarkable wave of popular emotion, that the calmer heads in the community prophesied a violent reaction. It so happened that the New South Wales contingent had but little opportunity of real service. Its achievements and casualties were alike insignificant, and on its return it disembarked under most unfavourable conditions in pelting rain. Nevertheless the reception of the troops on their return was almost as great as the demonstration at their departure. The prodigality displayed in equipping the force had provided scoffers with a text, whilst the huge patriotic fund had but few claimants upon it and remained a monument of what appeared to many in more sober moments unnecessary liberality. But none the less the majority of the colonists were glad that they had done what they had ; indeed, were England on a future occasion to appear in imminent peril, it is not at all improbable that Australians would again be found ready to aid her with their fortunes and their lives.

XII.

PRESENT CONDITION OF THE COLONY.

(1892.)

PASTORAL industries are still the mainstay of the country, and the pastoral inhabitants of the present day owe a heavy debt to the early pioneers who drove their flocks and herds out over the unknown wilds of Australia. It is curious to look back on the very small beginnings of the enormous pastoral interests existing now. When the first expedition landed at Sydney Cove, the live stock which had been obtained with such difficulty at the Cape, comprised only one bull, four cows, one calf, one stallion, three mares, three foals, twenty-nine sheep, twelve pigs, and a few goats; but the suitability of the country for pastoral pursuits soon induced enterprising men like Macarthur and others to commence breeding sheep and cattle and to start a trade in wool. Captain Macarthur, by systematic selection, and the purchase and importation of the best sheep procurable, greatly improved the strain of his flocks, and produced a fleece of very fine texture, which, being appreciated by English manufacturers, immediately found a remunerative market. The difficulties of transport in these early days were very great, but numerous importations were made from India and elsewhere. Some rams and ewes of a very fine breed, which had been presented by the King of Spain to the Dutch Government, were successfully brought from the Cape, and some additional specimens of the same strain were afterwards obtained by Macarthur from the royal flocks in England. When it had once been demonstrated that fine wool could be successfully grown in New South Wales, this became the most important industry of the country, and the number of sheep depastured increased very rapidly. Were it not for the losses occasioned by droughts, the flocks would perhaps before this have reached the limit which the pastures could carry, for they double themselves in four years if all goes well. The loss, however, from drought and disease is sometimes very heavy. In 1884, for instance, it is estimated that owing to the absence of increase from lambing, and the extraordinary mortality among breeding stock, the loss through the adverse season must have amounted to at least 8,138,000 head. This figure shows how important a regular rainfall is ; at the same time the liability of the Colony to the disastrous effects of dry seasons is being reduced each year by systematic water conservation, artesian boring and irrigation, and the cultivation of drought-resisting plants and shrubs.

The climate is so genial, that there is no necessity to house stock, which may be safely left in the open air, even during the winter months ; but the old way of tending sheep, which was to place them under the charge of a shepherd, has been superseded by new methods, for it has been found that a station can be more economically worked, and that better fleeces and a higher percentage of lambs can be obtained by the subdivision of the runs into paddocks. When the sheep are sheared, the wool is packed at the station in bales, weighing 450 lb., from 4 feet 6 inches to 5 feet 3 inches in length. The ramifications of the pastoral interests are so extensive, that the fluctuation of a penny per lb. in the value of wool in the consuming markets greatly influences the national prosperity. The enormous sum which a fall in price involves will be realised better when it is stated that if the prices of 1884 had ruled in 1886, the growers of New South Wales would have secured nearly £2,000,000 more than they actually received ; and, although in 1888 about 48,000,000 lb. more wool was exported than five years previously, the sum received was fully half a million less. There is annually a large exportable surplus of sheep for meat, amounting to about 4,850,000 head, but as yet but little has been done to utilise it, though there is now every prospect in the immediate future of a large export of frozen and tinned meat. The profitable returns afforded by sheep-breeding induced many pastoralists to substitute sheep for cattle on their properties, though in some districts there are signs of a change back to cattle.

The variety of soil and climate to be found within New South Wales is very great, and consequently almost any kind of crop can be successfully cultivated. On the banks of the northern rivers sugar-cane is

BATHURST.

grown, and there is every reason to believe that coffee, tea, and other semi-tropical products would do equally well. Maize flourishes in the valleys of the coast district, and cereals and other crops of cold and temperate climes thrive on the high plateau of the great dividing range; but hitherto the attractions offered by stock-raising have caused agriculture to be somewhat neglected.

It is not improbable that the next few years will see great changes in the system of land occupation. So far all attempts to induce a people to settle on small areas have failed. The results of even the most liberal laws have been insignificant, and the flocks of a semi-nomad pastoral population have monopolised the greater part of the country. But the continually falling values of meat and wool, and the incursions of rabbits, are rendering a change in old systems imperative, and it is impossible to appreciate the full effect of the change on the social organisation when it comes. A sparsely populated, but wealth-producing interior, has hitherto supported an enormous aggregation of people in the metropolis, in pursuits which are not directly productive; when, therefore, stock-raising as at present carried on succumbs, as it must inevitably sooner or later, to the more advanced methods of utilising the soil, the army of agents of all sorts and descriptions who are now dependent on the pastoral industry will have to find new avenues for the employment of their energies.

In 1884 a new Land Act was passed which, though differing widely in many important particulars from previous legislation on the subject, maintained free selection before survey, but at the same time gave greater security of tenure to the Crown lessees. The whole colony was divided into districts, which were placed under the charge of local boards and land agents, and a special tribunal for the settlement of disputes in regard to land has since been established. The present condition of settlement may be briefly summarised as follows :—

Estates of	Estates of various classes per cent.	Estates occupied by owner per cent.	Estates rented per cent.
1 to 30 acres	0·25	0·15	0·10
32 to 400 acres	9·73	7·85	1·87
401 to 1,000 acres	10·73	9·36	1·37
1,001 to 10,000 acres ...	28·63	24·57	4·07
Upwards of 10,000 acres	50·66	46·62	4·04
	100·00	88·55	11·45

The mining industry still gives employment to a large number of men, and a large variety of minerals have been discovered. In the Barrier Range district, which lies to the west of the river Darling, near the border of South Australia, and which will be remembered as the neighbourhood of Sturt's hardships and mishaps in 1844, silver deposits extend over about 2,500 square miles. The deposits worked by the celebrated Broken Hill Proprietary Company are phenomenally rich. A complete smelting plant on the latest and most approved principles has been erected, and the services of competent managers whose experience has been gained in the silver mining centres of the United States have been obtained.

MONUMENT TO CAPTAIN COOK.

From the commencement of operations in 1885, to the 31st of May, 1892, the Company treated silver and silver lead ores, which yielded 36,512,445 oz. of silver, and 151,946 tons of lead, valued in London at £8,252,138. Dividends have been paid amounting to £3,880,000, bonuses amounting to £592,000, and properties have been parted with valued at £1,744,000 ; so that the total payments made to shareholders have reached £6,216,000. Many mines which give great promise are not yet fully developed, and a large increase in the production of silver, should there be a recovery in price, is not improbable.

The railway system of the country is divided into three main arms, each being really a distinct system. The southern line, which is the most important of the three, branches at Junee, running from Sydney, 454 miles, to Hay, the principal town of the fertile district of the Riverina in one direction, and 412 miles to Jerilderie in another. There are also several minor branches which drain into the main line, while a line connecting the southern and western systems, from Murrumburrah to Blayney, gives almost direct communication between Melbourne and Bourke. Goulburn, a large town nearer to Sydney, will also be the recipient of several feeding branches. The southern line places the four chief capitals of Australia—Brisbane, Sydney, Melbourne, and Adelaide—in direct communication ; and the mails from Europe can now be landed at Adelaide and forwarded overland to all parts of Victoria and New South Wales. The Western system crosses the Blue Mountains by zig-zag lines, and enters the Bathurst Plains, connecting the metro-

GOVERNMENT HOUSE.

polis with rich agricultural districts, while a branch
from Nyngan to Cobar taps a mining and pastoral
country. There are also other short lines which feed
the western trunk line. The Northern system originally terminated at Newcastle, but the connection is
now complete with Sydney, the Hawkesbury River
being spanned by an iron bridge 2,896 ft. long. This
line runs through the Hunter Valley, to the rich district of New England, and traverses pastoral and
agricultural country until it joins the Queensland
system on the border beyond Tenterfield. Various
branches are projected besides the three systems mentioned, and there is an independent line to the Illawarra district, a country rich in coal and agricultural
produce.

There is but little more to record in connection with
New South Wales which can rightly come under the
name of history, for although the internal development
of the country, and the growth of national sentiment
have steadily progressed, there have been but few
events to mark an epoch during the last twenty years.
The aspirations and difficulties which used to affect the
provinces individually are rapidly losing their purely
provincial significance, and the interests of each colony
are so inextricably interwoven with those of its sisters,
that great questions must in future be decided more
and more in accordance with the interests of the
commonwealth as opposed to the inclination of a
particular member of the group.

TASMANIA.

XIII.

THE SETTLEMENT AT THE DERWENT.

(1803–1837.)

RUMOURS that the French intended to form colonies in the South Pacific again gained credence in 1803, and the Governor of New South Wales promptly took steps to prevent, if possible, the landing of foreigners on Australian territory. With this end in view Lieutenant John Bowen was despatched to Van Diemen's Land with "sealed orders not to be opened except on the appearance of French vessels," and with him were sent some soldiers and convicts, to form a settlement on the banks of the Derwent. A whaler named the *Albion* and the *Lady Nelson* acted as transports; after a tempestuous voyage Bowen, in the former, cast anchor off Risdon, in the Derwent, on the 12th of September, the *Lady Nelson* having reached her destination a few days previously. The new settlement was named Hobart after Lord Hobart, the then Secretary of State for the Colonies, and Bowen

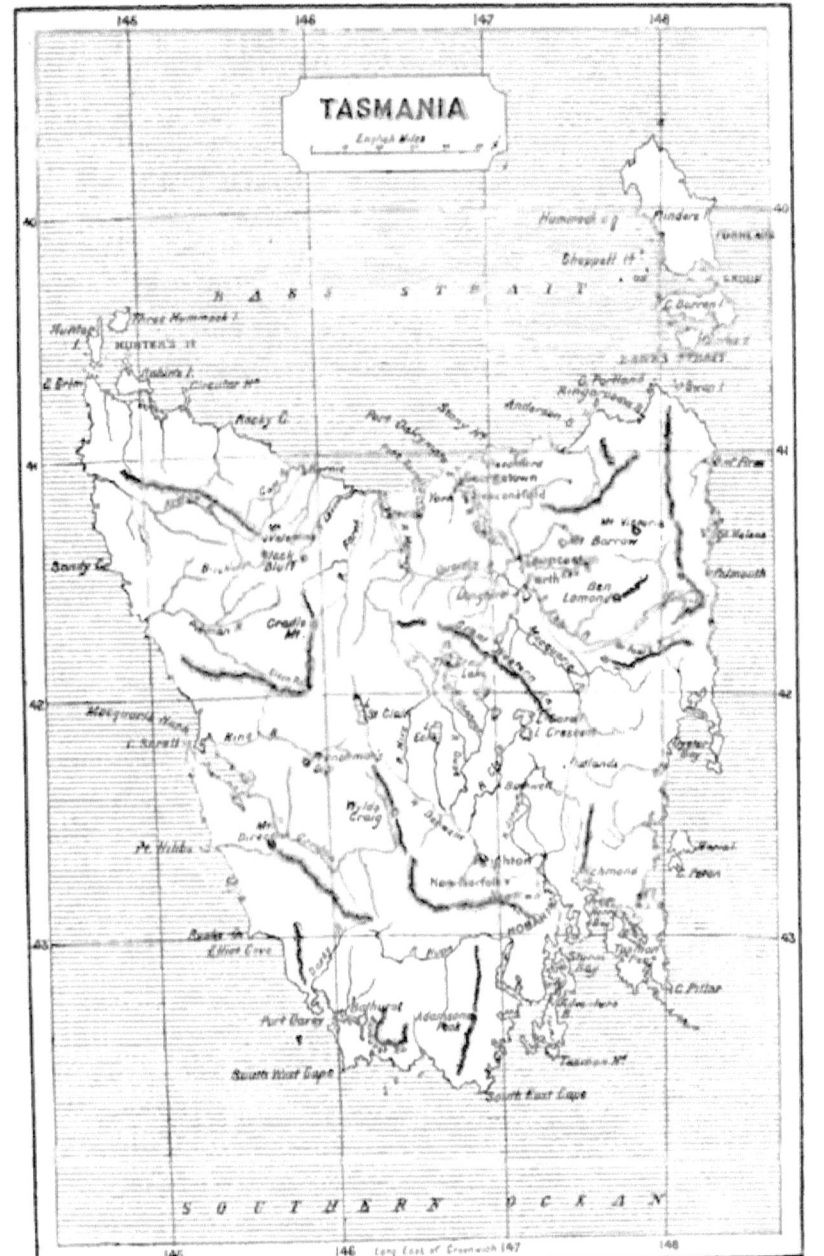

expressed himself as delighted with the site selected
for the town and the country generally. In the same
year Van Diemen's Land was inspected by Mr.
Collins, who had been despatched by Lieutenant-
Governor Collins to seek a spot to which the settlement at Port Phillip might be advantageously
removed. The Tamar was first visited, but did not
favourably impress the explorers, and the Lieutenant-
Governor, having obtained King's permission, decided
to transfer his colony to the Derwent. He would
appear to have been difficult to please, for on arrival
in the river he was not satisfied with Bowen's choice,
but landed and pitched his camp on the southern
side of the Derwent at Sullivan's Cove. Bowen, who
was subordinate to the Governor of New South
Wales, though he had been instructed to hand over
his command to Collins on that officer's arrival, for
some time was unable to obey ; for Collins was
unwilling to undertake fresh duties incurring increased work ; the cares of the settlement were
numerous, food was scarce, and both soldiery and
convicts made frequent attempts to rob the public
stores. At last King was compelled to peremptorily
command Bowen to return to New South Wales, as
it was impossible longer to tolerate the absurdity of
two distinct governments within eight miles of each
other, and Collins perforce took charge of the combined settlements. Although Port Dalrymple had
been rejected by Collins, it appeared expedient to
form a colony in that part of the island, and in 1804
Colonel Paterson, acting under instructions from
King, landed at George Town on the Tamar ; but

TASMANIAN NATIVE.

a better site for a town being discovered at York Town, the camp was moved to that place. The detachments were quite independent of each other, and Paterson was careful to get his jurisdiction defined before leaving New South Wales, the line of demarcation between the two commands being determined at the forty-second parallel of latitude.

Society in the island settlements was very much like society in Sydney, only on a smaller scale. The population consisted almost entirely of convicts and their guards, and the assignment system, by which the few free settlers who there were benefited by bond labour, was almost at once introduced. These new colonies were, however, better off in some respects than Sydney had been at its foundation ; for King, who had had every opportunity of seeing the difficulties surrounding the foundation of new settlements, and had suffered a bitter experience of the results of neglect and want of foresight, kept a watchful eye on the affairs of the young communities. Cattle were brought in considerable numbers from India and Ceylon, and all that could be done to render the settlements in Van Diemen's Land self-supporting was at once undertaken. Unfortunately the same miserable misunderstanding with the natives which so stains the early records of the continent led to bloodshed in Van Diemen's Land. On Bowen's first arrival he had been anxious to avoid any collision, and had taken no steps to open up communication with the aboriginal inhabitants. The black fellows, for their part, appeared to bear the intruders no ill-will, and, indeed, when intercourse had been established, as was inevitable sooner or later, they were on all occasions friendly and harmless. In March, 1804, a notice appeared in the *Sydney Gazette* in which it was stated that the natives about the Derwent were "very friendly to small parties they meet accidentally, though they cannot be prevailed upon to visit the camp;" but two months later this happy state of peace was rudely broken. Bowen was still in command of the settlement, but during his temporary absence, when Lieutenant Moore was acting for him, the first unfortunate affray occurred. A large body of natives, with women and children, appeared close to the camp (as was afterwards discovered) on a kangaroo hunt; and Moore, anticipating an attack, and being ignorant of their customs, assumed that their intentions were hostile. The soldiers were called out, and the order given to open fire, and some fifty blacks, men, women, and children, fell victims to the fear and stupidity of the officer in command. From this moment hopeless, relentless war commenced. Confidence was destroyed, and the native races disappeared with incredible rapidity before the lust and cruelty of the white man. Soon after the massacre at Risdon, Patterson on the other side of the island had also to use firearms, and the next few years of Tasmanian history are overshadowed by deeds of unexampled brutality. In 1805 an addition was made to the inhabitants by the arrival of some of the settlers from Norfolk Island, who had been offered land at either Risdon or Port Dalrymple, instead of their former holdings, when it had been determined to evacuate the island prison,

The time selected for the transfer was unfortunate, for the four following years were most disastrous. The Van Diemen's Land settlements suffered terribly from the period of famine which afflicted all the Australian colonies on account of the destruction of crops in New South Wales by floods, and the failure of harvests in the year following. Matters got worse and worse, until kangaroo meat was the only animal food obtainable. Seed wheat rose to £3 and £4 per bushel, and at length the public stores being exhausted, the prisoners were turned out into the woods to seek for food in any shape in which it could be found. In 1810 the strain was somewhat relieved by the arrival of breadstuffs from India, and with the return of fair seasons and an increase in cultivation the prospects of the colony improved. Governor Collins died suddenly at Hobart in March, 1810, and pending the appointment of a new governor, Lieutenant Lord, Captain Murray, and Lieutenant-Colonel Giels, all in turn administered the government. Macquarie crossed the Straits during the interregnum, and indulged his craze for naming or re-naming places. He was well received by the inhabitants, and after a short but pleasant visit returned to New South Wales. In 1811 Colonel Davey was appointed lieutenant-governor, in succession to Collins, and the two settlements of Hobart and York Town were brought under one control.

The arrangements for the administration of justice in Van Diemen's Land had hitherto been remarkable, for absolutely no Court had been established, and the most trivial offences could only be dealt with legally by reference to Sydney. Collins had brought out a judge-advocate with him to Port Phillip, but this gentleman's commission was not regarded as valid for Van Diemen's Land. He therefore declined to do any work, and contented himself with confining his labours to drawing his salary regularly for ten years. That a community of about three thousand persons should so long have put up with a judge who may have been ornamental but was certainly absolutely useless, is a remarkable fact; but in 1814 the inconvenience of having to go to Sydney to settle any trivial civil dispute became too great, and a "Lieutenant-Governor's Court" was established at Hobart Town with a jurisdiction extending to personal matters under the value of £50. Any dispute of greater importance, and all criminal trials, were still to be dealt with in Sydney; but the concession, so far as civil actions were concerned, was complete, for the disputants evaded the limit by dividing all their claims into amounts which the local court would be competent to try. After the arduous labours of Bates, the Judge-Advocate already mentioned, it would have been unfair to require him to undertake the new work which the establishment of this court created, so Macquarie appointed Captain Abbot to act as deputy Judge-Advocate, and this officer, although ignorant of law, seems to have given litigants fair satisfaction.

During Davey's administration of the government much solid progress was made in industrial development. Wheat was exported to Sydney in 1816, and

the inducements held out to immigrants, in the shape
of extensive free grants of land, produced a considerable influx of excellent colonists, many being
possessed of the capital which was so much required.
The finest portions of the arable land were about
this time alienated, and settlement would probably
have been even more satisfactory had not the country
been overrun by bushrangers, who plundered and
terrified the farmers.　The civil and military authorities were incapable of dealing with the outlawed
robbers, who found safe retreat in the mountain
fastnesses, and at last things assumed such a serious
aspect that Davey proclaimed martial law.　Abbot,
the Judge-Advocate, protested that such a step was
illegal, and Macquarie, who would have been obliged
in any case to ratify the proclamation, refused absolutely to sanction so extreme a course, and made
representations to the English Government which
resulted in the recall of the Lieutenant-Governor.
In 1815 the knowledge of the island had been
materially increased by the explorations of Captain
James Kelly, who discovered Port Davey and
Macquarie Harbour, and traversed a large portion
of the south, west, and north coast.　A rather
amusing incident is connected with Kelly's explorations.　When, after weeks of rough travelling, the
little band of pioneers reached the settlement at
York Town, the inhabitants, frightened by the wild
and ragged appearance of the men, turned out in
force to repel an attack from what they supposed to
be a party of bushrangers; and it was only after
mutual explanations that the weary travellers were

permitted to enter the town and obtain the refreshment and rest which they so much needed.

Colonel William Sorrel was appointed Davey's successor, and immediately on his arrival set to work to check the growing terrors of bushranging. Rewards were offered for the capture of bushrangers, and by this means many convicts and soldiers, the first inspired by a hope of obtaining their liberty, the latter by the prospect of more material gain, were induced to hunt down the robbers. Some of the stories concerning the capture of the leaders are of thrilling interest, and the daring and coolness displayed by both pursuers and pursued make the records of this period read more like sensational novels than sober official documents. The history of Michael Howe is, perhaps, the most dramatic. Howe, a sailor by profession, was convicted of highway robbery in 1812, and transported to Hobart Town, where the old instinct soon asserted itself and drove him to the bush. He took a leading part in the boldest raids on settlers, but escaped all his would-be captors by the aid of an aboriginal girl, who guided him to hiding-places almost inaccessible to white men. A price was put upon his head, and a party of settlers were eager in pursuit ; but when the bushrangers comprising his band were at length overtaken, the colonists were defeated and five of their number killed. This was not, however, sufficient retaliation for Howe's party, who made an attack on the homestead of the leader of the settlers, in the hope of wreaking vengeance ; the house in the meantime had been filled with soldiers, and the robbers

HEAD OF TASMANIAN NATIVE.

met with a warmer reception than they had anticipated. Many of the bushrangers were killed, and
amongst them Whitehead, one of the leaders of the
band. Howe thereupon severed the head from the
trunk of Whitehead, and, bearing it with him, successfully fled from the arm of the law. He again
formed his band, and, styling himself the "Governor
of the Ranges," continued to commit crimes even
more atrocious than before.

But the notoriety gained by Howe caused his
capture to be regarded as of the utmost importance,
the reward offered being exceptionally high. Worral,
a convict who longed for his liberty, pressed him hard.
Flying for life through the rocky mountains, the
black girl, worn and sick, lagged behind, and Howe,
moved by no feelings of affection or pity for the
woman who had followed him so faithfully, turned
and shot her, in the hope of preventing all possibility
of betrayal, should she be taken by his enemies. In
his haste his pistol was ill aimed, and the woman was
wounded but not killed, and henceforth one more was
added to Howe's pursuers—one who was the most
formidable of them all, for her motive was revenge,
not gain, and all his hiding-places and habits were
known to her. Once Howe was captured and bound,
but he slipped his bonds and slew his two captors.
At last Worral and a soldier named Pugh tried
artifice, and, concealing themselves in a hut, they
persuaded a former friend of Howe's to entice him
into it. His enemies sprang out upon him, and a
desperate fight began. Howe beat off his assailants
and turned to fly. But if they could not take him

alive, they were at any rate determined that no one else should ; clubbing their muskets, they dashed out the bushranger's brains.   This story will give some idea of the wild life led by many of the colonists, who slept with loaded firearms by their pillows, ready at any moment to repulse an attack by robbers who were already so steeped in crime that the taking of a life more or less could add nothing to the penalty already earned.

The war waged against the bushrangers was at length successful, and confidence was restored amongst the farmers.   Some pure Merino sheep from Macarthur's Camden flock were imported, and both stock-breeding and agriculture were energetically pushed forward.   Reform was also effected at this time in the management of convicts.   Musters were instituted, and stringent regulations governing the movements of assigned servants promulgated, while a penal settlement was formed at Macquarie Harbour, in which the worst of the prisoners were closely guarded.   Sorrel by these means afforded no opportunity to the prisoners of absconding into the bush without their flight being at once discovered. In 1822 the first church, St. David's, was completed, but no schools were as yet in existence, and the standard of morality was exceedingly low.   In Hobart there was a population of over 1000, but the town was little more than a collection of mean-looking wooden huts.   Trade had nevertheless greatly increased, and the colony showed promise of better things.   Sorrel left Australia in 1824, and was succeeded by Colonel George Arthur.   Shortly after Van

Diemen's Land was proclaimed an independent colony, and Local Legislative and Executive Councils were appointed. The first consisted of seven members, all nominated by the Crown, and the second of four nominees, mostly officials. One of the first acts of the new legislature was to pass a law to regulate the currency, which had become bewilderingly confused, paper, more or less worthless, and foreign coin, being the common circulating mediums. The anomalous condition of the administration of justice had in the year before been remedied, and a judge had been sent out from England bearing a charter establishing a Supreme Court of Van Diemen's Land. The Acts with regard to juries which were in force in New South Wales applied to the island, but Pidder, the new judge, read the law differently from Forbes, and rigorously excluded the emancipated class from the jury-box. During the previous ten years the social conditions of the community had greatly changed, and the evidences of the presence of a free population began to force themselves upon the Government. The most important of these was in regard to the press. After many unsuccessful attempts, a paper called the *Hobart Town Gazette* had been established in 1816, under official patronage, and subject to the Governor's control; this periodical still lived when Governor Arthur took up the reins of government. But Bent, the editor, longed to be free from restraining influences, and soon fell out with the imperious Arthur. The result could be only one way. Arthur triumphed, and the *Hobart Town Gazette* and *Van Diemen's Land Advertiser* ceased to appear for a

TASMANIAN NATIVE.

(Coal River Tribe.)

time, and a Government publication, under the first half of the old title, took its place. In the following year Arthur took steps to suppress the liberty of the press, and succeeded in passing an Act imposing a license fee and a stamp tax of threepence per copy on all newspapers. A penalty of £100 was incurred by any one publishing a paper without first having obtained a license, and (as was apparently intended) Bent soon fell a victim to the new measure, and posed as a martyr in gaol. But Arthur had gone too far, and his action gave life to a movement in favour of popular institutions. The King and Commons were petitioned for trial by jury on a more extended scale, as well as for government by representation ; an agitation at once commenced, which steadily increased till the boons craved were granted. General dissatisfaction was expressed at the harshness of Arthur's press law, and the prohibitory character of the stamp duty, and so strong was popular feeling that the Act was amended in the direction indicated.

But although Arthur was scarcely prudent in some of his measures, he did much to improve the internal organisation of the colony. Under his direction the whole island was divided into police districts, each under a stipendiary magistrate, and no convict was permitted to travel from one district to another without having first obtained a permit from the magistrate in charge. The commercial and financial affairs of the country also received attention, and Arthur recognised that the usury laws of England were very inappropriate to the very different circumstances of Van Diemen's Land. The question was a serious

one ; for, had the usury laws applied, 99 per cent. of
the transactions of the ordinary commercial life of the
community would have been legally punishable with
severe penalties.   Arthur took the bull by the horns,
and boldly declared the usury law not to apply.
The country was rapidly becoming more settled.
Mr. Henry Hellyer in 1827 traversed the banks of the
Arthur and Hellyer rivers, and named the Surrey and
the Hampshire hills.   The fertility of the soil, and
suitability of the colony for agricultural and pastoral
enterpise on a large scale, attracted the attention of
English capitalists.   In 1825 two large companies
were formed with the object mainly of sheep farming.
The Van Diemen's Land Company obtained by
charter a block of 250,000 acres in the north-west
portion of the island, and shortly after another
100,000 acres near Emu Bay and Circular Head, and
commenced operations in 1828.   The Van Diemen's
Land Establishment received a smaller grant of
40,000 acres in the Norfolk Plains District, and both
companies set to work energetically to import stock
and improve the breed.   Although bushranging had
been considerably diminished, there were still at large
many reckless and daring robbers.   In two years
there were no less than 103 executions, and in the
sparsely inhabited districts crime was very prevalent.
The convicts were ever on the alert for opportunities
of escape, and in a few instances met with success.
The most remarkable case is perhaps that of some
prisoners who, while being conveyed to Macquarie
Harbour—the destination of the most incorrigible
offenders—seized the *Cypress* and sailed away to

China and Japan. On arrival near port they abandoned their ship, and landed in an open boat, representing themselves to be shipwrecked seamen; and, their story being believed, they were liberally assisted with money to enable them to reach London. On their arrival in England, however, their identity was discovered, and some were hanged, while others were sent back to servitude in Van Diemen's Land.

But the convict and bushranging difficulties had sunk into insignificance compared with the all-absorbing question of the natives. The aboriginals had become more used to the manners and customs of the white population, and had profited by their intercourse. They now waged war in a far more scientific way, and their depredations were more frequent and extensive. When attacking a homestead they usually adopted the following tactics :— First, a feigned attack was made to induce the settlers to fire their guns, and then, before their arms could be reloaded, the black men rushed upon their victims and pierced them with their spears. There was no room for doubt that the cause of the hostility of the natives was to be found in the brutal treatment they had received at the hands of escaped convicts, and stockkeepers on distant runs. Governor Davey declared that "he could not have believed that British subjects would have so ignominiously stained the honour of their country and themselves, as to have acted in the manner they did towards the aborigines." Before a commission appointed by Arthur in 1830, blood-curdling stories of cruelty were freely told. One man had been punished for cutting off the

finger of a native, because he wanted it for a tobacco
stopper; while another had murdered the husband of
a black woman he coveted, and had compelled the
woman to follow him with the bleeding trophy of
the man's head hung about her neck. Could it be
wondered at that the natives regarded a race who
produced such inhuman brutes as these as a fitting
object for just vengeance? Governor after governor
had enjoined peace and harmony between the two
people; but the proclamations were not worth the
paper they were written on, for the blacks could not
read them, and the whites totally disregarded them.
Sorrel reminded his subjects, in 1819, that in places,
far from settlement, the natives were unsuspicious
and peaceable, manifesting no disposition to injure;
they were known moreover to be equally inoffensive
in places where stockkeepers treated them with
mildness and forbearance.

The prosperity of the European population was,
however, regarded naturally as of overwhelming
importance, and all considerations of humanity
had to succumb to measures of expediency. The
day for conciliation had gone by, and Arthur's
efforts to appease the blacks by allotting them special
districts were unheeded. The idea had been to
capture all natives found outside the limits of these
districts, and replace them within the boundaries,
but the capture parties organised for this service, with
but few exceptions, murdered many more than they
took, and the extreme rapidity with which the natives
travelled enabled them to avoid their pursuers, and
strike terror into the breasts of the settlers in lonely

places. This dark page of Tasmanian history is
relieved by one bright spot. A bricklayer named
George Augustus Robinson, who was filled with
religious zeal, offered to go unarmed among the
natives, and endeavour to affect by peaceful means
what the Government had failed to do by force.
Robinson received some slight assistance from the
authorities, but his efforts were useless while all
round him the work of treachery and carnage was
continued by the capture parties. At last Arthur in
despair at the non-success of his more humane intentions with regard to his native reserves, determined
to make one supreme effort to settle the question
once for all. A huge body of settlers, soldiers, and
convicts was organised to drive the natives into
Tasman's Peninsula, the narrow neck of which was
to be carefully guarded as soon as all the blacks had
crossed. Twenty-six depôts for provisions were
formed, and eight hundred soldiers, as many convicts,
and about four hundred free settlers were enrolled
as beaters. What is known as the Black Line was
formed, and an advance steadily made across the
island. Gradually the line of beaters contracted, but
when the journey was finished the natives were
behind and not in front. By some means they had
eluded the vigilance of the white men, and £30,000
had been expended with no result whatever. All
that there was to be shown for the money was one
male native and one boy, who had been captured on
the march. This failure was perhaps fortunate; for
Robinson was now given a fair field in which to try
his scheme. In less than five years he successfully

accomplished his mission, and the small remnant of the native race were gathered by him into one place by means of mutual confidence and his friendly persuasion. There were only two hundred and three survivors, all told, and they were removed to Flinders Island. Here Robinson did all in his power for their comfort, but "they died in the sulks like so many bears," the heartbroken relics of a people who might under better treatment have been capable of a high degree of civilisation.

While these events were occurring considerable progress was made in other directions. A great meeting was held in 1831 to demand responsible government, but, like most movements of this character, the object aimed at was retarded by the want of reason and moderation displaced by its advocates at its inception. Free institutions in a bond colony such as Van Diemen's Land was at this time would have been grotesque. A commission was appointed to inquire into the titles of persons to landed property, and the boundaries of estates were properly surveyed and defined. A further concession was, moreover, made in connection with trial by jury; and, by an enactment of the local legislature, juries were permitted in civil actions on the application of either party to the suit. Education and religion advanced rapidly in the later years of Arthur's Government, and the population improved morally and socially.

XIV.

EVENTS PRECEDING CONSTITUTIONAL GOVERNMENT.

(1837–1851).

THE labour of convicts being used for public purposes, the construction of roads and bridges throughout the country was energetically proceeded with,
and by these means internal communication became
more regular and frequent. Ten years previously a
foot post carried the mails once a fortnight between
Hobart and Launceston, but now a mail cart ran
twice a week, covering the distance, one hundred and
twenty-one miles in about nineteen hours. Arthur
left the colony at the end of October, 1836, and
although his imperious nature and untiring energy
made many enemies, he achieved much for the community under his charge, and was generally regretted
at his departure. The duties of acting Governor
were performed by Lieut.-Colonel Snodgrass for a
couple of months, pending the arrival of Sir John
Franklin, in January of the following year. But
Snodgrass unwittingly sowed the seeds of dissension,
and Franklin on his arrival found himself placed in

a position from which he could not possibly extricate himself without giving offence to a large section of his subjects. It so happened that Snodgrass had been persuaded to convene a synod of Presbyterians to deal with a matter affecting the Scottish Church, but the recognition of any other religious denomination gave umbrage to the Church of England, which claimed to be the only body which should be acknowledged by the State. On the other hand, there was a prospect, should it be conceded that the Presbyterians were under Government direction, that other dissenting bodies might claim similar tutilage. Franklin fully appreciated the difficulty, and at once dissolved the Presbyterian Synod, but in order that this action might not be misconstrued, he adopted Bourke's measures for granting State aid to all denominations, which by their own exertions might place themselves in a position to claim it. Franklin's act was too liberal, and had eventually to be amended on account of the frauds committed in the name of religion; but the principle of tolerance contained in the measure has ever since been accepted throughout Australasia.

It would have been difficult to have found two men more unlike than Franklin and his predecessor. Arthur was essentially strong and relentless. He had no pity for crime or the criminal, and justice under his direction took an even, if undiscriminating, course. Franklin, on the other hand, was filled to overflowing with philanthropy. With him to err was but human, an opportunity for Divine forgiveness. The result can easily be imagined. All the officers

of the Government establishments had been trained
to Arthur's methods, and failed to discover in
Franklin's apparent weakness, the saving leaven of
humanity. From the Colonial Secretary downwards
they fought tooth and nail against the new order of
things, and early in the day Franklin was compelled
to get rid of his private secretary, Maconochie, whose
theories on criminal treatment were a burlesque of
Franklin's methods.

But if for various reasons his reign was not an
administrative success, Franklin nevertheless left an
indelible mark on the social life of the island. An
extraordinary impetus was given to science, literature,
and all the arts. The promotion of higher education
and the general improvement of the conditions of
society were an object of constant attention. The
little meetings of the Tasmanian Society in the
library of Government House, when papers on scientific and philosophical subjects were read and discussed, were the beginning of the present Royal
Society of Tasmania, which has done much good
work. A national museum and a college, which was
intended to be a nucleus of a university, were founded.
The popular interest in science was increased by visits
from the French discovery ships in 1839, and the
Erebus and *Terror* in 1840. Strzelecki, too, who has
already been mentioned in connection with the discovery of gold in New South Wales, made a long
stay in Tasmania. Her Majesty's ship *Beagle* was
making a detailed survey of the coast and rivers, and
the *Fly* about the same time was engaged in similar
work ; so that the interest of colonists took a much

higher plane, and an entirely new spirit pervaded society.

Politically, however, this period was a turbulent one. Transportation was resumed on a large scale in 1841, and, as the influx of criminals increased, the free immigration correspondingly fell off. The free settlers began to be alarmed. Property fell in value and trade was depressed. The fact that it became necessary to pass a new insolvency law throws a side-light on the commercial situation, and naturally enough, as the shoe began to pinch, the clamour for responsible government was renewed with vigour. But the claims of the islanders were disregarded. When partially representative councils were granted to the other colonies in 1842, it was pointed out by the Secretary of State that no constitution could be conferred on Van Diemen's Land, so long as the majority of its population was bond ; but as one of the principal hopes of the agitators for the boon was that if legislation were placed in their hands they would be able to stem the tide of transportation, the explanation was, to say the least of it, unsatisfactory. In August, 1843, Sir John Franklin retired. He would probably have stayed longer at the helm, but he fell a victim to the jealousy and intrigue which permeated the official life of the colony. Mr. John Montague, the Colonial Secretary, had been dismissed by Franklin for insubordination. He at once went to England and preferred *ex parte* charges against the Governor of incompetence and injustice, with the result that Franklin was recalled without a chance of stating his version of the trouble. The later history of Franklin is too well known to need more than passing mention here, for the voyage of the *Erebus* and *Terror* in search of the North-West Passage, and the untimely fate of the expedition, is familiar to all. Franklin was popular, but he was too honest and generous to be a success as the governor of a penal settlement. His memory is preserved in Hobart by a bronze statue, above life size, which stands in Franklin Square not far from the site of the old Government House, where he passed the troubled years of his uncongenial government.

Sir John Eardley Eardley-Wilmot, Bart., arrived before Franklin left, and entered on a short but stormy term of office. The colony was in a very unsettled state, and the fears of the free colonist were increased by the transfer of the convicts from Norfolk Island to Van Diemen's Land. The situation was aggravated by financial difficulties ; for the cost of maintaining the huge gaols and a large army of police, which had become necessary, was a burthen greater than the settlement could bear unaided. A debt of £100,000 had been contracted to meet these expenses, and on the other hand the public revenue had diminished, owing to the practical cessation of free immigration and the consequent decline in the receipts from sale or lease of Crown lands. The Governor was confronted by a serious problem, and he determined to solve it by raising the *ad valorem* duties on imports from 5 to 15 per cent., and by imposing certain rates and tolls. The introduction of the necessary Bills in the Council was, however, the signal for more pronounced opposition on the part of the colonists. It was protested that the police-and-gaols charge was essentially unjust. If the colony had to receive British criminals, the very least Great Britain could do was to pay something towards the cost of keeping them in order. A second string to the opposition bow was that no estimates of expenditure were furnished, and that it was ridiculous to expect the settlers to provide funds in the disbursement of which they would have no control. Although Wilmot may have sympathised with the arguments advanced, he was compelled to find the money somewhere to pay for the maintenance of the establishments ; and as no better system than that already proposed was suggested he was obliged to try and force the obnoxious Bills through the legislature, with the aid of the official members. Although there was much excitement outside as well as within the Council Chamber, there was every prospect of the Governor obtaining a majority, when suddenly six of the unofficial members withdrew from the Chamber, thus making a quorum impossible, and effectually blocking further business. After some time had been wasted in fruitless negotiations, the " Patriotic Six," as they were popularly called, resigned, and petitioned the English Government on the points at issue. They were regarded as martyrs to the constitutional cause, and made a triumphal progress through the country. Mr. Richard Dry, whose name will appear again in these pages, was met at Launceston by an admiring crowd, who took the horses from his vehicle and themselves drew it amidst the greatest enthusiasm through the streets of the town. The reception of the other ex-councillors was almost equally demonstrative, but the Governor, regardless of these popular expressions, gravely accepted the tendered resignations and filled the vacancies in the Council with persons who, if less able, were more tractable. The Bills were passed, but the Governor had made enemies who contrived his downfall.

The financial difficulty was before long solved by the English Government consenting to contribute two-thirds of the cost of maintaining the police and gaols, but the news of this decision came too late to relieve Wilmot in his unfortunate position. In October, 1846, he was suddenly recalled, on account of unfounded and cowardly accusations made against his private character by one of his political opponents, who had returned to England. The charges were indignantly refuted by those who were in the best position to form an opinion, and a petition in Wilmot's favour was signed by the Chief Justice and all the most prominent and respectable members of the community. The Secretary of State was compelled to withdraw the accusations, on which the Governor's recall had been based, but with a strange want of justice declined to do anything to recompense the accused for the injury done him. Wilmot remained in the island, hoping against hope that his innocence would triumph; but the strain and disappointment were too great, and before long he died broken-hearted. During his short tenure of office, substantial progress was made in many directions. In 1844 Mr. W. L. Kentish, an engineer, discovered the open and fertile plains in the north-west portion of the island, and a little later Clarke's Plains, situated more to the westward.

Religion and education, which had got a firm footing under the fostering care of Franklin, continued to advance, and in 1842 the colony was made an independent diocese, and the first Bishop of Tasmania arrived in the following year. Mr. Latrobe came across from Port Phillip to take charge of the Government between the removal of Wilmot and the arrival of his successor; in January, 1847, Sir William Denison landed and entered on what turned out to be the most eventful term of office which has fallen to the lot of any Governor of Tasmania. The Secretary of State for the Colonies had learnt something from Wilmot's financial dilemma, and an engineer officer had been chosen to fill the post of Governor, in the hope that he would succeed in rendering the labour of several thousands of convicts more useful than it had hitherto been. Denison at once took steps to pacify the ruffled feelings of the settlers, and the "Patriotic Six" were, after some slight difficulty with Wilmot's nominees, restored to their places in the Council; comparative quiet having been thus obtained the Governor pushed on energetically with road-making and other public works.

But the all-absorbing question of transportation soon disturbed the political atmosphere. One of the first despatches received by Denison from Earl Grey, the Secretary of State, contained the words: "I have to inform you that it is not the intention of Her Majesty's Government that transportation to Van Diemen's Land should be resumed at the expiration of the two years for which it has already been decided that it should be discontinued ; " and Denison, although personally favourable to the continuance of criminal immigration, promptly communicated this intelligence to the Council. Meanwhile, however, the English Government had changed its intentions, and both the despatch and Denison's announcement were repudiated. The colonists were indignant. An anti-transportation league was formed, and opposition to the continuance of the system was vigorously prosecuted. The efforts of the advocates of the abolition of transportation were strenuously seconded by the supporters of the claim for representative government, and the success of the latter was regarded as the death-knell of the existing convict system. In 1848 Earl Grey had expressed his intention of introducing a measure into the English Parliament providing for a representative Legislative Assembly for Van Diemen's Land, and, although Denison had urged that a single chamber would be dangerous as "an essentially democratic spirit actuated the mass of the community," and that on this account "a second independent chamber should be formed," it was determined to model the new Council on the lines of that existing in New South Wales. In 1850 a Bill was passed granting in some degree the boon craved by the Council, two-thirds of the members of which were to be elected by the people. The first election under the new arrangement justified the hopes of the opponents of transportation, for nearly all of the sixteen men returned to the Legislature were pledged to oppose as far as

15

lay in their power the further introduction of convicts. On the 30th of December, 1851, the Council met, and the first divisions taken were on the question which was engaging so much attention. An address to the Queen, protesting against the continual influx of criminals into the country, was carried by a large majority, and thenceforward the matter received constant attention until in a despatch, dated December 14, 1852, the Duke of Newcastle (Lord Aberdeen's Colonial Secretary) announced that it had been decided to finally abolish transportation immediately. The last ship carrying a cargo of criminals sailed on the 31st of December, 1852, and in May, 1853, an official notification appeared in the *Hobart Town Gazette* to the effect that the colony had ceased to be a receptacle for the victims of British crime.

The news was hailed with every manifestation of delight. The Governor was asked to proclaim a public holiday to commemorate the event, but, although he declined to do this on the grounds that it would be an acknowledgment of class antagonism, the holiday was nevertheless held. The Anti-Transportation League, which had during the struggle become a most powerful organisation, was dissolved in 1854, and next year the prayer of the Council, that the name Van Diemen's Land should be buried with all its unsavoury associations, was granted, and the colony after half a century of troubled life entered a new and happier era as Tasmania.

XV.

UNDER THE NEW CONSTITUTION.

(1851–1893.)

EVENTS soon occurred to still further purge
Tasmania of the criminal taint; the enormous emigration of adult males, consequent on the discovery
of gold in Victoria, induced a large proportion of the
ticket-of-leave men and pardoned convicts to cross the
straits; and, although in 1852 payable gold was found
near Fingal and Town Hill Creek, the phenomenal
richness of the Victorian fields dwarfed all other
discoveries, and the current of emigration continued
to set steadily away from Tasmania. Those in
authority at length became alarmed at the extent of
the exodus from the island, and the Governor was
urgent in his appeals to the English Government to
replenish the exhausted labour market by sending
out large numbers of free immigrants. Prices of the
commonest commodities had risen to a fabulous
height, and those whom duty or necessity tied to
the colony underwent an exceedingly uncomfortable
experience. In spite of the unpromising outlook and
the great reduction in the adult male population,

public interest in the movement in favour of representative government was unabated. The Legislative Council drew up a scheme for a new constitution the principal characteristics of which was the establishment of an Upper Chamber, which it was suggested should be elected by the whole colony on a £25 freehold franchise. In the mean time the existing Council was increased in number from 24 to 33, the proportion of nominated to elected members remaining the same as formerly, and negotiation and discussion between the Governor and the Council continued with regard to the details of the proposed alterations. At the close of 1854, Sir William Denison retired from office, and was succeeded by Sir Henry Edward Fox Young ; shortly afterwards the royal assent was given to an "Act to establish a Parliament in Van Diemen's Land, and to grant a Civil List to Her Majesty." The new House of Assembly was to contain thirty members, elected on what was practically manhood suffrage, and the colony had been divided by the old Council into electoral districts for this purpose. An Upper Chamber was also formed under the title of Legislative Council on the basis mentioned above, the number of members being limited to fifteen. Considerable interest was taken in the first elections, but in most cases the same men who had occupied seats in the partially nominee body were again returned as elected members of the new parliament.

The first Premier was Mr. William Champ, who had been Denison's Colonial Secretary, but for some little time the life of successive ministries was extremely short, and the legislature did not settle down to steady work until the reins of government were taken by Sir Francis Smith. The material prospects of the country had during these years greatly improved, for the irresistible attraction of the gold-fields had somewhat waned, and there had been a steady immigration of a superior class of persons acquainted with agricultural pursuits. The signs of reviving vitality and expansion soon manifested themselves. In 1856 the expediency of constructing a railway between Hobart and Launceston was seriously discussed, and in the following year Hobart was lighted by gas, and a good supply of water was obtained for Launceston by the completion of extensive works. Two years later a submarine cable was laid to Cape Otway from Circular Head and King's Island, and the principle of self-government was extended by the creation of rural municipalities to look after local affairs. In 1860 active efforts were made to develop the mineral resources of the country, and prospecting expeditions were equipped by the Government, and placed under the direction of experienced geologists. Coal had been discovered ten years previously in the neighbourhood of the Don, but, as the seams had not hitherto been extensively worked, experiments to test its quality were now undertaken.

The advance of education kept pace with material development. In 1854 a Central Board of Education had been appointed, consisting of the Executive and Legislative Councils, but three years later the question of public instruction again attracted attention, and efforts were made to found a Tasmanian university. Matters were, however, scarcely far enough advanced to make this desirable ; so a compromise was effected. The old Board was dissolved, and an Act passed appointing a Council of Education with authority to grant the degree of Associate of Arts, and also to vote annually to suitable students two scholarships worth £200 each to be held for four years at an English university. The same difficulties which had been felt in New South Wales, in connection with State aid to religion, about this time called for consideration. The democratic spirit of the colonists was opposed to the maintenance or recognition of any established church, and it was impossible to render assistance to all denominations from the public treasury, first on account of the continued friction and jealousy which would be certain to result, and, secondly, on account of the heavy strain which such a charge would be on the finances of the colony. A Bill authorising the Government to raise a loan of £100,000, to provide funds to commute the annual aid then paid to religious bodies was passed in 1859, but the measure which finally freed the treasury from claims on account of religious endowment was delayed by one cause or another until 1869, when it at last received the royal assent.

During the next few years there is little to record beyond the efforts made to push on public works. The demand of the people for roads and railways, and a liberal public works policy became imperative, so that in 1864 Parliament voted no less than £106,000 for roads and bridges. But the cry for railways was not appeased. A proposal brought forward to construct a line between Launceston and Deloraine in this year was rejected, on the grounds of extravagance ; but the persistence of the promoters at length gained the day, and in 1868 the first sod of the new line was turned by the Duke of Edinburgh, who was then cruising in Australian waters. The railway was to be constructed under peculiar conditions, which soon proved unworkable. The Launceston and Western Railway Company were the nominal proprietors ; but of the total capital required the company only provided about one-ninth part, and the Government advanced the rest, the interest on the £400,000 thus lent being a first charge on the profits of the undertaking. Should the line be worked at a loss, it was agreed by the landholders of the district to be served that a rate should be levied to meet the obligation to the Government. Contrary to expectations, for the first two years after it was opened, the traffic receipts of the line barely paid working expenses, and consequently the landowners were called upon to make good their promise with regard to the interest on the £400,000. The attempt to levy the tax was met with violent opposition, the contributors asserting that the agreement had been rendered void by a concession which had been made to the Main Line Company subsequent to their signing it. Legal proceedings were instituted to compel payment of the rate, whereupon sixty-five of the magistrates who dwelt in the northern district petitioned the Governor, requesting him to intervene and cause the suspension of prosecutions. This Mr. Du Cane—the then Governor—

declined to do, and **twenty-six of the** petitioners consequently resigned **their** positions on the commission of the peace. · The agitation continued for some time, until at length the Government agreed to take over the line from the company, and the angry landowners were relieved from the terms of the contract with regard to the special rate. The Tasmanian Main Line Railway Company, although started under much more favourable conditions, fared little better than the Launceston and Western. The concession to construct a railway from Hobart to Launceston was granted in 1870, but the line was not completed for traffic for six years. After a troubled existence, on account of disputes first as to the route chosen, and then other points of disagreement, the railway was recently bought by the Government for £1,106,500, payable in 3½ per cent inscribed stock.

The practical failure of private companies induced the Government to itself undertake railway construction, and from 1885 to the present time not a year has passed without some material improvement in the railway service of the colony. The increase in railways was accompanied by an equal activity in road-making, jetty-building, and telegraph extension, and these public undertakings are perhaps one of the surest indications of the industrial progress of the people.

Allusion has already been made to the discovery of coal as well as the prospecting expeditions which were equipped at the time when the Governor dreaded the depopulation of the island on account of the rush to the Victorian gold-fields. In spite of the efforts

MOUNT BISCHOFF.

then made, nothing of any very great importance resulted, nor had the mineral possessions of Tasmania much influence upon its property until the discoveries of tin at Mount Bischoff in 1871. When the lodes were worked, Mount Bischoff proved to be one of the richest tin mines in the world, and its opening was the commencement of much greater activity generally. In the following year iron ore, which abounds over a very large area, was worked by a strong company, which erected a fine plant and expended a considerable sum of money. But unfortunately it proved impossible to produce a marketable article, owing to the extreme hardness and brittleness of the iron, due to the presence of chromium in the ore. It is quite possible, however, that this difficulty will be overcome, with the result that the iron deposits will be one of the most valuable possessions of the colony. Other metals, including gold, silver, and copper have been found, and to some extent worked, and there is every reason to believe that Tasmania, like her neighbours, contains enormous mineral wealth.

The constitution, as originally devised, had on the whole worked admirably. There were of course now and again slight conflicts between the two houses, but in most instances the business of the country had not seriously suffered, and matters had been arranged by mutual concessions and co-operation. In 1870, however, the democratic spirit—with its inherent antipathy to any privileges or claims based upon the possession of property—gained the ascendency, and an amendment of the Constitution Act was carried, reducing the leasehold franchise from £10 to £7, and extending the elective right to all in receipt of salary amounting to £80 per annum. At the same time the number of members in the Council was increased by one, and in the Assembly by two. The change did not make any very great difference in the character of the Legislature, and the Council continued to act as a wholesome check to the Lower House. This body frequently displayed an ambition and enterprise involving large expenditure of money which, if not carefully watched, would probably have landed the colony in serious difficulties. The extravagance of the Government did, indeed, reduce the finances to a very unsatisfactory condition by 1879, and led to the most heated contest between the two houses which has yet taken place. The estimates of expenditure in that year, as passed by the Assembly, greatly exceeded the estimated revenue, and the Council, when the necessary measures came before them, declined to sanction appropriations to meet which there would apparently be insufficient funds available. The Government were indignant, and disputed the right of the Council to amend "money bills;" but the Upper House stood firm and refused to pass more than six months' supply unless the estimates were brought into harmony. The fight was long and bitter, and as no money could legally be spent until the Appropriation Act was passed, the Council, after six months of the year had gone by, relented so far as to grant supply for eight months, so that ordinary engagements could be met; and Parliament was then prorogued. Ministers were urgent in their prayers for a dissolution, but as the Governor refused to grant it and could not be persuaded to coerce the Council, the Government resigned, and, a new ministry being formed by Mr. Giblin, the strife was ended by the imposition of fresh taxation, which brought the estimated income to approximately the same sum as it was desired to expend. The new taxes comprised a duty of 9d. in the pound on the annual value of real and personal estate, a revision of the charges at the customs house, and an excise duty of 3d. per gallon on beer. The feeling of the people was one of relief that a solution of the difficulty had been found before matters reached the extreme point which had caused so much inconvenience and misery in Victoria. The comparatively even tenor of public affairs was resumed ; no further important conflicts between the two branches of the Legislature took place, and no alteration in the Constitution was demanded for the next six years. By this time a rearrangement of electoral districts had become desirable, for some of the old divisions were unsuited to the changes which had taken place in the distribution of the people within recent years. The opportunity was seized at the same time to enlarge both branches of the Legislature, and consequently the Council was raised to eighteen and the Assembly to thirty-six members, while the general democratic tendency of the country asserted itself by still further reducing the franchise, although what was practically manhood suffrage had already been established.

It was also thought desirable that the country should have its own representative in London, and, therefore, in 1886 an Agent-General was appointed to transact the business of the colony in England.

Possibly from the fact that hitherto the island has not been convulsed by any sudden flood of immigration, and that the public imagination has not, to the same extent as elsewhere in Australia, been excited by the unexpected acquisition of treasure, Tasmania bears much greater resemblance to the old world than any of the other colonies. Lying to the south of Bass Straits its climate is cooler than that of the mainland, and the fruits and shrubs of the mother country grow luxuriantly. Agriculture, instead of stock-raising, is the main industry of the people, and the cultivation of English fruits has become an extensive and lucrative business. The life of the inhabitants is quiet and uneventful, and the stone-built farm houses, the hawthorn and sweetbriar hedges, the hop gardens and sunny wheat fields, remind the immigrant of home. Indeed, the general appearance of Tasmania is that of some particularly fertile country district of England, which has been bodily removed and set amid the blue waters and smiling skies of the far south.

VICTORIA.

XVI.

FIRST SETTLEMENT.

(1803–1839.)

At the beginning of the century, the activity of the French in the South Pacific caused King grave concern; and he was earnest in his representations to the British Government that no time should be lost in taking effective possession of the land to the southward of Sydney. An expedition was therefore fitted out in England and placed under the command of Colonel Collins, who has already been mentioned as the first Judge-Advocate of New South Wales; in April, 1803, the little band set sail in the frigate *Calcutta* and the storeship *Ocean*. After a comparatively uneventful voyage the vessels arrived off Port Phillip in October, and Collins, before landing his charges, spent two days in examining in small boats the land round the bay. But he was unfortunate in the spots visited, for he found sandy soil and shallow shores with an absence of fresh water at all the points inspected, and the reports of the other officers, whom he sent out to make explorations, only increased the unfavourable impressions he had formed. It is true that good land and fresh streams were believed to exist farther up the bay ; but Collins had a morbid fear of the natives, and the announcement that they had been met with in large numbers near the most promising country was quite enough to make him cling persistently to the coast. After a few days spent in fruitless search, as he had received peremptory orders to discharge the storeship without delay on his arrival, the convicts, soldiers, and settlers were landed on a narrow neck of country forming the southern shore of the bay about five miles from its entrance. The only fresh water to be had at this place was obtained by sinking perforated casks in the sand, while the soil appeared quite unsuitable for cultivation, and the nearest good timber was fourteen miles away. Collins was very much disgusted and took a gloomy view of the future ; but as his settlement was subordinate to the Governor in Sydney, he was unable to move until advice and instruction from King had been obtained. An open boat was therefore immediately sent round to Sydney with a despatch pointing out the failure of the efforts to find a suitable spot for the new colony, and asking leave to transfer the settlement bodily to Van Diemen's Land. Meanwhile, in compliance with the orders he had received before leaving England, Collins proceeded to discharge the *Ocean ;* but the work progressed slowly, for the wretched sailors and prisoners, who spent most of their time up to their waists in the sea, carrying cargo ashore, soon became

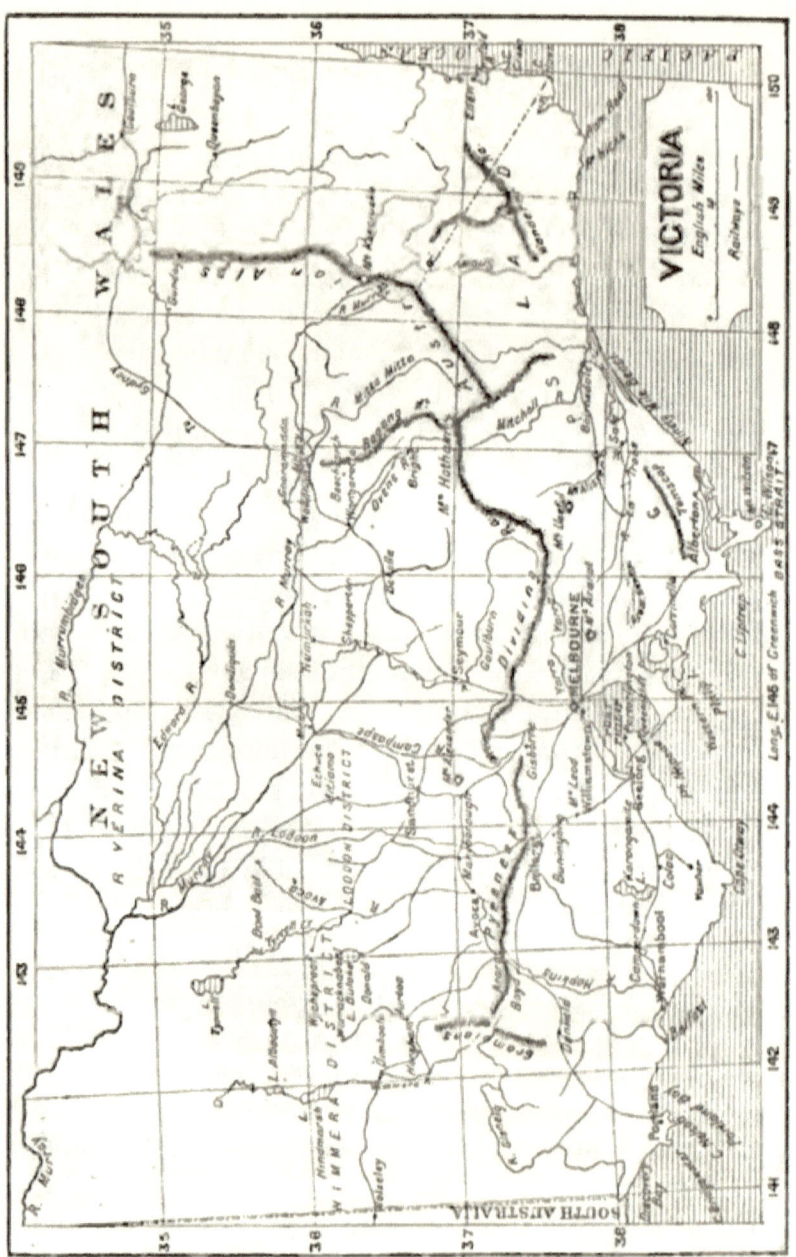

sick from the brackish water, which was all they could get to drink from the casks.

The *Ocean*, when empty, sailed for Port Jackson, picking up on the way the boat previously despatched by Collins ; her captain was thus able to corroborate the complaints which Collins's letter contained. Governor King had but little choice in his decision. Collins's prayer for permission to abandon Port Phillip was so urgent, and contained such a disparaging description of the country, that it was impossible to refuse ; at the same time, had he been instructed to remain, it would have been necessary to strengthen the military guard under his command to relieve him from fears of the natives, whilst at this moment it would have been madness to weaken the garrison at Sydney. King, therefore, though fully impressed with the desirability of establishing a settlement in that part of the country, reluctantly gave his consent, offering Collins the choice of Port Dalrymple in the north or the Derwent in the south of Van Diemen's Land. The *Ocean* was sent back to take the party across the straits, and the *Lady Nelson* sailed with her to render such assistance as might be needed. These two vessels arrived at the camp in December, 1803, and the *Calcutta* at once left for Sydney.

With all possible haste Collins packed his baggage and stores, and turned his back on a country of unpleasant memories ; but several trips had to be made before the whole party could be embarked, and the territory was not entirely vacated till the end of January, 1804.

The convicts during Collins's occupation had behaved fairly well. Twelve absconded, but all but two returned, who had, it was supposed, fallen a prey to the natives. One, however, William Buckley, was found thirty years afterwards living on friendly terms with the aborigines. For more than twenty years the Port Phillip district was strangely neglected, and it was not till the glowing reports of the explorations of Messrs. Hume and Hovell, and further rumours of an intended French colony, had been received in Sydney, that the formation of a settlement in the country was again attempted. Unfortunately Hovell instead of Hume had the ear of the authorities, and the mistake he had made between Port Phillip and Western Port was the cause of another failure. Captain Wright, with a small party of prisoners and soldiers, and Hovell to guide them, landed at Western Port, but a more unsuitable spot, barren and unapproachable as it was, on account of the mud-flats lining the shores, could scarcely have been chosen; when it was found that the French had already landed and departed, permission was given to the commander to withdraw, and Victoria was for the second time abandoned as useless and uninhabitable.

It is not probable that after two such failures the Government would have made any further effort, had not their hands been forced by the enterprise of some colonists from Van Diemen's Land. In very early days there had been small permanent whaling stations along the coast; but in 1834 the Henty Brothers were so favourably impressed with the appearance of the pasture lands behind Portland Bay that they determined to cross the straits from Launceston and cultivate the unoccupied territory. Their father was one of those who, in 1828, had been attracted by the scheme for settling Western Australia, and, being a man of means, had obtained a large grant of land in that colony. But when one of his sons had seen the barren wastes which were being lavishly granted to immigrants, he reported so adversely that the destination of the Henty family was changed to Van Diemen's Land. The father and eight sons all followed farming pursuits, but before long the restricted pastures of the island became too small for the flocks and herds, which had multiplied rapidly. Edward Henty, therefore, went in search of a new home, and settled at Portland Bay. After he had been living there some little time, two of his brothers joined him, and agriculture, stock-raising, and whaling were prosecuted with great success. There was, however, one serious drawback ; for the Secretary of State, when applied to, refused to grant the Messrs. Henty any title to the lands of which they had taken possession. In this particular case no serious inconvenience was experienced, for other claimants did not appear ; but a similar enterprise, which was undertaken a few years later, brought matters to a crisis, and forced the authorities to abandon the idea of confining occupation to the districts immediately surrounding the chief seat of government.

In 1834 a company was formed in Tasmania to acquire land and engage in stock breeding at Port Phillip. John Batman, the promoter and leader of the enterprise, was a remarkable man. A native of

New South Wales, he had crossed to Van Diemen's
Land when little more than a boy, and there had
distinguished himself in the chase and capture of
bushrangers, and later by the marked success which
attended his efforts to subdue the aborigines by
peaceful means. For some years he farmed, but his
adventurous spirit was always craving for fresh
excitement, and in 1827 he applied to the Governor
of New South Wales for permission to occupy the
country around Western Port. This request could
not be granted; to authorise detached settlements
would have been directly contrary to the instructions
of the Secretary of State. But the refusal in no
way quenched Batman's aspirations, and in 1834 he
became one of an association of eight members
which had determined to obtain possession of the
fertile country at Port Phillip without the sanction or
aid of the Government. The roll of Batman's little
company contained the names of many prominent
and influential men in Van Diemen's Land, and the
fact that Batman himself was to be the pioneer was
sufficient to assure reasonable prospects of success.
A little vessel of fifteen tons burthen, the *Rebecca*,
was procured, and John Batman, taking with him
some New South Wales blacks and a few white men,
set sail for Port Phillip. Bad weather was met with,
and the passage took nineteen days, but at last, on
May 29, 1835, the weary, uncomfortable voyage was
finished, and the little party of adventurers landed at
Geelong. Batman was in possession of the chart
made by Flinders of the bay and its surroundings,
and early on the morning after his arrival he started

off to explore on his own account. As he trod the
rich pasture lands comparatively free from timber he
became more and more elated, and the prospect from
the top of the Barrabool Hills increased his favourable
opinion of the country.

But Batman's special mission was to purchase
land from the natives, and on the second day after
landing he set off in quest of some of the aboriginal
inhabitants. Fires had been seen in the night
some distance away, so at daybreak all haste was
made to the spot, but the blacks had already
left. Batman started in pursuit, and after a tiring
journey overtook a party of about twenty women
and a large number of children. They at first
showed signs of fear, but appeared to understand
the expressions of amicable intentions which were
made by the New South Wales natives, and allowed
the visitors to approach. The usual presents of
trinkets, looking-glasses, &c., were made, and Batman,
having sown the seeds of friendship, returned to his
camp. Explorations were continued for the next few
days, and then the *Rebecca* was brought further up
the bay and moored off the mouth of the Yarra.
With fourteen companions armed for any emergency,
Batman commenced to walk along the left bank of
the river, but after he had travelled a little way his
course was interrupted by a tributary stream. Two
days they marched along through glorious pastures,
and towards the close of the second day, to their
delight, saw the smoke of fires ascending in the
distance to the south-east. Eagerly they pushed on
in the hope of coming up with the natives, and before

many miles had been covered overtook a man, woman, and three children. To their satisfaction they learned that the previous intercourse with the women had been discussed, and when the natives led them to the main camp of the tribe, on the banks of the Merri Creek, they were received with manifestations of friendship. After spending a night amongst the blacks, Batman next day proceeded to business, and had little difficulty in effecting an advantageous purchase. Skeleton parchment deeds had been made out in Hobart before starting, so only a few descriptive details had to be added, and then a contract between Batman, three brothers called Jaga-Jaga, and the chiefs of the Dutigalla tribe was duly signed and sealed by the persons interested, and Batman obtained possession, as he thought, of all the country from Indented Head to Merri Creek, or about 600,000 acres of fine pasture, in exchange for some trinkets and an annual tribute of blankets.

Having accomplished his mission, he bade farewell to the natives, and started to retrace his steps, but before he had travelled far he was confronted by an extensive swamp and, being overtaken by darkness, had to pass the night on its borders; in the morning, while making a circuit to avoid it, he came upon the Yarra, and eventually reached the *Rebecca*. The next day was spent in an examination of the river, and Batman selected the present site of Melbourne as the best place for a village. On his return the *Rebecca* was taken down to Indented Head again, where three whites and the New South Wales natives were landed to retain possession of the newly-acquired property and commence cultivation. The remainder of the party sailed for Hobart to give a report of their proceedings to the other members of the association, who were anxiously awaiting their return. Batman's account of his experiences created a great sensation in Van Diemen's Land, and many of the colonists at once commenced to formulate schemes for following his example and settling in the fertile country across the straits. The members of Batman's association were not, however, quite easy in their minds, and all along they appear to have had doubts of the validity of the formidable looking parchment deeds which represented their title to the land. These deeds had been prepared and signed in triplicate, and one copy was sent to the Governor on the 25th of June with a request, which was influentially supported, that he should do all in his power to cause the claim of Batman and his friends to be recognised by the authorities. On the 3rd of the following month Arthur gave his answer. In the first place, he pointed out, Port Phillip was outside his jurisdiction, so that, even were he willing, he could do but little to help them ; and he further warned them that the total disregard of any proprietary interest of the natives, evinced by the legislation in regard to South Australia, was pretty conclusive evidence that a claim based on an alleged sale by the natives would command little respect in England. At the same time, Arthur wrote strongly to the Secretary of State, requesting immediate attention, and some definite instructions with regard to the novel problems which were presenting themselves to the Government.

But, although ownership of property acquired in Port Phillip was questionable, this unsatisfactory circumstance was not sufficient to prevent many persons from going there. The most important expedition was arranged by John Pascoe Fawkner, who had been one of the children in the party which landed at the time of Collins's abortive attempt to form a colony in 1803. Fawkner's idea was to pursue at Western Port much the same policy as Batman had followed at Port Phillip, and a schooner, the *Enterprise*, was procured and loaded with stock, implements, seeds, fruit trees, and plants, and everything else which appeared necessary to equip a small agricultural and pastoral station. On July 27, 1835, the *Enterprise* left Launceston, but she almost immediately fell in with very bad weather, and after knocking about for three days was still close to the Tasmanian coast. Fawkner by this time was so worn out with sea-sickness that he was put ashore, and the voyage was resumed under the command of Captain Lancey. Western Port was at length reached in safety, but, as the intending settlers were displeased with the appearance of the place, anchor was again weighed, and the *Enterprise* headed for Port Phillip. Captain Lancey sailed his ship right up to the Yarra's mouth, and then, entering a rowing boat, proceeded up the stream. They first went up the Saltwater, but retraced their course, and, again entering the Yarra, camped at the spot which Batman had marked as a suitable site for a village. The place seemed to exactly meet their requirements, so next day the *Enterprise* was warped up and made fast to the trees,

and the cargo carefully landed. The whole party at
once set to work to clear the ground and prepare it
for cultivation; they were busily engaged in this
way when they were suddenly interrupted by the
appearance on the scene of Mr. Wedge, one of
Batman's partners, who informed them that they
were trespassing on the company's property. Wedge
endeavoured to prove his title, but Captain Lancey
ridiculed the deed, and fell to work again at clearing
and ploughing. Wedge, being then unable to do
anything more, retired, but in a few days returned
with his whole party to forcibly assert his claim to
the land which Lancey was occupying. Matters
began to assume rather a serious aspect, when the
rival companies camped side by side, but at length
the first-comers prevailed upon Lancey to accept £20
and cross to the other side of the stream. Not long
afterwards, however, Fawkner arrived with more men
and materials, and as by this time the events which
are about to be recorded had upset Batman's claim,
the river was once more crossed and the old site
again occupied.

Although Fawkner was the principal, he was not the
only man who determined to make the Port Phillip
district his home, and numerous little bands settled
on the territory within twelve months of Batman's
return to Van Diemen's Land. The prospect of
grave difficulties arising unless some proper system
of survey and sale of land were immediately introduced, caused the Governor of New South Wales,
Sir Richard Bourke, to issue a proclamation without
waiting for the decision of the Secretary of State,

in answer to Governor Arthur's despatch from
Van Diemen's Land. Batman's treaty with the
natives was, Bourke declared, void as against the
rights of the Crown, and all persons occupying land
in the Port Phillip district were trespassers unless
they were possessed of the ordinary license from the
Government. The situation was a perplexing one,
for a proposal of Bourke's to form a small settlement
at Twofold Bay on the south coast of New South
Wales had just been rejected by the Secretary of
State, on the grounds that the endeavour should be
to concentrate the population and not to scatter it
over a wide area, principally for the reason that
if the limits of occupation were restricted it was
believed the cost of the administration of justice and
general government would be smaller. Of course it
was simple enough for a governor to refrain from
forming new posts ; but what was to be done when the
new posts formed themselves, and then demanded the
protection and administrative benefits enjoyed by the
rest of the community ? As Bourke pointed out to
the Secretary of State, the question had now become,
how best to direct this new development in colonisation, not how to prevent the settlement of the
territory. Pending other arrangements, the inhabitants had themselves selected one of their number as
arbitrator in disputes, and the need for some action
by the executive was so evident that Bourke sent
down a magistrate, Mr. George Stewart, to report,
and (on his recommendation) appointed Captain
Lonsdale resident magistrate, supplying him with a
small detachment of soldiers to enforce his awards

and maintain order. This done he awaited despatches from the Secretary of State, which in due
course arrived, and were practically to the effect that
the English Government were at a loss as to the best
method of dealing with a question so "novel and
peculiar," and were content to leave the matter to
his discretion. Under these circumstances, Bourke
thought it advisable to visit the new dependency
himself, and accordingly in 1837 he journeyed to Port
Phillip. The settlers who now numbered from sixty
to seventy families, welcomed him with enthusiasm,
and he laid out and named the streets of a town
which he called Melbourne, in honour of the Prime
Minister of the English Government. Bourke was
impressed with the prospects of the Port Phillip
colony, and on his return recommended the Secretary
of State to appoint a Lieutenant-Governor or Commandant, advice which was before long followed. At
the same time he considered that if the inhabitants
desired legislative representation, they should be required to elect members to attend the sessions of the
Council in Sydney.

XVII.

THE ADMINISTRATION OF MR. LATROBE.

(1839–1852.)

UNDER the title of Superintendent, Mr. Latrobe was sent out in 1839 to take charge of the Port Phillip settlement. For the population had been largely augmented by immigration, and new towns at Geelong and Williamstown had been formed. Evidences of the rapidly increasing trade and social requirements of the people were to be found in the fact that two Sydney banks had opened branches in Melbourne, in addition to the establishment of a local bank, and two newspapers, under the titles of the *Melbourne Daily News and Port Phillip Patriot* and the *Port Phillip Gazette*, had succeeded a very primitive journal called the *Advertiser*. Latrobe's position was not an easy one, for administrative difficulties were continually appearing in the Government of a community which more than doubled itself annually. The most unsatisfactory matter was the inability of the authorities to keep pace in survey with the demand for land. In June, 1837, the first sale of half-acre town allotments took place, by the direction of Bourke, when the average price obtained was £35, and a few months later a second sale was held, at which values were about the same. By these means the immediate needs of the urban population were met, but the staff of surveyors and draftsmen at Latrobe's disposal was quite incapable of keeping pace with the applications for runs, while the frequent changes in the orders-in-Council relating to the sale and occupation of Crown lands, threw matters into still worse confusion. Port Phillip did not escape the consequences of too great prosperity, and for a short time had to submit to the chastening influences of depression caused by reckless speculation.

But nature was too bountiful to permit the stagnation to last long, and the rapidity with which the settlement grew almost justified the settlers in giving way to the temptation to speculate. It is needless, here, to follow the frequent and often unreasonable changes in the land laws which took place about this time, for all the colonies were treated with a diluted " Wakefield system," but in doses too weak to give a fair trial to the theory, and applied with a singular want of discrimination. In 1842 an Act had been passed in the English Parliament granting the inhabitants of Port Phillip authority to elect six representatives in the Legislature of New South Wales. But although this arrangement met every reasonable requirement, it was not sufficiently liberal to satisfy the ambition of the new colony. An agitation for total separation from New South Wales had commenced in the very infancy of the community, and in 1844 this movement took concrete form in a resolution submitted by Dr.

Lang, one of the members for Port Phillip in the Legislative Council in Sydney. Dr. Lang moved that the immediate erection of the Port Phillip district into a separate colony was advisable, but the motion was rejected by a very large majority, and the inhabitants understood that they would get little aid from New South Wales in their efforts at dismemberment. Having failed to obtain their way in a decorous manner, by an expression of opinion in the legislative chamber, a section of the population determined to call the attention of the authorities in England to their grievance in a somewhat remarkable fashion. It was intended to spurn their right of representation in Sydney as useless and worthless, and to nominate no one for the positions at the next election. This plan was, however, frustrated by the appearance of one candidate, duly proposed ; as he declined to withdraw, and would be elected were no opposition offered, the policy of the malcontents was suddenly changed, and "the Right Honourable Henry Grey, Earl Grey, in the peerage of Great Britain," the then Secretary of State for the Colonies, was nominated as his opponent. The burlesque was successful, and Earl Grey obtained a majority of 193 votes in a total poll of 397 ; but such a ridiculous result could hardly be expected to be gravely accepted by the Governor, and Sir Charles Fitzroy promptly declared the election void, and issued a fresh writ making Geelong instead of Melbourne the place of nomination. An attempt was made to re-enact the same farce on this occasion, and the Duke of Wellington, Lords Palmerston, Brougham, and Russell, and Sir Robert Peel were named as candidates ; but, fortunately, some local men were also nominated and returned at the head of the poll. But the comedians had in a measure achieved their end, for the attention of the Secretary of State was called to their complaint, and a select committee appointed to inquire into the matter, which recommended that the provinces should be separated. Earl Grey promised to give effect to their recommendation, but the Government of which he was a member going out of office, the necessary legislation was delayed, much to the disgust of the impatient agitators in Melbourne. At length, in 1850, an Act was passed authorising the division which was so much desired, and news of the intended step was welcomed throughout the Port Phillip district by general public rejoicing. Mr. Latrobe was appointed first Governor of " Victoria," as the new colony was called and the preliminary arrangements necessary for establishing a local legislature were placed in the hands of the Sydney Council.

Shortly before independence had been effected, the discoveries of gold in New South Wales threatened to depopulate its ambitious offspring, and Latrobe found his subjects rapidly diminishing in numbers. It seemed that the only hope of counteracting the superior attractions of the mother colony was for gold to be found in Victoria also ; and public meetings were held in Melbourne, at which a " Gold Discovery Committee " was formed to encourage search for the mineral within the boundaries of Victoria, by offering £200 as a reward to any one who should bring the first news of the existence of a payable gold-field within two hundred miles of Melbourne. The inducement was sufficient to cause many people to start out on prospecting expeditions, and before long the precious metal was discovered in several places. Rumours of the presence of gold in Victoria had been heard previously, and a man who described himself as a shepherd had in 1849 brought to Melbourne a rich quartz specimen, which he alleged he had obtained on the Pyrenees Range; his story, however, was discredited, and the matter was never followed up. Mr. Campbell, while staying with a friend at Clunes, found gold in March, 1850, but kept the matter secret until July, 1851, when gold was obtained in the Yarra Ranges, at Anderson's Creek, and in the quartz rocks of the Pyrenees. In August the famous Ballaarat fields were discovered, and in the beginning of September news of the finds near Mount Alexander was made public. By the end of September, 1851, the tide of migration had completely turned, and thousands of greedy fortune-seekers poured into the colony by land and sea. As the extraordinary wealth, first of Ballaarat, then of Mount Alexander, and a little later of Bendigo, became known, the crowds which trudged along the muddy, dusty tracks to these places rapidly grew larger and larger. In the autumn of 1852 fully seventy thousand men were grubbing for gold, and at the diggings the soil for miles had been plundered of its treasure. Before there was any diminution in the stream of immigrants from the other colonies, the flood was swollen by hundreds of thousands of men who came from Europe and America. In 1840 there had been under 10,300 people within the limits of Victoria; by 1850 the fertility of the soil had attracted about 76,200 ; but five years later the population had grown to 364,300, consequent upon the rush to the gold-fields. At this time there were nearly twice as many men as women in the country, and the accession to the population comprised many very undesirable elements.

The situation in Victoria was very different to that in the parent colony. For one thing, in Victoria the original population at the time of the discovery of gold was far smaller, so that it was more difficult for the government to suddenly be adjusted to meet the changed circumstances. The gold-fields in Victoria, moreover, were much more compact, and being nearer to the coast more easily reached. Consequently, shortly after the first rich finds, enormous numbers of people collected in comparatively restricted areas. On the banks of the Yarrowee at Ballaarat, for instance, there were at one time about forty thousand men encamped. About twenty-five thousand more were round Mount Alexander, and at the Bendigo diggings fully forty thousand miners had gathered. The machinery of government very soon proved utterly inadequate to the duties it was called upon to perform. Had the inhabitants of these camps been ordinary orderly citizens, the administration of affairs would have entailed organisation and care, but in communities so strongly leavened with criminals and reckless vagabonds, the maintenance of order and the law became hopeless. While Tasmania was purged of the worst portion of its crime-stained inhabitants by the gold-rush, the motley crowd, which swarmed like ants over the mud-heaps at the diggings, contained even more unruly characters than the Tasmanians. Latrobe seems from the first to have realised the gravity of the situation; but he had no really capable men at hand to help him, and, however great his personal exertions might be, the formation of governing machinery out of nothing, for a population that doubled itself each year, was a task beyond his powers. From the commencement the regulations and licensing arrangements which had been formulated by Deas Thompson for New South Wales were adopted by Latrobe, but though they might be satisfactorily worked with a comparatively small collection of men, they were quite unsuitable to the turbulent crowds which had gathered at Ballaarat and Bendigo. The monthly inspection of the licenses of forty thousand unwilling men is a by no means light task, and the system adopted was open to very great abuse in its application. Those who had licenses objected strongly to being constantly required to produce them to satisfy suspicious officials, while those who had not licenses had but little difficulty in secreting themselves and evading the activity of troopers. Acts of riot and lawlessness were before long not infrequent. Bushranging became common. The gold escorts were waylaid and robbed after the troopers who were protecting them had been shot. Even vessels in the harbour were attacked and plundered.

Much of this crime was traced to the Tasmanians, and special legislation was passed to protect the

colony from further inroads from this quarter. By
the Convicts Prevention Act of 1852 all persons
coming from Tasmania were required to prove that
they were not convicts before they were permitted to
land, and the captain of any vessel which conveyed a
convict to a Victorian port was made liable to a fine
of £100. But it was too late to take protective
measures; the harm had already been done; and all
the undesirable people from Tasmania who could by
hook or by crook get a passage across the straits had
arrived. A spirit of discontent was inseparable from
the miner's occupation. The very good fortune of
some bred dissatisfaction in the breasts of others, and
the anger of those who had toiled all day in the heat
to wash out next to nothing was but natural when
they were pounced upon by the police and commanded to show their license. Some men of course
were doing well, and at one time probably many
were winning from £40 to £50 worth of gold a day;
but for every stroke of luck there must have been
many bitter disappointments. The life of a miner
was rough in the extreme, and a large proportion of
those who flocked to the diggings were quite unpre-
pared for the hardships and discomforts with which
they had to contend.

The crowd at the gold-fields was comprised of men
of every class and nearly every nationality. The
banks of the Yarrowee presented a strange appearance, with the eager line of men standing shoulder
to shoulder, washing in the muddy water the dirt
brought them from time to time by a companion.
A little further back the earth was cut into in-

numerable holes, flanked by great mounds of red soil,
in and around which men busily ran or dug with
feverish energy. At night the scene was even more
weirdly curious, for the glaring lights of the theatres
and grog shanties joined with the flaring torches and
fires of the miners in throwing into strong relief the
shadows of the tents and their wild surroundings.
Above all rose the hum of a city, broken now and
again by bursts of noisy revelry. Wealth easily won
was as readily squandered, and the lucky digger
showered gold with a free hand. Prices were exorbitant, for the miner drunk with fortune seldom asked
for change, and the style of living generally was recklessly extravagant.

The oppressive prosperity of their neighbours, however, caused discontent on the part of those on whom
fate had not yet smiled, and the feeling of irritation
against the authorities was augmented by the scramb-
ling, inefficient administration of the law. Twice a
week "digger hunts" were held by the police, and all
miners who could not produce their licenses were
seized and taken off to the commissioners' camp,
being usually chained to the surrounding trees, until
that official was ready to deal with them. Often
their tents were burnt by the police, and not infrequently mistakes were made and flagrant injustice
perpetrated upon those who had hitherto obeyed the
law. While the feeling at the gold-fields was in this
irritable state, the Government blindly endeavoured
to double the license fee, which even then was costing
more than its value to collect. Latrobe's new executive council considered that in view of the large

extra expenditure involved in the regulation and maintenance of order at the gold-fields, the sum of thirty shillings per month was not a sufficiently large contribution to the public revenue by those who were so rapidly winning fortunes from the soil. Oblivious of the unfortunates who had suffered and toiled in vain, Latrobe was urged to raise the monthly fee for a permit to dig for gold to £3. A notice was therefore promulgated in the Government *Gazette*, in December, 1851, to the effect that from the commencement of the following year the increased rate would be demanded. It was also hoped that by this step many would be induced to desert the diggings for more settled occupation ; for all other industries were crippled by the dearth of labour, and prices and wages in the towns and indeed throughout the settlement had risen to unheard-of figures. Even at the ruinous rates offered it was impossible to obtain servants, so that every one, the most wealthy included, had to perform the meanest domestic offices for themselves ; while it was probable that, unless some change were effected, the coming harvest would remain ungarnered, and the flocks unshorn. Communication with England and elsewhere was almost completely suspended. No sooner did a vessel let go her anchor in Hobson's Bay than the crew deserted and went to try their fortunes at the diggings.

All sorts of strong measures to prevent the depopulation of the towns were urged upon the bewildered governor, but they were all impracticable, and the raising of the license fee was the only expedient which could be resorted to with the remotest prospect of success. But at Bendigo, Ballaarat, and elsewhere there were men only waiting for a favourable opportunity to defy a government which they knew was weak, and towards which they had no feelings of loyalty or respect. A few days after the publication of the *Gazette* notice meetings were held near Mount Alexander, and language was used which augured ill for the maintenance of order in the future. So hostile did the mining population appear that the Government was filled with apprehension, for in the case of any serious opposition being offered to the collection of the tax there was not sufficient force available to compel it. Latrobe's advisers wavered. On the 15th of December a meeting numbering from twelve to fourteen thousand persons was held at Forest Creek, and a few days afterwards a similar gathering assembled at Geelong. The proposed fee was denounced as exorbitant and tyrannical, and the exaction of any fee whatever from miners was described as an imposition of an iniquitous "capitation tax on labour." This turned the scale, and the Government on the 13th of December withdrew the notice which had produced the storm.

Latrobe recognised the serious blow that had been struck at the authority of government, but he was thankful for the comparative peace which followed capitulation. By this time the population had increased enormously, and the extravagance of the miners had made trade so profitable that many were induced to forego the diggings and cater for the wants of their inhabitants. Prices remained high, but a development of other industries took place more commensurate with the growth of the community. The flood of immigrants continued to flow as strongly as ever towards the shores of Victoria, and the hotels and accommodation houses in Melbourne were quite insufficient to provide shelter for the crowds of newcomers. In the reserves and open spaces the adventurers pitched their tents, but as at these canvas towns there were no sanitary provisions, and no proper control, cleanliness and even ordinary decency were an impossibility. At length the miseries of the immigrants, many of whom found themselves on landing in the midst of surroundings utterly different to anything they had expected, excited the pity and benevolence of the other residents. Temporary shelters were erected to house the families who could find no accommodation, and hulks in the bay were secured for the use of single women. The cost of these arrangements were partly borne by the Government and partly defrayed out of private contributions.

XVIII.

THE EUREKA STOCKADE.

(1852–1857.)

IN 1852 a despatch was received from the Secretary
of State for the Colonies announcing that the English
Government had determined to hand over to the
various provinces the revenue derived from gold,
since it was thought that the increased cost of government on account of the gold-fields would make it
necessary for all the colonies affected to largely
increase the charge for police, as well as the expenditure for general purposes. At the same time
Latrobe's prayer for reinforcements was complied
with, and fifty police were despatched from England
and a man-of-war ordered round to Hobson's Bay.
These additions to the local forces were sorely needed,
for the difficulty of guarding the traffic on the roads
to and from the gold-fields had been increased by
the opening of the Oven's diggings in June, and the
spirit of resistance, which had grown greatly since
the concessions with regard to the increase to the
license fee, made it necessary for the authorities to
be continually in readiness to quell anticipated out-

breaks. Latrobe longed to be free from the necessity of collecting a tax which was expensive and odious to its contributors, and, with this end in view, recommended that an export duty on gold should be substituted for the license fee, only such an amount being charged for a license as would ensure the registration of those authorised to dig for gold. The Export Duty Bill was introduced, and got as far as the second reading in the Council, but at the diggings the Governor's actions were misrepresented and used as a further incentive to riot. Meetings were held at Forest Creek, at which it was determined to refuse to pay any license fee at all if an export duty were charged ; and at other places, more especially at Oven's, crowds began to get alarmingly insubordinate. Members became frightened, and the Bill, which was the beginning of the disaster which clouded Sir Charles Hotham's rule, was shelved.

A serious disturbance took place early in the following year at Forest Creek. It was caused by a mistake on the part of the police, who burnt the tent of an innocent man under the impression that he was engaged in illicit selling of spirits. His friends and associates were justly indignant and the ever ready agitators saw their chance. Meetings to denounce the authorities were held. Inflammatory notices were posted all over the diggings, but it was evident that a desire for a rupture with the Government was quite as strong a motive with the leaders as any sympathy with the sufferer. The man whose tent had been destroyed was compensated ; but further signs of discontent followed.

At the beginning of **August, a** deputation **from** Castlemaine and Bendigo waited upon Latrobe **to** make certain complaints and requests, which were very like threats and **demands.** The license fee they said **must be** immediately reduced to 10s. a month, paid monthly or quarterly **at the option of** the licensee ; **facilities should be** given to miners for the purchase **of** land **for** cultivation, and **the mining** population **should be** directly represented in **the** Legislature. **Latrobe said he would** consider what they had laid **before** him, **but the** deputation, disappointed **at not having obtained some definite** undertaking from **the Governor, called a** public meeting in Melbourne, which **was largely attended, and was** characterised by speeches **of greater violence than** wisdom. At Bendigo it was decided to take united action to force **a** reduction of the fee. It was determined that a **few men** should tender 10s. to **the** Commission for the **September license,** and that **the** others **should abstain from taking out** any license at **all until a** favourable decision **by the** Government had **been arrived at.** On **the day on** which the fees were payable, Latrobe promulgated a lengthy reply to the **deputation.** He **pointed out** that whereas the direct **cost of administering** the gold-fields had amounted so far **to £600,000,** the revenue derived from licenses and gold export had only amounted to a little over £460,000 ; so that the demand for smaller taxation was unreasonable, while, moreover, **it was** not in his power to alter **the amount until a** law had been **passed by the Council.** Latrobe appears to have **been sanguine that his** reasoning would be heeded, and expressed to the Secretary of State a belief that "the license for September, notwithstanding all the parade of resistance, would be taken out without any extraordinary compulsory measures being had recourse to."

Nevertheless, he thought it desirable to at once send reinforcements to the disaffected district, and as a further sop to the aggrieved diggers a resident of Bendigo was nominated to the Council. But this gentleman was unfortunately repudiated by those whom he was supposed to represent, and resigned. On August the 27th, a procession containing about two thousand persons marched by the Commissioner's camp, and fired shots into the air as a menace, while those deputed to tender the 10s. fee performed their part. Their attitude was determined, and the Chief Gold Commissioner and the Chief Commissioner of Police sent off in hot haste to Latrobe to report what had occurred, and to urge that "the reduction of the license fee, if not its abolition altogether, is inevitable." That the miners would bitterly resist any attempt to collect the prescribed 30s. was evident, and the scared officials trembled to think what would happen "if blood should once be shed." With such advice from those whose duty it would be to enforce the law, Latrobe yielded. Instructions were sent hurriedly to Bendigo that no attempt was to be made to assert the power of the Government. If the miners refused to pay the fee no steps were to be taken to compel them, although Colonel Valiant, with one hundred and fifty of the 40th Regiment was sent to take command so that fully four hundred and fifty police and soldiers were on the field. To take the places of the soldiers thus withdrawn from Melbourne the *Electra* landed marines and blue jackets to guard the gaol, and Latrobe appealed to Sydney and Hobart for reinforcements. In both cases, men were promptly despatched to his aid, but as by the time they arrived the diggers and not the Government ruled the colony, they had but little to do. A meeting was held in Melbourne, at which the Governor was grimly congratulated on his surrender, and affairs lapsed into the ominous tranquillity which preceded a more violent storm. Latrobe had long come to the conclusion that he was unsuccessful. Although he had bravely done his best, he was not strong nor determined enough for the difficult position which he occupied ; and when permission to retire from the Government was granted, he gladly left a charge which was beset with financial and revolutionary difficulties.

Sir Charles Hotham, a distinguished officer, was appointed to succeed him, and arrived in the colony in June, 1854.

There were many matters requiring Hotham's immediate attention. The financial position was critical. The estimates of expenditure for the year exceeded the anticipated revenue by a third, and already there was a deficit of over £1,000,000. Even the estimate of revenue showed no likelihood of being realised, unless great reforms were introduced. In all the public departments, the most scandalous waste and mismanagement was going on, and although there were fully 60,000 men at the diggings, only

14,000 licenses had been taken out for June. In July the Chief Commissioner was directed to pay more attention to the collection of the fees, and a substantial increase took place, but the sum obtained was still under one-third of what might reasonably have been expected. In September, Hotham urged the Commissioner to make a further effort, and ordered that the Assistant Commissioner should twice a week "search for unlicensed miners"; and he himself made a tour of the gold-fields to see with his own eyes the people and the officials with whom he had to deal. Wherever he went he was enthusiastically received, but hardly had he returned to Melbourne when a drunken brawl produced the outbreak which had been hovering on the horizon for years.

A miner named James Scobie fell out in the early hours of the morning of the 6th of October with one Bently, a Tasmanian ex-convict, who kept a disreputable publichouse at Ballaarat, known as the Eureka Hotel. In a scrimmage Scobie was killed. Bently, his wife, and a man named Farrell were arrested and tried before the local bench of magistrates, of which Mr. Dewes was the chairman. They were acquitted, although the evidence against some of them was strong, and the apparent perversion of justice aroused a tumult in which the friends of Scobie swore that they would themselves punish Bently for the murder since the law courts were corrupt. On the 17th of October, thousands of infuriated men surrounded the Eureka Hotel, which was quickly pillaged and burnt to the ground. The inmates narrowly escaped destruction, and were only saved from the vengeance of the mob by the military and police. Hotham saw that something must be done at once to allay the irritation, and offered a reward for the capture of Scobie's murderers, and appointed a commissioner to inquire into the charges against Dewes. Bently and two other men were again arrested, and this time convicted and heavily sentenced ; and three of the rioters at Bently's Hotel also suffered short terms of imprisonment for their share in the riot. Hotham remembered La-trobe's experience at Bendigo, and determined to make preparations for the worst, as in the present temper of the miners it was difficult to foretell how serious the worst might be. By October 21st, 430 military and police had been collected at Ballaarat, under Captain J. W. Thomas of the 40th Regiment, who was instructed to enforce the law " when called upon to do so, without regard to the consequences which might ensue." At the diggings the storm was gathering rapidly. A " Reform League " was formed, and a deputation despatched to the Governor to " demand " the release of the three imprisoned rioters. But Hotham was not so pliable as Latrobe, and the menace implied in " demand " had no effect upon him.

A commission had already been appointed to make full inquiry into the administration of the gold-fields, and Hotham referred the miners' delegates to that body promising to give effect to its recommendations. In other matters brought before him he expressed a desire to meet the views of the mining population, so far as it was legally possible for him to do so, but he was firm in his determination to refuse any favours which were sought with threats. The delegates returned to those who sent them with the Governor's reply, but the motley crew who had become aware of their strength at the Bendigo trouble in the previous year were intolerant of control, and resented the firmness and strength so unexpectedly shown by the executive. Their words and actions became more violent. On the 28th of November a detachment of the 12th Regiment, when entering Ballaarat, was hustled, and a baggage waggon overturned, injuring a drummer-boy, and the next day a huge meeting was held on Bakery Hill. Open revolt against the authorities was decided upon ; a flag was hoisted and a bonfire made of licenses. Hotham was in constant communication with Thomas, and messages in cypher passed rapidly from one to the other. Open defiance of the law could not be tolerated, and a crisis was inevitable. Hotham therefore directed that the licenses should be inspected as usual, and on the 30th of November a commissioner with a police escort set out to perform the duty. They were received with showers of stones, and even when reinforced were unable to quell the disorder, so that the Riot Act was read and the military called to disperse the miners, several of whom were taken prisoners.

The insurrectionary movement had now assumed definite shape. It was fitly described by the Gold Commissioner as "a strong democratic agitation by an armed mob," and the license was only the occasion, but not the cause of the outbreak. On the evening of the 30th of November, drilling was commenced by the insurgents on Bakery Hill, and Peter Lalor was elected leader. Arms, stores, horses, and ammunition were forcibly seized, and the roads to Melbourne and Geelong watched with a view to intercepting reinforcements, should they be sent to the authorities. On the 1st of December shots were fired into Thomas's camp, and it was thought advisable to take special precautions at night as an attack was anticipated early in the following morning. The troops were therefore continuously under arms. At 4 a.m. a detachment was sent to disperse an armed body which had assembled on Bakery Hill, but the mob retired before the military. Later in the day, the camp was surrounded by about two thousand armed men, who threatened but eventually withdrew. On the same afternoon Mr. Amos, a gold commissioner, reached Captain Thomas with the tidings that an entrenchment was being formed at Eureka Hill, and that he had been attacked and plundered. Reinforcements had left Melbourne on the 1st of December, under Major-General Nickle, but Thomas saw that his opportunity had now come, for by attacking the Eureka position at night or in the very early morning he would probably find all the insurgents collected in one spot and so be free of fears of an assault on the camp in his absence.

At 2.30 a.m. on Sunday, the 3rd of December, 1854, the soldiers and police were mustered. One hundred mounted men, seventy of whom were police, and 196 foot (152 belonging to the 12th and 40th Regiments), comprised the attacking force. At 3 a.m. they left the camp, and in about thirty minutes reached the stockade, which had been described by Amos. Their movements had, however, been perceived, for the warning shots of sentries were heard before they got far from their camp. When the soldiers were within about a hundred and fifty yards of the entrenchment the diggers opened a brisk fire, which was returned by the military and police as they gradually closed on the rebels. The engagement was short but sharp. With one rush the soldiers carried the barricade. The insurgents' flag was torn down, and all who were found within the stockade were captured, while many others were intercepted by the mounted force as they fled down the hill or endeavoured to hide themselves behind anything which appeared to offer shelter. No fewer than a hundred and twenty prisoners were carried back to Ballaarat, but the losses on both sides were heavy. Captain Wise, of the 40th Regiment, received a fatal wound, and thirteen more of the military were wounded most severely. On the day after the engagement, Captain Thomas wrote, "I have reason to believe that there were not less than thirty killed on the spot, and I know that many have since died of their wounds." The effect of the reverse on the mining population was immediate. In the same despatch which is quoted above, it was stated "that the police now patrol in small bodies the length and breadth of the Ballaarat gold-fields without threats or insult."

18

The general feeling at Ballaarat seems to have
been one of relief. The administration of the
ordinary law was bad, but the terrorism of the rebel
leaders was infinitely worse. By this bold stroke
on the part of the executive, the law had been
vindicated, but it soon became apparent that the
sympathies of the bulk of the people were with the
miners, and the commission which Hotham had
appointed reported that the diggers had genuine
cause for complaint. The same feeling which had
been shown in Melbourne in favour of the rioters at
Bently's Hotel appeared again in support of the
rebel leaders, who were now to be tried for high
treason. Public meetings were held in different parts
of the colony, at which resolutions exonerating the
offenders from blame were unanimously passed. The
failure of the prosecution was a foregone conclusion,
although the evidence in support of the charge was
exceptionally strong ; for no jury was likely to convict in the face of the open threats which were freely
made in the press and elsewhere. Early in 1858 the
case in the criminal court commenced. Thirteen
prisoners were in the dock, but each one was in turn
acquitted and received with wild huzzas by a mixed
crowd within and outside the building as he regained
his liberty.

Sir Charles Hotham lost no time in redeeming his
promise to the deputation from Ballaarat, that he
would give effect to the recommendation of the commission. An Act was passed by the Council abolishing the license fee, and substituting "Miner's Rights,"
the payment for which was only twenty shillings per

annum. A miner's right also carried with it representation in the Council, and two members each
were allotted to Bendigo, Ballaarat, and Castlemaine,
and one each to the Avoca and Oven's gold-fields, so
that, although beaten at Eureka, the miners got their
way, obtained freedom from taxation, and gained
representation in the Legislature. In December, 1854,
municipal institutions had been established, and a
large measure of local government having been
granted to the inhabitants, the complaint of unpopular and tyrannical government was for ever
removed.

XIX.

THE NEW CONSTITUTION.

(1857–1863.)

THE troubles of Sir Charles Hotham did not end with the capture of the Eureka stockade, and the completion of the labours of the gold commission. Years of reckless extravagance and incompetent financing had reduced the treasury to the verge of bankruptcy, and although surrounded with the insurrectionary difficulties which have already been described, the Governor did his utmost to remodel the administration of public finance, with the result that his labours were crowned with complete success. The way in which matters were being conducted by the existing ministers can be gathered from the fact that the estimates for 1855, as presented to Hotham for his approval, showed an anticipated expenditure of no less than £2,226,616 in excess of the probable revenue. The Governor personally examined the various items, and then appointed a committee of finance by whose help he was enabled to reduce the estimates of expenditure by over two millions, and so to reorganise the whole system of audit and disbursement that at the end of the year the actual deficit was not more than £53,668. The revised regulations proved effective, and by the end of 1857 all fears of impending national bankruptcy were removed, the surplus in the treasury standing at no less than £609,638. Meanwhile a select committee had been appointed, as in New South Wales, to consider Sir John Pakington's despatch, with regard to the proposed new constitution.

A Bill was drafted, providing for two houses, both of which were to be elected by the people. But one was to be founded on a higher property qualification, and was to be more especially representative of those persons who were in possession of large property interests within the colony. The Upper House, or Legislative Council, was to have a life of ten years, but in order that the electors should have a constant opportunity of expressing their views, it was arranged that every two years, a certain number of members were to retire in rotation, and again submit themselves to election. The Legislative Assembly was intended to be an entirely democratic body, and on the suffrage designated every adult male, including the unstable mining population, had a vote; so that an absolute majority could always be obtained by the labouring classes. There was one very great difference between the powers of the Council in Victoria and those of similar bodies in the two adjoining colonies; for, whereas both at Sydney and Adelaide under the terms of the Constitution Acts the Legislative Council and the Assembly had equal authority in regard to Money Bills, with the one exception that such Bills to be introduced in the Lower House, in Victoria, on the other hand, the Council was given specifically the power to reject, but not to alter Bills involving expenditure or the imposition of taxation. This difference is more especially worthy of note as, before the new Parliament had been long in existence, it led to some of the greatest constitutional difficulties which have ever been experienced in any of the Australian colonies. The measure as drafted by the local Council was agreed to in England, and on the 23rd of November, 1855, the new Constitution and responsible government were proclaimed.

The attainment of political freedom was clouded by the death of Sir Charles Hotham, whose labours on behalf of the colony had been too much for his health. In 1855 he died literally in harness, overwhelmed by the onerous duties of his responsible office. For some months affairs were administered by the military commander, and then Sir Henry Barkly arrived to take charge of the Government. Being possessed of much tact and ability, he was able to steer the new Parliamentary bark through its early difficulties. In the first year of its existence a heated dispute arose over a suggestion to conduct the election for both houses by secret ballot, and a measure embodying this arrangement was eventually passed, though the ministry succumbed in the conflict. Before the Constitution had had a fair trial, the democratic party commenced to tinker it; in 1857 the property qualification of members of the

Assembly was abolished, and universal suffrage for electors at the same time established.

The restless enterprise of the people showed itself in other ways than political conflict, and they entered heartily into the work of opening up the interior of the continent.

In 1860 a Melbourne merchant offered £1,000 for the furtherance of exploration, and the Royal Society of Victoria undertook to organise an expedition to cross the continent. A sum of £3,400 was soon subscribed, and the Victorian Government granted £6,000, and brought twenty-six camels from Arabia at a cost of £3,000 more. The most complete arrangements were made, and Robert O'Hara Burke was appointed leader, with G. J. Landells as second in command. W. J. Wills was to make scientific observations, and two other scientific men and eleven subordinates were also sent, together with twenty-eight horses to carry the baggage. On August 20, 1860, the long train of horses and camels left Melbourne amidst great enthusiasm, and all went well until the Murrumbidgee was reached. Here Burke quarrelled with Landells, and the latter, in consequence, resigned. Wills was promoted to be second in command, and the party then starting again, kept together until they came to Menindie, on the Darling, where Burke left a man named Wright, with half the expedition, and himself pushed on rapidly, instructing Wright to follow more leisurely. With six men and half the horses and camels, Burke and Wills set off, and on the banks of Cooper's Creek, finding fine pastures and plenty of water, formed a depôt, and waited for Wright, who, however, did not appear. After some time had been lost, Burke determined to wait no longer, but to make a rapid journey to the Gulf of Carpentaria. He therefore left four of his men, with six camels and twelve horses, at the depôt, instructing them to remain for three months, and if he did not return within that time to consider him dead and return to Menindie.

On the 16th of December, Burke, Wills, and two companions started, taking with them six camels and one horse, which carried provisions for three months. After following Cooper's Creek for some way, they struck off to the north, till they came to Eyre Creek, but soon finding that it turned eastward, they left its banks and marched due north, keeping along the 140th meridian. The country was covered with forests of boxwood, alternating with rich and well-watered plains, and after a few weeks they came upon a fine stream, running north, the Flinders, which entered a large river, on whose banks was most luxuriant tropical vegetation. Burke now hurried forward so fast that one by one the camels sank exhausted, and leaving the two men to look after them, Burke and Wills set out by themselves on foot, and walked till they reached the shores of the Gulf of Carpentaria. Their little store of provisions was exhausted before they regained their friends, but they found the horses and camels greatly improved by their rest, and ready to move southwards. But the heat and exertion had told severely on the constitutions of all. Towards the end of March their provisions began to fail; a camel was then shot

and its flesh dried, but in a month this too was gone,
and the horse was killed. One of the men died a
day or two after, and the remaining three were
almost broken down. Four months and a half after
leaving the depôt they reached it again, but it was
still deserted, though they found a notice stating that
their friends had left that same morning. The word
" dig " was cut on a neighbouring tree, and buried
beneath it they discovered a small supply of provisions. The three deserted wanderers rested for a
couple of days, and then started for Adelaide, because
at Mount Hopeless, where Eyre had turned back in
1840, there was now a large sheep station, and it was
thought that it could not be more than one hundred
and fifty miles distant. Wills opposed this plan, but
Burke prevailed, and they set out for Mount Hopeless.
Till it was lost in marshy thickets, they followed
Cooper's Creek, and then they had to shoot their last
camel and dry its flesh, while they took a short rest.
They then turned southwards, but when within fifty
miles of Mount Hopeless they gave in, and turned to
go back. After a weary journey they once more
reached the banks of Cooper's Creek, and Burke set
out to seek some natives, who, when found, received
him kindly, and showed him how to gather the seeds
from a kind of grass called Nardoo. But it made
them sick, and failed to nourish them. Whilst they
were thus camped on Cooper's Creek, below the
depôt, the rest of the expedition returned to seek
them, for instead of following closely on Burke,
Wright had remained at Menindie for over three
months, and the party from the depôt was halfway

back to the Darling before it met **him.** Again they just missed obtaining help, for finding no signs of Burke and Wills at the depôt, and concluding that they had perished, their friends hastened homewards. Shortly after they had left, Wills set out by himself for the depôt, on the chance of help having arrived, but upon reaching it he found it was still deserted ; he therefore turned back to rejoin his companions. He was rapidly dying of hunger when he met some natives, who received him in a friendly manner, helped him to their camp, and gave him food. For four days he rested with them, and then started once more to fetch his friends. The journey was necessarily very slow, and when the three men returned the blacks' camp was deserted. They staggered on a little further, and then, as Wills was completely broken down, they left him in a hut, and placing near him enough Nardoo to last eight days, started off again in quest of the natives. On the first day they travelled a fair distance, but early on the second Burke gave in. He prayed his companion not to leave him till he was dead, for he felt he could live no longer. A few hours after dawn on the following day, Burke died. The only survivor wandered on, and coming across an abandoned native camp, found a bag of Nardoo which would feed him about a fortnight, and with this prize he hurried back to the hut where he had left Wills. But the life of his friend was already ended, and once again he set out and found a tribe who were hospitable and permitted him to stay with them. When the rest of the expedition returned to Victoria with the news that Burke and

Wills were lost, in all the colonies parties were organised to go in search of the explorers. The Royal Society of Victoria equipped a small party, under A. W. Howitt, to examine the banks of Cooper's Creek, and from Queensland an expedition was sent to the Gulf of Carpentaria by sea, and another from Rockhampton to the Gulf of Carpentaria overland, while from South Australia a party was despatched from the direction of Lake Torrens, and thence to Cooper's Creek. At length the Victorian party, after tracing the course of Cooper's Creek down-stream from the depôt, came across tracks of camels, and before long some natives led the way to a camp where the only survivor was found, but so weak that he could scarcely speak. The blacks were rewarded for their kindness with gifts of looking-glasses, gay pieces of ribbon, and other articles, and the search party returned homewards. Later on the Victorian Government sent an expedition to bring the bodies of Burke and Wills to Melbourne, where they were accorded a public funeral.

XX.

UNDER RESPONSIBLE GOVERNMENT.

(1863-1893.)

In 1863 Sir Henry Barkly retired, and his place was filled by Sir Charles Darling, who, on his arrival, found the country in a very unsettled condition, and ripe for disorder. The crowds of people who had been attracted by the diggings were still nominally engaged in the search for gold, but by this time most of the alluvial workings had been exhausted, and the golden treasure could only be won from the quartz reefs after severe toil with the aid of expensive appliances.

Those of the new-comers, therefore, who had a knowledge of other trades began to look about them for suitable employment, and amongst the artisans, who were seeking some outlet for their knowledge and energies, the idea became popular that if once the importation of English and foreign-made goods were to be checked, the demands of the inhabitants of the colony would soon create the local manufacture of all sorts of articles with it, and a profitable market for the labour of all who desired to quit the diggings.

In other words, a protective policy was advocated by the unemployed, and there were plenty of persons in the Lower House who were easily convinced by any suggestions offered by their constituents. A Bill was consequently introduced by the Ministry of Mr. McCulloch, imposing heavy duties on all articles which it was thought could be made on the spot, and passed by the Assembly by a considerable majority. But when it came before the Upper Chamber it was unceremoniously rejected. The Ministry were indignant, and the relations between the two houses became anything but cordial. Still the course taken by the Council had been entirely constitutional, and the Assembly had no legal remedy or justifiable cause of complaint ; but Mr. McCulloch was not to be beaten. When the Appropriation Act was prepared, the whole of the Customs Duties Bill was incorporated in it, and again passed by the Legislative Assembly, and the Council were thus placed on the horns of a dilemma. By the special provision of the Constitution Act, they had no power to amend Money Bills, but if they rejected the Appropriation Act as it stood, it would mean that the Government would be utterly deprived of funds to meet the ordinary current expenses of administration. After seriously considering which was the better course to take, it was determined to refuse to be tricked in this way, and the Appropriation Act, with its obnoxious addition, was rejected.

The whole city was at once thrown into a ferment, and the Government began to collect customs duties without waiting for the sanction of the Upper House.

This course was pronounced illegal when an appeal was made to the Law Courts, and a dissolution followed. In the new Assembly the number of members in favour of protection was materially increased, and the Duties Bill was again passed and forwarded to the Council, but only to again meet with the same fate which it had previously suffered. The Ministry, therefore, resigned. Meanwhile, the absence of any Appropriation Act was causing much hardship and discomfort. Public servants could not receive their salaries, and public creditors of all sorts had to do without their money. But the Council showed no signs of yielding, and cast the responsibility on the Government, which in its turn vilified the Council. But the same ingenuity which had suggested the expedient of tacking the Customs Bill to the Appropriation Act suggested a way of obtaining funds without parliamentary sanction. Application was made to the Bank by the Government for an advance with which to pay the public servants, and after some difficulty £40,000 was obtained and promptly handed to the various creditors. No sooner had the money been spent than the Bank demanded its return, and at once brought an action against the Government to recover the amount. No defence was offered, and a verdict was given in favour of the Bank, whereupon the treasurer was enabled legally to pay money from the public coffers to meet the judgment of the Supreme Court. The same trick was resorted to over and over again, and Darling acquiesced in the proceedings, or, at any rate, did nothing to stop it. This contrivance reduced Parliamentary government

to a farce, and the Council, which had some sense of
the dignity of Parliament, seeing that they were being
beaten, suggested a conference, and eventually passed
the Appropriation Act and the Customs Duties Bill
separately.

The Imperial Government were displeased with
Darling's action, and pointed out to him that he
should have taken steps to protect the Constitution
from this burlesque ; he was summarily recalled, his
place being filled by the Right Honourable F. H. T.
Manners-Sutton. For a moment there was a lull in
the conflict, and it seemed as if there might be some
chance of parliamentary government proceeding in a
fairly orderly manner, on constitutional lines. But
the fighting instinct having once been aroused it was
hard to allay it, and out of the old feud a new one
sprang. McCulloch brought forward a proposition to
vote £20,000 to Lady Darling to compensate her
husband for his loss of office, and the censure which
had been passed upon him by the Secretary of State.
The Assembly readily agreeing to this arrangement,
the money was duly voted. The Council thought that
Darling had only met with his deserts, and refused
absolutely to pass the Bill when it came before them.
Again the obnoxious vote was tacked to the Appropriation Act, and again the Appropriation Act was
thrown out by the Council. The new governor would
not permit the tactics which had been winked at by
Darling, and the whole machinery of the country was
brought to a sudden standstill. Fortunately at the
critical moment the difficulty was solved by Darling
himself, for McCulloch received a letter from the

ex-governor, saying that he had been amply compensated for his loss of office by the Imperial Government, and that he could not accept the money which it was proposed to vote to Lady Darling. The Appropriation Act was therefore passed by the Council without the £20,000, and the political life of the colony settled down for some years, into comparative peace and quietness. There were still constant changes in the ministry, but beyond this the only important alteration in the Constitution was the reduction of the property qualification of both members and electors of the Upper Chamber. Numerous measures for the internal development of the country, and for the education and general welfare of the people were passed, without serious friction between the two houses.

But in 1873, Sir James Ferguson Bowen took office as Governor, and was shortly confronted by a similar difficulty to that which wrecked Darling, and which had been so happily solved in the time of his immediate predecessor. A Bill had been passed on this occasion by the Assembly, granting a salary of £300 per annum to all members of the two houses, the principal object being to enable any man, however poor, to enter the political arena. At this time Mr. Graham Berry was Premier, and when the Payment of Members Bill was rejected by the Council he followed the course which had been taken by McCulloch ten years previously, and embodied it in the Appropriation Act for the year. The Upper House once more asserted its privilege, and threw it out, and once again the country was involved in a constitutional crisis. The Government was powerless against the Upper House, so they vented their spleen upon unoffending public officials. On Wednesday, 8th of January, 1878, a *Gazette* notice appeared, dismissing many hundreds of public servants, and consternation was spread in the Civil Service from the highest to the lowest ranks. After a considerable interval, however, which was occupied in mutual recriminations, the Appropriation Act, divested of the amounts for payment of members, was passed by the Council, and the mutilated public service was able to breathe again. A petition was made to the Imperial Government to help the colony out of its continually recurring constitutional difficulties, and representatives from the Assembly hastened to England to attempt to justify their action. The appeal was nevertheless fruitless, for it was pointed out that ample machinery was then in existence for the settlement of all ordinary disputes, and that no intervention from outside could be more effective than ordinary intelligence and moderation on the part of the local legislature. The decision of the Secretary of State remained unshaken by the eloquence of Berry, and he asserted that the Imperial Parliament would never consent to alter the constitution of Victoria at the request of one house only.

Sir George Bowen was recalled, and succeeded by the Marquis of Normanby, and parties in Parliament being more equal, there were for some years no violent political disturbances. In 1880 a compromise was arrived at on the vexed question of the payment of members, and the Council passed a Bill giving salaries to the Lower House, and throwing out a measure intended to confer the same remuneration upon themselves. During all these years, although the Parliament of the country had spent much of its time in internal squabbles, many useful measures dealing both with social and industrial questions had found a place in the Statute Book. The wonderful natural wealth of Victoria had caused enormous expansion in agricultural settlement, and a large amount of both English and local capital had been invested in undertakings promoting manufacture. A progressive railway policy was followed, almost all lines being constructed by the state with funds borrowed in England, and the colony is now covered with a network of lines which is rather in advance of its real requirements. The sudden accession of enormous quantities of foreign money seeking investment caused values to rise as suddenly, and Victoria entered upon a period of extreme inflation, which produced the ordinary accompaniments of reckless speculation and gross extravagance. The formation of a coalition Government removed in a great measure the check of a strong opposition, and although many measures of popular utility were passed, the Government augmented the general tendency to gamble by a profuse expenditure of public money, especially upon the creation of many heavily endowed local bodies, such as harbour, irrigation, and water trusts. Apart from the recklessness of some of the financial operations of the colony, both public and private, the people of Victoria have shown commendable enterprise in the development of the wonderful natural resources of the country. When

the return from the gold-fields fell off, a great proportion of the diggers resumed their regular occupations
many became permanent settlers, and commenced
the cultivation of the soil. The rich tracts, which
won for the colony the name *Australia Felix*, are
now for the most part utilised for tillage and stock-
raising. Much has also been done to bring the
unwatered portions of the country into use by means
of irrigation, and Victoria claims the distinction of
having been the first of the Australian group to in-
stitute a public system of water conservation and
irrigation upon a large scale. The extensive works
undertaken are perhaps somewhat in advance of the
present necessities of the colony. But there can be
no doubt that in the time to come Victoria, from the
great fertility of its soil, the wealth of its mineral
deposits, and the energy and enterprise of its inhabitants, will maintain a position as one of the greatest
of the Australian States.

WESTERN AUSTRALIA.

XXI.

EVENTS FROM 1826 TO 1874.

THE territory which now forms the colony of Western Australia was first occupied in 1826, at the time when the scare of settlement by the French was at its height. Sir Ralph Darling, who was then Governor of New South Wales, contented himself with sending a small military detachment to King George's Sound, and no effort was made to occupy the country for pastoral or agricultural purposes. In the following year, however, Captain Stirling, while cruising along the western coast, was much struck with the beauty of a large river which had been discovered by the Dutch in 1697, and called Swan River on account of the number of black swans which covered its waters. Stirling wrote an enthusiastic description of the place, and as in England at the moment land-hunger was very prevalent, the idea of forming a colony on entirely new principles in the country received considerable support, and was soon put into execution. Captain Freemantle was despatched with a few men to do the pioneering work,

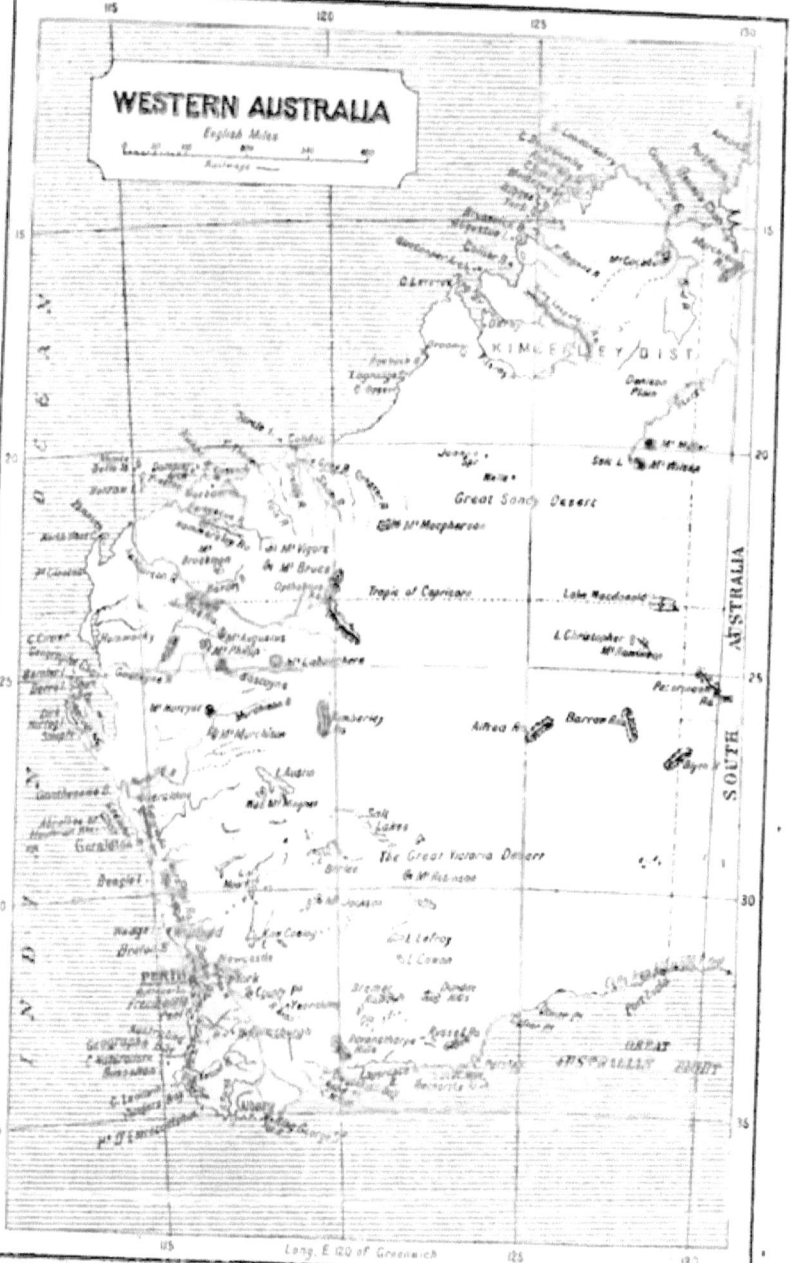

and Captain Stirling followed with some eight hundred of the intending settlers.   So far all went well; but Freemantle, on his arrival, found that the land which had appeared so fair from the sea was in reality little but a barren, sandy waste, covered with dense scrub.   He could find no harbour and no good site for a town, and when Stirling arrived at the beginning of June, 1829, practically nothing had been done. For lack of a better situation, the emigrants landed on a bleak spot called Garden Island, and set to work to make temporary shelters out of anything which came to their hands.   The misery of these first few months it would be difficult to describe ; and added to discomforts of the new-comers was the hopelessness of the future, engendered by the gloomy reports of the exploring parties, which were constantly being sent across to the mainland to seek a site on which it would be possible to form a town.   At last a spot on the Swan River, where it broadens into large shallow lagoons, was decided upon; but it was many miles from the sea, and the river was useless for navigation, as its mouth was blocked by a bar which made it impossible for a vessel of any size to enter.   Freemantle, which was little more than an exposed roadstead, had to be used as a port, and the goods of the settlers were landed on the beach and then carted miles across the sandy waste to Perth, as they called the proposed capital.

The emigrants to Western Australia had been attracted by an indiscriminating desire to become large landed proprietors, and the whole scheme of the colony was based on the principle of barter in land.

The Governor and officials were paid in land ; land was offered in huge tracts to all who brought property to the country. The introduction of a piano carried a claim for so many acres ; and the first fleet was loaded with every imaginable article, a great proportion being absolutely useless to people intending to do pioneering work in a new country. Before the end of 1830, about a thousand new arrivals had reached the colony, in thirty ships loaded with " property," and then began a scramble for the promised estates, for almost all held land orders. The claimants for the largest areas had first choice of localities and promptly selected land as near as possible to the city, so that as the area became lower the intending farmers found their estates vanishing over a distant horizon. Blocks were granted, and marked off on a map which was remarkable on account of its extreme simplicity ; for beyond the fact that, owing to the general run of the coast line, it was reasonable to suppose that land was there, no one knew anything about it, and it might have been an Eden or a wilderness. As a matter of fact it was the latter, and moreover it was already inhabited by black natives who were not prepared to recognise the title granted by the lavish Governor and generous officials in Perth. Under the scheme, for every £3 worth of goods introduced into the colony, forty acres were given, but the fee simple was not to be had by the grantee until 1s. 6d. per acre had been expended on its improvement.

Human beings, if over ten years old, were assessed at 6s. each, and one man, Mr. Peel, was granted

250,000 acres, with a possible extension to one million acres, at the rate of two hundred for each person whom he brought out answering to the above description. This gentleman had a very unfortunate experience. He took three hundred servants and £50,000 worth of goods and stock with him, intending to follow agricultural and pastoral pursuits on a large scale. His calculations were upset, however, by the quality of the soil, his servants deserted him, and his implements lay rusting unused, while the valuable live stock wandered off over the vast estate, many falling victims to a poisonous shrub which abounded in the district. Mr. Peel lost everything; but his case, although the amount at stake was larger, is only typical of what was going on all round. The persons with smaller properties were no better off; and the more venturesome, who tried to reside on their distant estates, met their deaths for the most part from starvation or disease, far from their fellow-men, while not a few were sacrificed to the spears of the native tribes.

The prospects of the colony could not have been much more gloomy, and all who had the means returned to England or sought in the other provinces the fortune which there seemed no hope of finding in Western Australia. Immigration of labourers fortunately ceased as soon as an account of the real state of affairs reached England, and Governor Stirling was compelled to seek aid from the Secretary of State for his almost starving subjects. Although no convicts had been directly sent to Western Australia previous to 1843, and the intention had been to keep

this settlement at any rate free from the criminal
taint, many ticket-of-leave or freed men from Tasmania found their way to the new colony, and produced the same troubles with the native inhabitants
which darken the pages of early Tasmanian history. Acts of brutal cruelty provoked barbarous retaliation, which was in its turn punished by the law,
although the white men, the original transgressors, were
seldom called to account. When Governor Hutt succeeded Stirling, in 1838, the Government made an effort
to improve the relations between the aborigines and the
settlers ; and while persons committing outrages on
the natives were, if possible, severely treated, substantial remissions of purchase money for land were
made to those who for two years continuously employed a native in some useful office about their
farms. Persons were also appointed to specially
guard the interests of the black men, and to try and
prevent collisions between the two races. But the
humane efforts of the Governor were greatly crippled
by want of funds.

There is but little to record of the first fifty years
of the history of Western Australia. Attempts
were made to induce settlement by exceptional facilities for acquiring land, one of the special features
of the arrangements being the issue of leases of Crown
land, entitling the holder to cultivate, and carrying a right of pre-emption at the expiration of the
term of lease. The amount of good land near Perth
was very limited, and the hope of discovering better
pastures, and the great difficulty of getting away from
the colony when once landed there, alone kept it

from being totally deserted. **The first** change of importance occurred in 1848, when a proposal was made
by the English Government that Western **Australia**
should receive convicts.   Five years previously, boys
from a penitentiary had been sent out ; but they were
not regarded as criminals, and their assignment was
called " apprenticing."   In 1845, a similar suggestion,
that the tide of transportation should be directed to
Western Australia, had been rejected **by the inhabitants ;** but three years of hopeless stagnation had
produced a change, and Earl Grey's offer was, in 1848,
readily, although not unanimously, accepted.   It was
hoped that **the expenditure of** Government money,
which a convict establishment and its **guard would**
involve, would infuse a little life **into** the drooping
energies of the settlement ; while the farming element
in the population thought that some relief from their
difficulties might be obtained by the use of cheap
convict labour on their **estates.**   These anticipations
were to some extent realised, and **a market was provided for the pastoral or agricultural** produce of the
colonists.   **The slight advantage** obtained was, how-
ever, dearly bought, for the colony soon became little
but a gaol, and the freaks of the convicts **caused
society, such as it was, to be in a continual** state of
apprehension.   Industries **gradually came into existence, and** a trade in timber became **valuable ; for the**
magnificent jarrah forests and the sandal wood yielded
a store which was always **saleable.**   Pearls, lead, and
guano were also discovered ; but **even** in the development of these gifts of nature a lack of enterprise and
the want of capital made the results insignificant.

In 1845 Governor Hutt retired, and the government was for twelve months administered by Colonel Clarke, and, on his death, for another year by Colonel Irwin. When, in 1848, Captain Fitzgerald, R.N., arrived to take command, two expeditions were being prepared to search for new pastures, and the success of one, which found a small plot of good land near Champion Bay, raised the spirits of the colonists. So great was the excitement, that the Governor himself journeyed to see the new prize; but his trip was marred by an unfortunate encounter with the natives, in which some of the aborigines were killed. Immediately on the Governor's return, an expedition was organised to settle at Champion Bay, and work a lead mine which had been found on the Murchison River; but Fitzgerald was reminded by the Secretary of State that the Imperial Government would bear no expense on account of any further occupation of territory, and it was only after earnest representations that consent was given to the despatch of a small military guard to protect the pioneers. The condition of the main settlement at this time may be gathered from Fitzgerald's communication to Earl Grey in connection with this incident. "So great was the prevalent despondency and depression," he wrote, "that the flocks were to a great extent thrown out of increase and prepared for the cauldron, all classes of colonists were daily leaving as opportunities occurred, and were it not for the hope which the discovery of this new land diffused, my conviction is that every flock-owner in the colony who had it at all in his power would have boiled down his sheep and abandoned the colony for South Australia."

The convicts were not a desirable element in the population, and the lax control exercised over them sometimes led to strange scenes. Once, in 1852, during a race meeting at York, about thirty prisoners, armed with clubs, absconded and made their appearance on the course. The magistrates present thought it necessary to suspend the festivities, and swear in special constables to look after the visitors, while from fifty to sixty natives were prevailed upon to assist the authorities by becoming temporary warders. Nevertheless, when, in the following year, a rumour reached Western Australia, to the effect that the English Government contemplated ceasing transporting to the colony, the suggestion aroused what Fitzgerald described as "one universal feeling of alarm and despair" in the minds of the settlers. Public meetings to protest against such a step were largely attended at Perth and Freemantle, and petitions in favour of the continuance of transportation were transmitted to the Secretary of State. Their prayer was granted, and more convicts were poured into the colony; but when it was hinted that if they were so glad to have them, the inhabitants could hardly grumble if asked to pay something towards their keep, an angry remonstrance was the answer, the colonists refusing to pay anything at all, and claiming immigration of free settlers assisted by England, as some compensation for the acceptance of the bond. A compromise was effected. Governors Kennedy and Hampton followed Fitzgerald, and Hampton stayed at the helm till 1868, when transportation was finally and completely abolished, on account of a change in the prison policy in England.

The settlers meanwhile made every effort to open up and colonise the vast territory of the colony. In 1873, Major Warburton, with his son, two white men, and two Afghans to drive seventeen camels, left Alice Springs, on the South Australian Overland telegraph line, and after traversing terribly barren country, at last reached the Oakover River, on the north-west coast. Towards the end of the same year, Giles started on a similar journey, intending to cross from the middle of the telegraph line to Western Australia. But after going half-way, he abandoned the idea and returned. Three years later he renewed his attempt, and successfully accomplished the journey. In 1874, John Forrest, Government Surveyor of Western Australia, left Geraldton, to the south of Shark Bay, and, travelling 1,200 miles almost due east, reached the telegraph line. Alexander Forrest, the Jardine brothers, Ernest Favenc, Gosse, and Baron von Mueller, have also contributed to the exploration of Australia, and now only a small part of South Australia and the central portion of Western Australia remain unknown.

XXII.

CONSTITUTIONAL CHANGES.

(1875–1893.)

WESTERN AUSTRALIA has passed through several stages of constitutional development. Originally the whole responsibility rested with the Governor; afterwards a small executive council and a nominee legislature were created to aid him. Later, the same sort of arrangement as had for so long existed in New South Wales, came into operation—namely, a legislature partly nominated and partly elected. This system met all ordinary requirements for some years; but, in 1870, during the rule of Governor Weld, who followed Hampton, the Legislative Council was considerably enlarged. Signs of a desire for representative institutions had long been manifest, but up to this point the opinions of the inhabitants on the question had been pretty evenly divided, and, if anything, the advocates of a change were in a minority. When Sir William Robinson succeeded Mr. Weld, in 1875, the agitation for responsible government took a more active form, although the wiser heads of the colony still saw the impossibility of proper local administration in a community consisting of about three thousand free adult males and five thousand persons who had been at one time or another convicted criminals. When, therefore, in 1878, a resolution was moved in the Legislative Council, affirming that responsible institutions should be immediately granted it was lost by a majority of thirteen votes to five ; but, nothing daunted, its advocates continued to keep the question prominently before the public, although it soon became evident that the concession would be made by the Imperial Parliament only on the condition that the territory then known as Western Australia should be divided, and a comparatively small portion given up to the control of the very limited population. When, however, this determination became generally known, the idea of subdividing the colony was bitterly opposed, and for a time the constitutional question lost popular interest.

But, although temporarily obscured, the ambitions of the settlers were still alive, and it was determined to show the opponents of autonomy that the inhabitants of Western Australia, if few in numbers, were nevertheless capable of managing and developing their huge estate. Sir H. Ord, who had now become Governor, enthusiastically supported the enterprise of the people. Strenuous efforts were made to construct public works, with the object of opening up the country, and funds were raised for the purpose by the floating of loans on the English market. It was found, however, to be easier to devise large schemes than to carry them out. The field administration was careless, and the estimates of cost were loosely drawn up, so that when the time came to pay for many ventures the bill was much larger than had been anticipated. The result was a deficit of about £30,000, and this financial failure produced a general feeling of discontent amongst those who had to contribute to the revenue, and still further dimmed the prospect of obtaining responsible government. Sir Henry Ord left the colony while it was in this mood, and Sir William Robinson returned and entered upon a second term of office.

Public works were still carried on, however, but as it was clearly impossible for the Government to undertake the construction of a railway system for the whole colony, arrangements were made with an English company to build a line from Albany to Beverley, a distance of about 241 miles, on the land grant system, and later a similar concession was made to the Midland Railway Company, whose track was to run from a point on the Eastern Railway, near Guildford, to Walkaway, two hundred and sixty miles distant, and then was to join a Government line running to Geraldton. In each case the companies received twelve thousand acres of land for every mile of railway constructed, such property to be selected within forty miles of either side of the line, half the frontage to the railway being reserved for the Government. Various other lines, some belonging to the Government and some to private individuals, have already been made, and, considering its scanty and scattered population, Western Australia is possessed of fair means of internal communication. A telegraph line between Perth and Freemantle (a distance of about twelve miles) was constructed by a private company, and opened for the transmission of messages as early as 1869 ; the line was taken over by the Government two years later. Since then telegraphic communication has been entirely in the hands of the State, and great progress has been made. The alternative cable of the Eastern Extension Telegraph Company stretches from Roebuck Bay to Banjowangi ; Western Australia is thus possessed of a direct service with Europe.

The efforts to develop the natural resources of the colony had their effect. The people of Western Australia had shown that they were capable of sound progress, and when in 1887 a resolution was again brought forward in the Council affirming that self-government was desirable, it was passed by an almost unanimous vote, and the Governor was requested to take the necessary steps to carry the matter to a conclusion. But, as formerly there had been differences of opinion on the subject, it was thought wise, before such a fundamental change was made, that the voice of the inhabitants should be clearly given. So at the end of the following year the Council was dissolved, and early in 1889 a general election took place, at which the principal question before the constituencies was whether or not the Imperial Parliament should be approached with a view of obtaining for Western Australia the benefits of autonomy which had so long been enjoyed by the other provinces. The change in popular sentiment was apparent directly the new Council assembled, and resolutions similar to those rejected in 1878, and carried by a majority in

1887, were passed without a single dissentient voice. In April a Bill defining the new Constitution was prepared, and after but slight amendment was forwarded to the Secretary of State. As opposition to the transference of the Crown lands to the Colonial Government was anticipated, the Governor, Sir Frederick Napier Broome, and two prominent settlers were appointed by the Council to represent the affairs of the colony in England, and to do their utmost to steer the measure, on which so much depended, safely through the quicksands of the Imperial Parliament. As had been expected, clauses were introduced at an early stage which were highly distasteful to the West Australians, but on reference of the Bill to a select committee, all the obnoxious provisions were excised, and full control of their own affairs and of the whole of their huge territory was vested in the local legislature, which it was proposed to create forthwith. The Act received the royal assent on the 15th of August, 1890, greatly to the satisfaction of the whole of Australia. The new Constitution differed in detail but little from the measures under which the eastern colonies have been governed since 1855. An Upper House was established, containing fifteen members, the first holders to be nominated by the Crown, but with ample provision for making it elective so soon as the population of the colony shall have reached sixty thousand. To become a member, it is necessary to possess a substantial property qualification, but the qualification defined for the elector is extremely low. Members are elected to the Assembly on the basis practically of manhood suffrage, and provision is made for the representation of Crown lessees. The new system of government has not yet been sufficiently long in operation to make it possible to form an opinion as to its utility. But there is every reason to believe that Western Australia will in the future make as good use of its plenary powers of legislation as the other colonies have done.

From recent discoveries it would appear to be by no means improbable that gold will be as powerful a factor in the development of Western Australia as it has been in most of the other colonies of the Australian group. The progress of both New South Wales and Victoria was slow and uncertain until the news of the discovery of gold was noised abroad. Then, and not till then, did it begin to be realised what a land of promise this almost unknown country was, and from that date up to the present time the current of immigration, set in motion by the finding of the precious metal, has continued to flow steadily to Australian shores. Until quite recently, however, there seemed to be no prospect of the same fortune awaiting Western Australia, and by many persons competent to form an opinion it was generally considered that this portion of the continent was almost destitute of mineral wealth. But it has now been pretty well proved that this idea was entirely erroneous. Mining and prospecting are quite in their infancy in Western Australia, and the industry has there, as in most other places, met with many misfortunes at its commencement. Perhaps the most severe check to mining enterprise followed the first discovery of gold at Peterwangy, for, as soon as it became known that gold had been found, there was a rush from the other colonies quite unwarranted by the character of the discovery. The precious metal was never gained in payable quantities, and the disappointed diggers, finding nothing, left in disgust. The next venture was little better, for, although the assay of the ore from the Kendinup field gave a large return, the presence of a great quantity of arsenical pyrites caused such a loss both in gold and mercury, when the ore was treated on the ground, that no satisfactory return could be obtained. After this followed the rush to Kimberley ; here again the alluvial workings were shallow, so that they were soon worked out, and although Kimberley has now settled down into a reefing district, and some very rich finds have been made, confidence has not been entirely restored, and Western Australian mining enterprises are viewed with suspicion.

But further discoveries are continually being reported, and the reefs in the neighbourhood of the Yilgarn Hills, which stretch away from north to south, indicate that gold extends for a distance of at least fifty miles. Other reefs have been found at Peewah, and a little further east the alluvial fields of Pilbarra are being worked with a considerable amount of success, while the last discovery is in the vicinity of Austin's Lake, in the Murchison district. The presence of gold in Western Australia would appear to be conclusively established, and it would seem to be deposited over a very extensive area. It is not likely that gold mining will ever be the principal industry of the country, for at any rate more than a brief period, but those who are attracted by the prospect of an easily-acquired fortune on the gold-fields readily turn their attention to other pursuits, and to the development of other resources of the country, which are of a more permanent nature. Western Australia has the advantage of the experience of the other colonies to guard her from the dangers invariably attending any sudden accession of population. Once let the country get a fair start, and its progress cannot fail to be rapid, for, besides its large pastoral resources, and belts of good mineral country extending from one end of the colony to the other, gold is not the only mineral of which it is possessed. Very rich lodes of copper and lead have already been worked successfully for many years, but, the price of these metals having fallen, the mines have temporarily stopped. The Government have offered, as an inducement for the establishment of lead-smelting works, £10,000 for the first ten thousand tons of lead smelted in the colony. A ready market can be obtained for the metal both in China and Singapore. In addition to the above metals coal and tin have been found in considerable quantities, and there is every indication that in the near future, Western Australia will take, as a treasure-house of mineral resources, a high place among the colonies of the Australian group.

Hitherto this province has certainly been a laggard amongst Australian States, but now that political freedom has been consummated, and its immense pastoral, mineral, and agricultural possibilities are becoming more perfectly appreciated and understood, the country is certain soon to assume a position more in accordance with its vast natural resources.

SOUTH AUSTRALIA.

XXIII.

EARLY SETTLEMENT.

(1829–1840.)

THE colony of South Australia was founded in an entirely different way, and for totally different reasons, to any of the other provinces, and its origin and early history are of peculiar interest. In 1829 Mr. Edward Gibbon Wakefield, who had spent some years in New South Wales, wrote a pamphlet, which was published in London under the title of " A Letter from Sydney." The author described graphically the conditions of social intercourse in the penal settlement, dwelling more particularly on the absence of the opportunity for refined enjoyment and literary or artistic cultivation in a community in which nearly all were workers. How, he asked, could intellectual life flourish in a country where there were no gradations in free society? It was impossible for a man of taste and education to farm his property with the aid of free workmen, for the inducements offered to the labouring classes to become themselves proprietors were so

SOUTH AUSTRALIA

great that it was unreasonable to expect them to remain in service. For these reasons there must always be something wanting in colonial society built up upon the lines hitherto pursued. Instead of reproducing a nation strong both in its intellectual and physical parts—an extension, in fact, of the mother country—both good masters and good men would be absent, and their places would be taken by an unsatisfactory class of peasant proprietors, who would be able to do nothing to advance the higher life of the people, and who would be unable, from lack of capital, even to make the most of the land which they occupied. But Wakefield did not content himself with simply pointing out the poor results of existing methods of colonisation. He sought the cause of failure, and endeavoured to construct a scheme, free from the evils of which he complained.

The essence of this plan was that a " sufficient price " should be charged for the land, which should then be parted with absolutely to the purchaser, and that the supply of labourers by immigration, assisted by the revenue from land, should be as nearly as possible proportioned to the demand for labour at each settlement ; so that only possessors of capital should hold the land, and while capitalists would never suffer from an urgent want of labourers, labour would never fail to obtain well-paid employment. There is not space here to elaborate the details of Wakefield's plan, but it attracted much attention, and his theories were enthusiastically accepted in England by all sorts and conditions of men. In 1831 the first attempt was made to put the scheme into practice, and a South

Australian association was formed with the object, to use Wakefield's words, of " substituting systematic colonisation for mere emigration." The suitability of the southern portion of Australia for colonisation had been determined by recent explorations, and the association applied to the English Government for a charter granting them what amounted to sovereign rights over the whole southern portion of the continent. Objections were made to the surrender of legislative powers to an irresponsible company, and, although the promoters asked the Secretary of State for the Colonies to suggest modifications in their proposal, he declined to do so on the grounds that it was their business, not his, to formulate an acceptable scheme.

Two years later negotiations on the subject were again commenced, and in August, 1834, the English Government passed a Bill empowering the Crown to establish a province in South Australia, and to appoint colonisation commissioners to look generally after the affairs of the new settlement. Wakefield's theory was to be carried out, to a certain extent, and the minimum price of land was fixed at 12s. ; a price very much above that charged in the other colonies. The commissioners were authorised to borrow money, in anticipation of revenue from land sales, in order to promote immigration of the necessary labourers. The Act was a comprehensive measure, and there were other provisions to meet the requirements of the colony in the future, such, for instance, as the clause authorising the establishment of a constitution for local self-government in any province containing fifty thousand inhabitants. These arrangements, however, never came into operation, and the most important point was the formation and status of the commission, and the refusal of the English Government to afford any pecuniary aid. If the experiment were tried, they said, the promoters must find the money. Colonel Torrens, who remained in England, as chairman, and Mr. Fisher, Resident Commissioner in Australia, with nine others, formed the Board, and a governor, Captain Hindmarsh, R.N., and a Surveyor-General, Colonel Light, were appointed by the Government to guard the interests of the Crown. But the duties of Hindmarsh and Fisher were ill-defined, and apparently both were nominally entrusted with supreme power in the control of the colony's affairs.

The preliminary arrangements were soon completed, and the pioneer vessels, *Duke of York* and *Lady Mary Pelham*, sailed in February, 1836. After an uneventful voyage the ships arrived off the coast in August, and the emigrants were at once landed at Kangaroo Island, where a small whaling station already existed. But trouble began early, for when Colonel Light shortly afterwards arrived in the *Rapid*, he was dissatisfied with the island as a site for the capital of a settlement, and crossed to the mainland. Even then he had some difficulty in coming to a decision, and after examining Port Lincoln he returned to Holdfast Bay, and settled on the spot where Adelaide now stands. The position was admirable in some respects, but it was seven miles from the nearest harbour, and great inconvenience was experienced in landing the baggage which the colonists had brought with them. Con-

flicting opinions were freely expressed concerning
the proposed site for the capital, many wishing to go
to Encounter Bay ; but the supporters of Light prevailed, and the surveyors set to work to mark out the
plan of the future city. ˌAltogether, in 1836, nine
ships arrived, carrying about five hundred persons,
and amongst the number Governor Hindmarsh. Faith
in the future prospects of the settlement was strong,
and after the Governor had read the orders in Council
founding the colony, in a tent pitched in Glenelg
Plains, a banquet was held to commemorate the
event, and for the moment the cause of dissension was
forgotten.

But those who disagreed with Light's choice resumed active opposition, as soon as they discovered
they enjoyed the sympathy of the Governor. A
public meeting was held, at which Light was supported
by Fisher, the Resident Commissioner, and a majority
of the colonists ; but so much friction had been caused
that the administrative arrangement which, under the
most favourable conditions, would have been anomalous, became utterly unworkable. Nevertheless,
by March, 1837, the survey of the capital had been
completed, and the first sales of allotments took place.
The minimum price for land had been fixed at 12s.
per acre to commence with, with the intention of
raising it presently to £1, and at the first auction
town-lots sold for from £3 to £13 each—a fairly
satisfactory figure. But the colonists, instead of
taking up country lands, clung to the skeleton city,
and amused themselves by joining in the wrangle
between Hindmarsh and Fisher, which was daily

becoming more bitter. The utter absence of effort on the part of the pioneers to obtain anything from the soil is an extraordinary circumstance of the first few years of the colony's existence. The persons possessed of capital commenced to speculate in town allotments, which it was supposed would rapidly rise in value as population increased, and labourers who had been brought out with the idea that plenty of agricultural work would be readily obtained had to live as best they could, being unable to discover any men of means to employ them. The gambling in city property became wilder and wilder, while most of the money brought by the intending settlers was paid away for food and clothing instead of the purchase of estates. Matters looked serious; the Governor and Commissioner were useless as far as directing the energies of the people went, for whatever was done by the one, the other offered opposition to. At length news of the unsatisfactory condition of things reached England, with the result that Hindmarsh was summarily recalled, and Fisher dismissed, while Colonel Gawler was sent out to take control, combining in his own person the two vacant offices. In a despatch he describes the state of things which he found on his arrival. All the means of the colonists, he alleged, were vanishing in payment "for the necessaries of life." There were "scarcely any settlers in the country; no tillage; very little sheep or cattle pasturing; the two landing-places of the most indifferent description; the population shut up in Adelaide, existing principally upon the unhealthy and uncertain profits of land-jobbing." The public finances were in a hopeless muddle, and the expenditure authorised for the whole year, namely, £12,000, had all been drawn and spent in the first quarter. Each day the position was becoming more grave, for a poorer class of immigrants was arriving, under the expectation of obtaining work from those who had already been some time in the colony and were now practically without the means of sustenance. Prices rose rapidly. Breadstuffs increased in a short time from £20 to £80 per ton, and a strong desire to leave the miserable place was evinced by all who had not already squandered the money which might have taken them away. Gawler had to face a difficult situation, and his first care was for the starving crowds who had from no fault of their own been placed in this helpless position. If the private landowners could not or would not employ them, the Government must, in order to save them from an otherwise inevitable fate. Gawler at once commenced extensive public works. He managed to pay the destitute labourers, partly out of his own pocket, and partly by discounting bills on the English Treasury, but, apparently, on the principle that sufficient unto the day is the evil thereof, he quite disregarded the fact that there were no funds available to meet the cost of the work. The immediate pressure was removed, and the hungry mouths filled by the provisions which Gawler imported on the public account ; but his efforts met with no response from the more wealthy colonists, and the Government, having once accepted the responsibility of providing work for the unemployed, was unable to stop the expenditure until the demand for labour on the part of the public

relieved it of its burthen. Doubtless Gawler expected
that, if the immediate crisis were safely passed,
private enterprise would at length come forward to
develop the natural resources of the country, and he
is more to be pitied than blamed for the disastrous
consequences of his action. When he arrived he was
in a dilemma from which there was no escape.

The public works which were undertaken were, for
the most part, valuable of their kind. Extensive
wharves and warehouses were erected at the port, in
addition to a custom house, and a good road was
laid to the city. Other public buildings, including an
expensive residence for the Governor, were put up, but
still the crowd of labourers which clamoured for work
showed no signs of decreasing. Gawler had exhausted
his own fortune in the payment of wages, and no
revenue could be obtained from the colony ; so the
only course open was to draw bills on the English
Treasury for larger and larger sums. The first few
drafts were honoured readily enough, for the English
Government recognised the difficulty of Gawler's
position, and the sore straits in which he had found
the colony ; but when the bills became more frequent,
and amounts higher, Gawler was informed that no
more drafts would be paid. Already, however, he
had incurred liabilities amounting to nearly £400,000,
and as the warning from the English Government
was emphasised by the refusal to pay £69,000 worth
of bills on presentation, matters were abruptly brought
to a crisis. Speculation in land was immediately converted into an universal desire to sell at any price,
and the marketable value of real estate fell lower and

lower. A general exodus of all who could afford to
go away followed, but the supply of provisions had
ceased with the dishonour of the Governor's bills, and
in spite of the reduction in numbers, the community
was stared in the face by starvation.

But such a state of things inevitably produced its
own remedy. The famine prices of provisions made
people seriously entertain the idea of growing wheat
or rearing stock themselves, and the ridiculously low
figure at which land could now be bought enabled
those who previously had expected to earn wages to
become themselves proprietors. A large number of
sheep and cattle had moreover been brought overland
from Port Phillip and New South Wales, by the most
enterprising of the squatters, many of whom were so
well satisfied with the quality of the country in South
Australia that they determined to remain ; so that
both agricultural and pastoral pursuits were at last
systematically prosecuted.

The little settlement about this time presented a
curious spectacle. Society might be roughly divided
into three classes—first, the original immigrants, who
had started from England with a certain amount of
capital, which had been as a rule squandered in speculation ; secondly, the wretched, starving labourers ;
and last (but by no means the least important), the
" Overlanders " from the other colonies, who not
infrequently dissipated much of what they received
from their live stock in noisy revelry, which scanda-
lised the little town. These wild bushmen were the
only people who were contented or well-to-do, and
their prosperity stood out in greater contrast owing

to the misery and hopelessness of their surroundings.

Meanwhile the serious predicament in which the colony was placed by its practical inability to pay its debts had been occupying the attention of the English Government. Gawler appears to have been held entirely responsible for the trouble, and the difficulties which he inherited from his predecessor were overlooked in the desire to fix the blame for the failure of the colonising scheme on some one. As a matter of fact, the collapse was a natural sequence of the apathy and ignorance of the first batch of immigrants, for seeds were sown in the first few months of the occupation of the territory which could not fail to bear disastrous fruit, however capable might have been the administration of the Government. Gawler was the scapegoat, and in May, 1841, he was unceremoniously recalled. The English Government had determined to lend the colony sufficient to enable it to pay its debts, and to entirely remodel the system of administration. The Commission was abolished, and South Australia became to all intents and purposes a Crown colony.

Captain George Grey was despatched to take charge, and Gawler was surprised one day by a visit from this officer, who presented his papers, and immediately took the reins of government into his own hands. Grey was fortunate, for he reaped the full benefit of the lesson learnt by the people from past failures. As soon as farming was energetically prosecuted it was found that the land, which had appeared nothing but an uninviting wilderness to the first arrivals, was in reality extremely fertile, and admirably adapted both for agriculture and wool growing. The change wrought by a couple of years of steady work was wonderful. Butter and cheese were exported in considerable quantities, and the area under wheat had so broadened that the crop yielded a surplus available for export over and above local requirements. After the harvest of 1845 not only were the neighbouring markets fully stocked with South Australian breadstuffs, but there was a large balance remaining on the hands of farmers for which they could find no purchasers.

XXIV.

IMPROVING PROSPECTS.

(1840–1855.)

THE year 1840 is memorable on account of the efforts at exploration made by Edward John Eyre, who, with five Europeans, three aborigines, some horses, and a small flock of sheep, started from Adelaide, intending, if possible, to penetrate the interior and cross the continent. Journeying first to the head of Spencer's Gulf, he there received a fresh supply of provisions from a small vessel which had been sent to meet him, and then, after travelling some way through an arid desert, he turned to the west, and sighted what at first appeared to be a large lake, but on closer examination proved to be nothing but a dried-up bed, covered with a sheet of glittering salt. Boldly the explorers advanced on the treacherous surface, but at every step the coat of salt cracked, and their feet sank into thick black mud. For some miles they pursued their way, but at length the black ooze became so deep that they were compelled to retrace their steps, and seek some way round

ADELAIDE. *[By permission of Messrs. Chaffey Bros., 35, Queen Victoria St., London.*

the shores of the swamp. After much fruitless toil they were obliged to hasten back to the nearest stream, but, having procured a fresh store of water, they again faced the inhospitable interior, and twice their path was barred by the great salt lakes. At length, turning westward, they pushed forward, but were soon deep in a barren waste, desolate in the extreme. Again supplies ran short, and death from thirst stared them in the face, when their fears were removed by the sight of a fair-sized river in the distance. Hastening joyfully to its banks, they eagerly knelt to drink the water, but to their horror and despair found it salt, and hopelessly they turned back towards the head of Spencer's Gulf. Loath, however, to return to Adelaide without having accomplished something in the way of discovery, instead of turning homeward they travelled along the shores of the Great Australian Bight, with the intention of following the coast to Albany. The lack of water again greatly retarded progress. Three times they struggled round Streaky Bay, but as often had to return to obtain water to drink. At length Eyre made the whole of his party, with the exception of one man named Baxter and three natives, return to Adelaide, and, taking a few horses and a large supply of water and provisions, he and his four companions once more made an attempt to round the Bight. Day after day they struggled on through loose sand and burning rocks, all the time suffering greatly from the glare and the want of water. Once the whole party nearly perished. Even the horses fell down, unable to proceed any further. But after a long tramp Eyre with one attendant discovered several small holes, apparently dug in the sand by the natives, and gathering water hastened back to revive the exhausted animals. They camped at the water holes for a week, and then once more set out on their perilous journey. Again they passed a long stretch of desert waste, and two of the beasts died; consequently a large portion of the provisions had to be abandoned. But to turn back now was as hopeless as to go forward, and they despondently pushed on. Baxter, while Eyre was absent a short time from the camp, was murdered by two of the blacks, who looted the stores and ran away. The ground was too rocky for Eyre even to dig a grave in which to lay his friend's body, and, rolling it in a blanket, he left it on the scorched rock. With the remaining black he trudged wearily onwards, until at length a vessel was observed close to the coast, and signs made by Eyre were answered. Fresh clothes and food were obtained from the captain, and three weeks later they reached Albany, and were received with enthusiasm by the inhabitants. After remaining a short time, they returned to Adelaide, where Eyre's account of his travels created a deep sensation.

A very great change in the prospects of the settlement was about this time caused by the discovery of rich mineral deposits. During 1841 a man in charge of a team of bullocks was crossing the Mount Lofty Range, and, as the road was steep and rough, on reaching the summit he resorted to the common expedient of making a heavy log fast to the tail of the waggon to act as a drag, or brake, to prevent the

load from pressing too heavily on the bullocks. This
done, the journey was resumed, but as the waggon
went lumbering along over ruts and boulders the log
bumped and ploughed up the track in its rear, and
the eye of the driver, who had loitered a little behind,
was suddenly caught by the glitter of something in
the freshly disturbed earth. He picked it up and
examined it. It certainly was a very bright and
heavy piece of rock, and, what was more, the whole
surrounding country was covered with the same stuff.
Convinced that the stone contained some valuable
mineral, he gathered specimens, and made the best of
his way to Adelaide. On showing his find to persons in the city he learned that it was rich ore, and
shortly afterwards the land on which he had seen
it was opened up, and a quantity of silver and silver
lead obtained.

In the following year a still more important discovery was made on Kapunda Station, first by a son
of the proprietor, Captain Bagot, and shortly afterwards by an overseer named Dutton. Attracted by
the brilliant green colour of an outcropping rock, an
examination showed that the land hid extensive
deposits of rich copper ore. Captain Bagot saw his
opportunity, and, without allowing any suspicion of
the nature of his find to get abroad, applied to have
the eighty acres which embraced the lode put up to
auction. It was apparently rocky, sterile country, so
there was no competition, and it was bought by Bagot
for a minimum price of £1 per acre. As soon as he
had possession active operations were commenced,
with the most satisfactory results, and an enormous

return was obtained by the lucky owners. The
Kapunda mine became the great topic of conversation, and men and money began to flow into South
Australia from the other provinces. The search for
mineral wealth soon resulted in the discovery of
another rich copper reef, about forty-five miles from
Kapunda, and ninety miles from Adelaide. The
land on which it was situated was still the property
of the Crown, and as rumours of the find had got
abroad, keen competition was anticipated if the sections were put up to auction. There appeared only
one way to avoid this, which was for those anxious
to become possessed of the mine to combine and
avail themselves of the provision of the Crown Lands
Regulation which permitted specially surveyed blocks
of not less than 20,000 acres to be bought at the
minimum of £1 per acre without competition. Two
companies were hastily formed to purchase the land
on these terms—one consisting principally of Captain
Bagot's friends, and the other of merchants and
tradesmen in Adelaide. The rival parties watched
each other with jealous eyes, fearing that each would
forestall the other before arrangements could be completed.

But in a small community such as that in South
Australia £20,000 in gold was a large sum to find for
speculative purposes, and at length, as competitors
from Sydney were expected, the two companies
were forced to combine their forces in self-defence,
on the understanding that directly the land was
bought it should be equally divided between Bagot's
" Princess Royal Company "—or, as they were popu-

larly called, the "Nobs"—and the "South Australian Mining Company," commonly known as the "Snobs." After an enormous amount of trouble, the necessary £20,000 in gold was scraped together, the Governor refusing to accept anything in payment except coin, and the land was secured. It was generally supposed that copper was to be obtained from the whole of the property, but after the division had been made the expectations of the "Princess Royal Company" were by no means realised, while the Burra Burra mine, belonging to the "Snobs," yielded handsome returns. The copper deposits were actively worked, and before long there were fully five thousand persons on the field, and the roads to the new town were constantly traversed by hundreds of teams of bullocks, which plodded from the seaboard to the mines, carrying provisions and stores for the miners, or bringing the heavy ores to port for shipment to Europe.

The sudden acquisition of mineral wealth, perhaps more than anything else, raised South Australia from the slough of despond into which it had sunk, and Grey was enabled to put into force the principles which Gawler had wished, but had been unable to follow. At first his energetic administration provoked great opposition, and noisy meetings were held in Adelaide, at which violence was threatened if he persisted in his policy of retrenchment, and the Governor's recall was loudly demanded. The wages of men on public works were reduced from 1s. 6d. (with rations) per day to 1s. 2d., and everything that could be done was done to make Government

employment compare unfavourably with the offers
of private masters. Meanwhile the estimates of
expenditure which had been prepared for Gawler
were ruthlessly cut down, and strenuous efforts
were made to bring the public outgo to something
approaching the same figure as the legitimate
public income. The steps taken were successful,
and Grey, by his carefulness and determination,
soon produced order out of chaos, and prepared
the colony to reap the full benefit of its changed
prospects. In three years the expenditure was
brought to one-sixth of its former amount, and
meantime the revenue from local sources had materially increased.

Even while the outlook was most gloomy, the
inhabitants had been frequently pleading for
representative institutions. The settlement had
scarcely shown itself capable of properly managing
its own affairs, and the answer to the prayer of
the petitioners was that before the representative
principle could be conceded it must " be made evident
that the internal resources of the colony are fully
adequate to provide for its own expenditure." In
the meantime a nominee council, consisting of seven
members, was appointed to assist the Governor, and
take in some degree the place which had been occupied by the defunct commission. Grey had done
well, and the success of his administration won the
applause of many who were the loudest, shortly before,
in the denunciation of his methods. In 1845 more
meetings were held, but this time praise, not blame,
was showered on the head of the Governor, who at

the height of his popularity was transferred to New Zealand.

Colonel J. H. Robe was selected to fill Grey's place, but his career in South Australia was short and troubled, for although a fine, straightforward man, he was always out of touch with the feelings of his subjects. The chief difficulty arose from an attempt to tax the output of the mines, but the violent opposition which this measure excited was due as much to hostile feeling towards the Governor on account of his Religious Endowment Bill, as to any injustice in the proposition to impose a royalty on minerals. Robe had endeavoured soon after his arrival to pass a Bill affording State aid "to provide for ordinances of religion," and only carried his point in the Council after a bitter struggle. When, therefore, his next important measure, the Mineral Royalty Bill, came on for discussion, it created no surprise that even the Council deserted him. As he could not obtain legislative sanction to the tax, he endeavoured to impose it on the authority of royal prerogative. This step was obviously a mistake, and called forth a stormy and angry protest ; indeed, Robe's inability to get on with those under his charge became so apparent that the English Government recalled him.

The next Governor sent out was Sir Henry Young, who was possessed of just the qualities which Robe had lacked. He entered with enthusiasm into all the schemes of the settlers for the rapid development of the colony, and led the way with more energy than discretion in many attempts to open up the country. The event which is most intimately associated with his name is the navigation of the river Murray. It appeared to Young that great things must follow could the magnificent waterway of the Murray be used for navigation, and money was freely spent to attain this object. Large sums were expended in an attempt to remove the bar at the mouth of the river, and a prize of £4,000 was offered to the first person who should successfully navigate the Murray to the junction of the Darling in an iron steamer. Such a reward naturally produced competitors, and, after infinite trouble and expense, Mr. Cadell succeeded in accomplishing the feat ; but the £4,000 did not cover his outlay, and when he tried subsequently to create a carrying trade in wool from the stations along the banks of the river to the sea, his efforts ended in financial failure. The Governor was not more fortunate at Port Elliot. As fast as the sand was dredged away, fresh deposits of silt accumulated, until at last the attempt to form a harbour was abandoned, and the £20,000 or more which had been spent upon the work was practically thrown away.

The advance of South Australia received a check in 1851, when the discovery of gold in Victoria caused the greater part of the capital and enterprise which had worked such wonders to be suddenly withdrawn. A period of general stagnation followed, and it looked by no means improbable that the miserable times of Gawler were going to be repeated. The copper mines were still kept open, but only with great difficulty, for the gold-fields had attracted a very large proportion of the adult male population, and the properties could not obtain sufficient labourers. Agricultural and

THE MURRAY.
(From Murray Bridge Railway Station.)

pastoral pursuits suffered most, and for a short time the fields which should have been waving with yellow corn were bare and neglected, and the flocks and herds had to get along as best they could, unshepherded and uncared for. While Adelaide was languishing, Young's ears were filled with stories of the fabulous wealth and growth of Melbourne, until the Governor decided to make an effort to divert to the South Australian port for shipment some of the stream of gold which was flowing from the Victorian mines. An extremely well equipped gold escort was therefore established between Bendigo and Adelaide, and the advantages anticipated by Young were to some extent realised. As the excitement of the first rush died out, many of those who had deserted South Australia returned to their former homes, finding that it was a surer and more profitable enterprise in the end to supply bread and other necessaries to the miners than to join themselves in the feverish hunt which ended so much more often in failure than a fortune.

The returning population brought renewed prosperity, but the sudden exodus had produced some curious problems, which the Government had great difficulty in solving. The most remarkable of these was the complete withdrawal of all coined money from the colony by persons travelling to Victoria. Before the gold rush had been long in progress it was found that very grave difficulty was being experienced by merchants and others, owing to the want of a common circulating medium. There was gold in plenty, after the institution of the escort from Bendigo, but it varied in fineness, and was unsuitable for exchange purposes, on account of the opportunities its use afforded for fraudulent practices. The position was serious, for commerce showed signs of being paralysed by the difficulties thus created. The Governor had no authority to coin, and no plant for minting purposes, so he took the next best course, and issued little blocks or ingots of the precious metal of an uniform size and fineness. The expedient met the case, and relieved the commercial strain, but the action taken by Young was without doubt *ultra vires*, and he consequently received a mild rebuke at the hands of the Secretary of State.

Meanwhile the work of opening up the interior had been pushed ahead. John McDowall Stuart, who had been in Sturt's expedition to the Stoney Desert, was employed in 1859 by a number of squatters to explore new country, and, having found a passage between Lakes Eyre and Torrens, discovered fine pastures. In the following year, the South Australian Government offered £2,000 to the first person who should cross the continent from south to north, and Stuart started from Adelaide to make the attempt. With two men he travelled towards Van Diemen's Gulf, and penetrated to within four hundred miles of the coast ; but the natives were so hostile that he had to return. The next year he followed the same course, and got to within 250 miles of the northern shores, but want of provisions on this occasion made him again turn back. The report of this expedition was sent to Burke and Wills, and was received by them shortly before they left Cooper's Creek for the first time. In 1862, Stuart succeeded in reaching Van Diemen's

Gulf, and returned safely, but a shadow was thrown over his entry into Adelaide by the arrival on the same day of the remains of Burke and Wills, on their way to Melbourne.

XXV.

UNDER RESPONSIBLE GOVERNMENT

(1855–1893.)

SOUTH AUSTRALIA went through much the same stages of constitutional development as the other Australian colonies, and although the final measure conceding autonomy was based on more democratic principles than anywhere else, the political life of the country has been comparatively uneventful. In 1851, when the Legislatures of New South Wales and Victoria were altered, a Council consisting of eight nominee and sixteen elected members was provided. This arrangement, however, was of short duration. When the Council met in 1853, the Governor informed members that Bills had been prepared making the necessary provision for an alteration of the Constitution. The idea was that a nominee Upper House should be created, the seats in which would be tenable for life, and that an Assembly should be elected by the people on a low suffrage every three years. The authority of the two chambers was to be equal on all points, except that Money Bills should be introduced

in the Assembly; but the rather remarkable stipula-
tion was made that the latter body might, at the
termination of the third Parliament, pass a Bill
changing the constitution of the Council, and making
it elective without requiring the consent of that body
to the alteration.   But popular feeling was so averse
to a nominated body of any description, even with the
safeguards suggested, that these proposals were never
made law, and in deference to the wishes expressed
by the inhabitants the original Constitution Bill was
delayed in England, and eventually referred back to
the South Australian Council for amendment.   At
length, at the close of 1855, another measure, very
different in character, was forwarded from the colony
for the sanction of the Imperial Parliament.   The
Legislative Council in the second Bill was, like that
of Tasmania, elected by the colony as one constituency,
on a low franchise, and the province was divided into
districts for the election of members to the Assembly,
the basis of the suffrage being that each male adult,
above the age of twenty-one years, duly registered and
resident for six months in South Australia, should
have the privilege of one vote.   The Bill was passed
intact by the Imperial Parliament, and received the
royal assent in January, 1856.

From that time to the present but little constitutional change has been effected, and although the life
of successive ministries has been extremely short,
contests between the two houses have been rare, and
the public life of the colony has been singularly free
from violent upheaval.   With the attainment of
plenary powers of legislation, the history of social and

political development practically closes, and the only events to be described in the following years are the great efforts which have been made towards internal expansion and amendment of the arrangements affecting the disposal of the public estate. The legislation of the colony was adorned in 1858 by a measure of such obvious and universal utility that it has been generally adopted, not only by the other provinces of the Australian group, but in a large measure by the mother country. Mr. R. Torrens, who was a Government official before the inauguration of the new Constitution, and later a member of the first Legislative Assembly, became impressed with the extreme difficulty which existed in the transference of real estate. To remove these hindrances, he devised a method by which registration was combined with a system of endorsement on the original title deed of all changes made in the ownership of the land ; so that, instead of a long series of involved legal documents, the purchaser of real estate would only have to be satisfied as to the soundness of one deed. A measure of such sweeping reform could not be introduced without a large amount of opposition, but Torrens' Bill was nevertheless passed, and it has proved to be one of the greatest boons ever conferred upon the community.

Although, owing to the energy of Torrens, facilities for dealing in private property were greatly increased, the regulations affecting the public domain remained for some years much less satisfactory than those in force elsewhere. The early troubles of South Australia resulting from the half-hearted attempt to

put into operation the system of land alienation pro-
pounded by Gibbon Wakefield have already been
recounted. The early regulations were from time to
time modified, but no radical change was made in the
land laws until 1872. In the year named, an Act was
passed arranging for survey of all land before sale.
It was then put up to auction, those who expressed
the intention of residing on their properties being
given first choice. After this class had been satisfied,
non-residents were permitted to compete for the
remainder, and what was left was open to selection,
without competition, at a minimum price of £1 per
acre. The payments were easy and spread over
a number of years, and a certain value of improvement
by the purchaser was necessary before a title could be
obtained.

In 1888 the Act which has just been described
gave way to a new law which with slight amendment
is still in force. All metals and minerals are reserved
to the Crown, and special arrangements are made for
long leases for pastoral tenants, and sales by auction
for cash in some cases, and on deferred payments in
others. The mining industry is provided for by the
issue of specific or general mining leases, these last
being practically prospecting licenses. The conditions
to ensure the improvement and stocking of pastoral
properties are stringent, but an encouragement to
pioneers is given by the offer to *bona fide* discoverers
of new pastures of a lease at the rate of 2s. 6d. per
annum for each square mile of country occupied. A
special feature of the measure is the portion referring
to working-men's blocks. Under these clauses twenty-

acre lots in certain localities may be leased at a nominal rental to any one who gains his livelihood by his own labour ; but residence on the property is required. In all cases the rent and price of the land is determined by specially appointed boards, who classify the country under their direction and supervise all sales and other transactions.

The Northern Territory of South Australia, which lies within the tropics, is dealt with under a special Act, which was passed in 1882, and the inducements to settlers in this district are on an even more liberal scale. Permission is given for alienation of blocks of 1280 acres at the rate of 12s. 6d. per acre cash, or on deferred payments; for pastoral occupation leases of any area up to four hundred square miles are granted for seven years at 6d. and for a further eighteen years at 2s. 6d. per annum per square mile. In order to encourage the growth of tropical crops, extremely advantageous arrangements are made for the leasing or purchase of cultivation blocks. Hitherto no great progress has been made in the Northern Territory, although in 1864 a serious attempt was made to utilise the country which had lately been added by the English Government to South Australia, at the colony's request. Surveyors were despatched to the Gulf to mark out a town and chart the country preparatory to leasing or alienation, and land orders were offered both in England and Adelaide at a very low figure in the hope of inducing settlement. These first attempts were, however, far from successful. The surveyors quarrelled amongst themselves, and the greater portion of the staff deserted their chief and returned to Adelaide. After five years had been wasted Mr. Goyder, Surveyor-General, himself went north, and selected Port Darwin as the best site for a settlement, and a town called Palmerston had scarcely been laid out before the discovery of gold and the determination of the Government to construct a telegraph right across the continent from Adelaide gave the new settlement a fair start. Land in this distant region was offered at 1s. 6d. an acre, on deferred payment, and a bonus to encourage the cultivation of sugar was promised by the Government.

The life of the little colony in the Northern Territory has so much depended on the overland telegraph line, that it may be well here to refer to the work. This undertaking had long been contemplated, but the rather vague ideas on the subject were crystallised by an offer of the British Australian Telegraph Company, which contracted to lay a submarine cable from Singapore to Van Diemen's Gulf, if the South Australian Government would undertake to connect Adelaide with Port Darwin, by an overland wire, thus completing telegraphic communication with Europe. The proposition was favourably received, and the work entered upon with enthusiasm. Mr. Todd was placed in charge, and it was evident from the outset that enormous difficulties would have to be overcome. For one thing, over 1,300 miles of telegraph wire would have to be laid through practically unexplored country, a great portion of which was nothing but rocky sandy deserts, devoid of both pasture and water. The whole distance, some 2,200 miles, was divided into three sections, and while Mr. Todd entrusted the two extremities to contractors, he himself personally supervised the middle portion. The time for the completion of the work was the 1st of January, 1872, when the Cable Company had agreed to have performed their part; and before this date both the Adelaide end and the centre section had been finished. In the far north, however, the work had failed. There were no trees for posts, the difficulties of transport were almost unsurmountable, and the tropical heat was too great for the labour of Europeans. It looked at one time, indeed, as if the junction would never be made, and as the date agreed upon had nearly arrived, and the company threatened to sue the Government for damages if the line was then unfinished, there was much consternation in Adelaide. Mr. Todd hastened up to the Port Darwin end, to see what could be done. Coolies and Chinese were introduced, wells were dug along the route and iron posts provided where trees could not be obtained, and by great exertions things were pushed forward. A fracture in the submarine cable had meanwhile relieved the Government from fear, and in August the two ends of the overland wire were joined at Central Mount Stewart, and then the first telegraph message was flashed from shore to shore. By October the cable had been repaired, and telegraphic communication was established with the old world, Australians thus being able to read at their breakfast tables events which had occurred in Europe but a few hours previously. Before many years had passed, another telegraph line was carried along the arid shores between Adelaide and Albany in Western Australia, so that now there is direct communication between the four extremities of the Australian continent.

The construction of railways has also been considerable, but at present the railway system is confined to the south-eastern corner of the colony, with the exception of the track which runs northward towards Port Darwin. The first sod of the great transcontinental railway, which has its southern terminus at Port Augusta, was turned by the Governor, Sir William Jervois, in 1878, and it has since been extended 686 miles from Adelaide to Oodnadatta. The construction was also commenced at the Port Darwin end, and the line was carried to Pine Creek, leaving a gap about 1,140 miles still to be covered before traffic can be opened from the southern to the northern coast.

There is little more to be said with regard to South Australia, which has been singularly happy in an uneventful history. Gold has been discovered within its borders, but not in sufficient quantities to affect its destiny to any great extent. Nevertheless it is rich in minerals, and the copper deposits of Burra Burra have been eclipsed by similar discoveries at Moonta and Wallaroo. Agriculture has steadily progressed, and although the yield of wheat is light per acre, the cost of clearing and preparing the soil for tillage is proportionately small, and the South Australian harvest affords annually a large surplus of breadstuffs for exportation to Europe and the other colonies. This province is essentially one of great poten-

tialities. Much of the country between Adelaide and
Port Darwin, which was long supposed to be absolutely useless, and nothing but desert, has proved to
be not unsuitable for pastoral purposes, while many
of the rivers which flow into the Gulf of Carpentaria
are bordered by rich alluvial flats which probably
some day will be covered by extensive cotton and
sugar plantations. The great problem to be solved
is the supply of labour in the tropics ; but apart from
this, a very large portion of the country is as yet
practically unexplored, and until more perfect knowledge is obtained of its capabilities it will be rash
to predict what the future of South Australia may be.

QUEENSLAND.

XXVI.

THE MORETON BAY SETTLEMENT.

(1825–1851.)

THE colony of Queensland owes its origin to the report made by Mr. Bigge, on the state of the penal establishments—towards the close of the reign of Governor Macquarie in New South Wales—in which he recommended that some spot should be found to which the worst class of criminals could be despatched, where they would be far away from the temptations which were inseparable from a community partly bond and partly free. Surveyor-General Oxley was therefore sent in the cutter *Mermaid* to seek on the northern coast some place which would meet these requirements. Port Curtis was his original destination ; but after a careful examination ·he was dissatisfied with its qualifications, and turned southwards towards Moreton Bay. While lying at anchor, a party of natives was observed approaching the shore, and the attention

of those on board was turned towards one man,
who appeared to be possessed by an uncontrollable
delight at the sight of the ship. A boat was sent
ashore, and the copper-coloured savage turned out
to be one of a party of four Europeans, who had
left Sydney with the intention of sailing to the
Illawarra district (to the south of the capital of
New South Wales), but had been driven by storms
far out of their course, and had all nearly died from
thirst and exposure. After terrible hardships, under
which one of the number succumbed, land was
sighted, and the three remaining castaways beached
their boat at a spot where they perceived a stream
of fresh water. The intruders were soon surrounded
by natives, but were treated with extreme kindness,
and Pamphlett—who now told the tale to Oxley—
had remained with them ever since. The desire
for civilised life had been too strong for the others,
who had started off to walk home under the impression that they were south of Sydney. It is
needless to say that they were never heard of since.

With Pamphlett's aid a large river was discovered,
and Oxley at once rowed fifty miles up and made
a hurried survey of the country. On his return to
Sydney he gave a most enthusiastic description of
his discoveries, with the result that after considerable
correspondence between the Imperial Government
and the Governor—in which the reluctance of the
Secretary of State to found a new settlement was
apparent—Oxley was ordered in September, 1824,
to again set sail for the Brisbane River, in the brig
Amity. He had on board a detachment of the 40th

Regiment, in charge of Lieutenant Miller, and thirty
prisoners, who were to form the first penal settlement on the north-east coast. In the following year
Captain Logan was appointed to the command, and
in 1826 Sir Thomas Brisbane himself visited the new
depôt, which in his opinion met all the requirement
of · Bigge's report as it was far from all civilised
habitations, and it was practically impossible for
a prisoner to escape. Rapidly additions were made
to the convict population, but as no free settlers
were permitted to come within fifty miles of the gaol,
the early doings at Brisbane are buried in oblivion.
Sufficient, nevertheless, is known to show that the
Moreton Bay depôt rivalled in corruption and
brutality Tasman's Peninsula or Norfolk Island.
Tales of horrible cruelty and disgusting immorality,
both on the part of the convicts and the natives
amongst whom they were suddenly thrown, were
not uncommon ; and at length matters were brought
to a crisis by the murder of Logan. The deed was
committed either by convicts—in retaliation for some
of the ferocious attacks which had been made upon
them by the overseers—or else by the natives, who
had received almost equal provocation. Previous to
this tragedy, Logan had energetically explored the
country, with which he was almost as much pleased
as Oxley had been, and made also experiments in
cotton-growing and in the establishment of some
primitive industries.

From the date of Logan's death, the Governors of
New South Wales appear to have had a desire to
abandon Moreton Bay, and the criminal establish-

ment was gradually reduced. Meanwhile the discoveries of the explorers who had pierced the country between Sydney and the north, traversing the Darling Downs, had induced large numbers of stockowners to drive their flocks and herds on to the new pastures; and the out-stations of the most enterprising crept nearer and nearer to Brisbane. In 1839 it was determined to entirely abandon Moreton Bay as a penal establishment, and Lieutenant Gorman was sent up to remove the last relics of the gaol. The prohibition against free settlers on the Brisbane River was still in force; but, although not revoked for some time, it became a dead letter, and many more free men settled on the banks of the river. By 1841 a large portion of the Darling Downs had been taken up by squatters, and the settlement of the country further north had so far progressed that the Government considered it necessary to offer allotments in the towns for sale. Sir George Gipps came up from Sydney and laid out the plan of the town of Brisbane, on the Brisbane River, and another town further inland called Ipswich, while townships named Toowoomba and Drayton began to gather round two wayside inns, established for the convenience of travellers across the Darling Downs. The first auction of Crown lands situated in Brisbane was held in Sydney; sites met with ready sale, at prices averaging about £343 per acre.

In December, 1841, the ordinary machinery of government for a free community was provided; and Captain Wickham was sent as police magistrate,

BRISBANE.

[By permission of Messrs. Chaffey Bros., 35, Queen Victoria St., London.

while Crown lands commissioners were appointed
for the Darling Downs and Moreton Bay districts.
The pastoral industries of the province rapidly
increased ; but its otherwise satisfactory progress
was marred by the gross brutality displayed towards
the natives. The very early settlers seem to have
been inconvenienced but little by the depredations
or hostility of the aborigines, but soon the atrocities
committed by the shepherds and stockmen on out-
lying stations called forth acts of retaliatory violence
from the blacks, which were in their turn followed
by inhuman revenge at the hands of the white men.
The settlers were urgent in their appeals for more
police protection, and a body of native police officered
by Europeans, was formed to cope with the disorders
which were becoming more and more frequent. But
they only made things worse, for a member of one
native tribe displays savage enjoyment in the
slaughter of members of any other tribes, and the
native police soon developed into an armed force for
the extermination of the aboriginal inhabitants.

It is needless to record here in detail the disgusting atrocities, which are well known to all who were
connected with pioneering work in Queensland, but
a few instances will be sufficient to give an idea of
the manner in which the blacks were " civilised."
At the commencement of 1860, two partners in a
station complained in the papers that a party of
native police had shot and wounded a large number
of blacks, many of whose bodies were left to rot
unburied within a mile or two of the homestead.
Even those natives who had been employed pretty

constantly for many years by the owners did not escape, but friendly and hostile blacks had been indiscriminately shot down. A further instance is recorded in which a sub-inspector of police hand-cuffed a native boy, tying his arms to a high rafter in the verandah of the police barracks, and then flogged and kicked him until he was so maimed that he shortly died; while on another occasion some squatters rode down and shot no less than twenty-two natives, and after spending the night by a water-hole, walked round in the morning, and dashed out the brains of those who were not yet dead with one of their own clubs. The troopers showed little com-punction in murdering scores of the natives, and on one occasion, when a white man had been killed by two blacks, a body of police in the dead of night stealthily surrounded the tribe to which the culprits belonged. A korroboree was being held at the time; at a given signal the police fired a volley into the midst of the dancing crowd, and then rushed in to complete the work of destruction. A common method of freeing a run of the aborigines was also by wholesale poisoning. A barrel of flour, in which white arsenic had been mixed, was given with a smile as a present to the unsuspecting victims, and before long half the tribe would be writhing and screaming in agony, which at last terminated in death. Could it be wondered at if the blacks took revenge when they could?

But otherwise the settlers showed great energy, and entered with determination upon the work of opening up their immense territory. Captain Sturt, who had discovered the Darling and the Murray, offered to conduct an expedition into the centre of Australia ; and in 1844 a well-equipped party of sixteen persons started from the banks of the Darling, at the furthest point that had been reached in 1828. Following the course of the river they passed Laidley's Ponds and Lake Cawndilla, and then turned northwards for the interior, through a barren desert, until they reached a few hills which are now known as the Barrier Range. Fortunately for the party it was the winter season, and they could obtain a moderate supply of water, but by the time they had passed another chain of hills, which Sturt called the Grey Range, summer had come. The heat in 1844 was exceptionally intense, and in the sandy plains of the interior it was so great that the baked earth split the hoofs of the horses and quickly dried up the water from the creeks. One party found a stream, however, flowing in a rocky basin, and Sturt formed his depôt beside it, remaining there for six months. Several excursions were made during this period, and the creek on which they were camped was followed, but after a course of twenty miles it was lost in the sand. The wanderers suffered terribly from the heat, which was sometimes as high as 130° in the shade. The ink dried on their pens before they could touch the paper to write. Their combs split, their nails became brittle, and metal if touched burned their fingers. A hole was dug in the ground sufficiently deep to enable them to escape the dreadful glow of the sun, and day after day they prayed for rain. At last the party grew haggard and ill, and one being attacked with scurvy rapidly sank and died. But finally rain came, and as there was now plenty of water, the journey was continued.

After travelling northwards sixty-one miles a new depôt was formed, and excursions were·made into the surrounding country. But as they journeyed further north they came to a region of hills of a barren red sand, and lagoons of salt bitter water. For some time they toiled through this country, but when at length they reached the last hill and nothing was to be seen but a vast stoney plain, which Sturt called the Stoney Desert, summer was again at hand and water was failing. So they hastened back ; but their water was exhausted before they reached the depôt, and they were then in danger of being buried by shifting sand hills. Sturt made one more attempt to find water, discovering a magnificent stream which he called Cooper's Creek. But on again entering Stoney Desert, he was compelled to retrace his steps, and when he reached the depôt on his return he was worn to a shadow and the glare of the sandy waste had blinded him. His reports on the arid country gave rise to the idea that the whole centre of Australia was one vast desert, but this has since been proved to be an error.

All the north-east portion of the continent was left unexplored till 1844, when a young German botanist, Ludwig Leichardt, with five men, left Sydney, and, passing through magnificent forests and fine pastures, made his way to the Gulf of Carpentaria, discovering and tracing many large rivers as he went. At Van Diemen's Gulf a ship was waiting to bring

him home ; and on his return to Sydney he was
rewarded by a public subscription of £1,500, and a
grant from the Government of £1,000.   In 1847 he
again started to make further explorations in the
north of Queensland, taking with him sheep and
goats, which, however, so impeded his progress that,
after wandering over the Fitzroy Downs for many
months, he returned without having achieved anything.   In the following year he led a third expedition, with which he intended to cross the whole
continent from east to west.   A start was made from
Moreton Bay, and in two years he expected to reach
the Swan River settlement.   A large party set out,
and soon passed the Cogwoon River, and from this
point Leichardt sent a hopeful letter to a friend in
Sydney.   But no news has since been received of
him or his companions, although for many years
expeditions were sent out to search for him.

On Leichardt's return from his first journey, Sir
Thomas Mitchell set out northwards, and after discovering the Culgoa and Warrego, turned west,
travelling over a great extent of level country.   At
length he came upon a river, and followed the current
for 150 miles towards the heart of the continent,
and then returned.   Edmund Kennedy, who was
soon after sent to trace the course of the newly-
found stream, followed its banks for 150 miles
below the place at which Mitchell had turned back.
He, too, was then forced to return, through want of
provisions.   He had seen enough, however, to con-
vince him that this stream was only the upper part
of Cooper's Creek, which had been discovered by

Sturt. In 1848, Kennedy landed on the north-east coast with twelve men, and turning inland to the north-west, travelled towards Cape York, where a vessel was to meet him. Dense jungles and prickly shrubs barred his path, and tore the flesh of the travellers at every step, while vast swamps often made long detours necessary. Leaving eight of his companions at Weymouth Bay, he pushed on towards the north with three others and a black boy, Jackey. But one of them accidentally shot himself, and was unable to proceed. Kennedy, who was now only a few miles from Cape York, left the wounded man with the two other whites, and started, accompanied by Jackey, to obtain aid from the schooner. Before they had gone far, however, a tribe of natives attacked them, and a spear hurled from among the bushes pierced Kennedy in the back, and he fell from his horse. The blacks rushed forward, but Jackey fired upon them, and at the report for a moment they were frightened and fled. Kennedy soon died, and the faithful Jackey dug a grave and left him in the forest. Then with the journals and other papers he plunged into a stream, and walking along its bed with only his head above the surface, in this way escaped his enemies. As soon as he reached the Cape, and was taken on board the schooner, a search party was despatched for the wounded man and his companions, but it proved fruitless, while only two of the eight who had stayed at Weymouth Bay had survived starvation and disease, when relief arrived.

XXVII.

THE COLONY OF QUEENSLAND.

(1851–1893.)

QUEENSLAND was almost as hasty as Victoria in its demand for separation from the parent colony, and in 1851 a petition was forwarded to the Queen, praying for the same concession for the Moreton Bay district as had in that year been granted to Port Phillip. The petitioners were unsuccessful, but three years later they renewed their appeal, and met with a favourable reception. As a result, in 1855 an Act was passed by the Imperial Parliament giving the Government power to make a division of New South Wales, so as to form a new colony, when such a course was deemed advisable. But delays occurred, and in the following year the ministry went out of office, so that the matter received no attention for some time. At the close of 1859, however, the desired change was made, and the portion of New South Wales to the north of the 29th parallel of latitude was proclaimed a separate colony, under the name of Queensland. Sir George Bowen was appointed the first Governor, and the town of Brisbane, which then contained about seven thousand inhabitants, was chosen as the capital and seat of government. The new colony covered more than 670,000 square miles of country, but its inhabitants numbered only about twenty-five thousand persons.

Queensland was never as a separate colony under the nominee system of government, but commenced its career under the guidance of responsible ministers. The first Parliament opened on the 29th of May, 1860, the Legislative Council, which consisted of members nominated by the Governor for life, and the Assembly being elected by the people under what is practically manhood suffrage, the only qualification being six months' residence. Any person on the electoral roll is qualified to be a member. The duration of Parliaments is now limited to three years, and members of the Assembly receive a salary of £300 per annum.

In 1858 a rush took place to the banks of the Fitzroy River, in the far north, where gold was said to have been found. Ship after ship arrived in Kepple Bay, crowded with men bound for Canoona, a place about seventy miles up the river. Before long some fifteen thousand had collected, but it was found that the gold was to be met with over a very small area only, and many of those who had come to the place, having spent all their money on their outfit and passage, were unable to get away. Amongst the crowd thus gathered in this isolated spot, far from civilisation, terrible distress soon began to show itself, and for sometime the Fitzroy River was the scene of wretchedness and starvation. At length the Governments of New South Wales and

Victoria took pity on the unfortunate miners, and provided means of transport for the destitute who wished to leave the place. Some, however, at the time of greatest scarcity, had taken up portions of the fertile land on the banks of the river, and commenced farming. From these beginnings sprang what is now the thriving town of Rockhampton. The Government of Queensland was anxious to attract some of the immigrants who were coming in large numbers to Australia, and offered rewards, ranging from £200 to £1,000, to the discoverers of profitable gold-fields. A great impetus was thus given to prospecting, and during the following years many districts were opened up by parties of miners.

In 1867 a man named Nash, by accident, found extensive gold deposits at Gympie, a place about 130 miles from Brisbane. Nash kept his discoveries secret, and commenced to collect gold for himself before giving publicity to the news. He soon procured several hundred pounds' worth of the metal, and then, as it seemed impossible to avoid discovery (as a road ran close to the spot at which he was at work), and as it was not improbable that some one else would forestall him in reporting the field, he came down to Maryborough, and announcing his valuable find, received the Government reward. A rush to Gympie immediately took place, and the field proved to be exceedingly rich; a nugget, worth about £4,000, was found close to the surface. Other gold-fields have also been discovered from time to time. Far to the north, on the Palmer River,

rich deposits have been found ; and, in spite of the
hostility of natives and the tropical heat, great
numbers of miners are at work, including thousands
of Chinamen.

But the fields already described are insignificant,
when compared with the enormous yield of the
Mount Morgan mine, which has already paid
£2,750,000 in dividends. It is a huge mound of ore,
which is highly ferruginous, and contains gold to the
extent of several ounces to the ton, its peculiar
formation, in the opinion of the Government geologist
of Queensland, being due to the action of the thermal
springs. The story of its discovery is peculiar. It
is situated near Rockhampton, in the very district to
which the diggers had rushed with such ill-luck in
1858. A young squatter had bought a selection
of 640 acres from the Government, but it was on a
rocky hill, and he found that for grazing or cultivation it was useless. Accordingly, when the offer was
made of £640 by three brothers named Morgan, he
gladly closed the bargain ; but soon after the transaction the fortunate purchasers found that the dirty
grey rocks, of which the whole was composed, contained so much gold that £20 or £30 worth of it
could be extracted with rude appliances from every
cartload of stuff. Work was immediately commenced,
and before long Mount Morgan turned out to be the
richest gold mine in the world. A year or two later
the hill which had cost £640 was sold for £8,000,000.
It is now calculated that it is worth at least double
that sum, and the shares of the company which possess it have reached a figure equivalent to £18,000,000.

But gold-mining is not the only industry which has been followed in Queensland. In the northern districts tropical products are successfully grown, and about 1861 the cultivation of cotton was commenced. No very great progress was made for the first three years, but when the American war cut off that source of supply, the enhanced price of both cotton and sugar (the cultivation of which was commenced in 1865) more than compensated for the comparatively higher cost of white labour in the Queensland plantations. As long as the price of cotton and sugar remained high, the question of labour on the plantations was not of such importance as to seriously interfere with the industries. But when, on the close of the war, these articles fell to their normal level, the American product again coming into competition, and the planters of Queensland finding it necessary to effect some radical change in the management of their estates, it was proposed to substitute the cheap labour of coolies from India for the more expensive Europeans; but there were difficulties in the way, and eventually Chinese were introduced. They did not come up to expectations, and planters were at their wits' end. At length a sugar planter named Towns conceived the idea of bringing labourers from the South Sea Islands, and as he was also the owner of ships which traded to the islands, he had no difficulty in putting the scheme into practice. The Kanakas (as the islanders were called) were apt pupils, and soon became expert plantation hands. They also met all requirements as to cheapness, for a few presents of finery seemed to satisfy them for years of labour.

Towns' example was speedily followed by his neighbours, and the practice of employing Kanakas on the plantations instead of white men became general. The islanders as a rule made engagements for one or two years' service, and then having received in payment, cloth, knives, hatchets, beads, &c., to the value of about £10, were sent back to the islands. A system such as this of necessity bred abuses, and unscrupulous masters resorted to all sorts of tricks to swindle the Kanakas out of their pay. Again, as the demand for island labour increased, the supply of volunteers was unequal to the requirements of planters, and captains of vessels took to wholesale kidnapping, and to all intents and purposes sold their captives in Queensland to the plantation owners for so much a head. There were consequently frequent conflicts between the crews of labour vessels and the inhabitants of the islands. The white men would suddenly appear at the native villages and take as prisoners crowds of men and women; in revenge the natives, whenever they got a chance, attacked the vessels visiting the islands and murdered all they found on board. All sorts of devices for getting near the natives were tried by the kidnappers. Sometimes they disguised themselves as missionaries, and then when an opportunity occurred, on account of the trust inspired by their appearance, they fell upon their victims, and hurried them off to the ships. As a result, if real missionaries, suspecting nothing, approached the islanders, they were

frequently speared or clubbed to death, without discrimination.

The conflict in most cases was, however, onesided.
Labour vessels cut down the frail canoes, and while
the occupants were struggling in the water they were
secured, dragged aboard, and thrust into the hold.
The hatches were battened down, and when enough
of the poor wretches had been crammed into the ship,
sail was set, and but little attention was paid to the
passengers, who if they survived the terrible passage
in the filthy and confined holds were sold to the
planters or their agents. It must not be supposed
that all the planters engaged in the labour traffic
behaved like ruffians, but nevertheless such deeds as
those described were of common occurrence. At
length these scandals so aroused popular feeling that
in 1868, the Queensland Legislature passed an Act to
regulate the island labour traffic. The Polynesian
Labourers Act provided that no islanders were to be
shipped to the colony unless the captain of the vessel
could produce a document, signed by some responsible person, to the effect that those whom he brought
had shipped without compulsion. At the same time
special Government agents were appointed to ac-
company every vessel engaged in the trade, and to
exercise a general supervision over the islanders on
the voyage. The minimum payment to Kanakas on
the termination of their service was fixed at £6 worth
of goods for each year's work, and other minor
provisions were also enacted for the general regulation of the trade.

These rules were right enough as far as they went,

but the whole system was such that it was impossible to make a law which could not be in one way or another evaded. Without doubt the new Act effected much good, and the island traffic lost many of its most objectionable characteristics. But frequently the clauses which made it necessary for a document to be produced showing that the Kanakas were voluntary immigrants were little but a dead letter. Nothing was easier than to bribe the chief of any tribe by a present of a few trinkets, to compel a certain number of his people to go before a missionary and express their desire to ship to Queensland, although really they may have been most averse to the proposal. Again, while the Government agent was put to watch the captain, and the captain was only too happy to watch the agent, there was always the danger of collusion, and cases have been brought to light in which the deeds of the crews of labour vessels have been a blot on our civilisation. There is evidence, however, that now the abuses have been reduced to a minimum ; one of the best signs of the great improvement which has been effected is that islanders who have served a term in Queensland very often re-engage when the opportunity offers, and bring with them their friends and relations. The whole traffic is nevertheless undesirable, and it is almost impossible, even with the best intentions, for the Government to ensure that only volunteers are brought to the colony, and — what is more important — that expirees are sent back to their proper destinations. It has frequently been asserted that Kanakas have been landed at the wrong islands to save trouble, and this practically means handing them over to be murdered by hostile tribes. The whole question is surrounded with difficulties, and the proposal to re-introduce the system, after a temporary suspension, is at present calling forth an animated controversy between its friends and its opponents. In all branches of material development Queensland has made rapid progress, and under liberal land laws and state-assisted immigration the population has rapidly increased. An agitation has for some been on foot in favour of a subdivision of the huge territory, for it is hoped that in this way the friction may be avoided which the very conflicting interests of the North and South must under existing arrangements inevitably produce.

Like most of the other colonies, Queensland became intoxicated with its own prosperity, and plunged headlong into extravagance in its public expenditure, but, although this course has been followed by the usual reaction, the natural resources of the country are so enormous that the depression is unlikely to be of long duration or to seriously dim the brilliant promise of the future.

NEW ZEALAND.

XXVIII.

FROM THE FIRST SETTLEMENT TO THE RECALL OF GOVERNOR FITZROY.

(1791–1846.)

LONG before any systematic attempt was made to colonise New Zealand there had been intercourse between the Maori population and the whaling ships, which visited the coast in large numbers. As might have been expected, these meetings often led to misunderstandings, and the cruelty and immorality of the sailors was fully counterbalanced by the acts of revenge perpetrated by the natives, in accordance with their ancient customs. Occasionally large numbers of passengers and seamen fell victims to the misbehaviour of earlier visitors. Thus, in 1809, a ship called the *Boyd*, on her voyage to England, touched at Whangarua, in order to obtain spars, and, while the captain and many of the crew were ashore, the Maoris made a descent upon them, and having killed and eaten all who were to be found, attacked the ship, leaving only one woman and three children

to tell the tale. The survivors, who had hidden themselves when they saw the Maoris coming, were eventually rescued by the crew of the *City of Edinburgh*, aided by a friendly native named Te Pahi. Several events of a somewhat similar character attracted the attention of Australians and Englishmen to the barbarous islanders, and the Rev. Samuel Marsden, the chaplain in New South Wales, urged the establishment of a mission station at the Bay of Islands, which had been the seat of most of the outrages, in the hope that the missionaries might be able to improve the relations between the two races. His suggestion was carried out, and a small settlement formed, while at the same time one European and three chiefs of the native tribes were appointed magistrates for the district, and were instructed to use their utmost efforts to diminish the continually recurring collisions. In spite of these precautions, murders and other atrocities continued. Every vessel that cruised in New Zealand waters had boarding nets, and, should any mishap drive a luckless ship upon the coast, the probable fate of all on board was only too well understood. In 1816 two ships were wrecked and their crews killed and eaten. In 1823 the Imperial Parliament at last realised that it was necessary to take some steps to mitigate these evils, and, in order to control at any rate the European settlers and visitors, the jurisdiction of the Supreme Court of New South Wales was extended to residents in New Zealand.

Much of the trouble which had arisen and subsequently occurred between the two races was due to the ignorance and want of appreciation of the Maoris and their customs shown by the Europeans. As a race the natives were vastly superior intellectually to any savages with whom Englishmen had previously been in contact in the Southern hemisphere. Guided largely by tribal traditions and native customs, their actions were often inexplicable to the white strangers, and as a result

A MAORI CHIEF.

there were many collisions which a better acquaint-ance on either side would have prevented. For instance, it was a gross offence to touch any article which was *tapu*, that is, which for some reason had been placed under a ban, or which had been declared sacred from the touch or eye. Constant and un-conscious breaches of the Maori law were made by strangers, and indeed it was only by great care that they could be avoided. Any flagrant digression

demanded *utu*, or atonement, which was only procurable too frequently by the death of the offender.

Hence many barbarous and incomprehensible acts
of apparently inhuman revenge, for trivial matters,
were perpetrated, which in reality were instigated by
native customs that the Maoris felt constrained to
blindly obey.

One of the survivors of the crew of a brig which
was seized on the east coast in 1816 was killed for
lending a knife to a slave and afterwards breaking
the *tapu* which this had caused, by using the
same knife to cut food for a chief's mother. The
latter happened to die, and when the facts were made
know the *tohunga* (priest) had no doubt that the
breach of the *tapu* was the cause of her decease. A
council of the tribe was held, and the poor fellow was
sentenced to death, though the chief, who liked him
very much, did his best to save him. The *tohunga*
in an eloquent address, pointed out to the chief that
the gods would never be appeased if *utu* were not
exacted for breach of the *tapu*, and that the lot of his
friend was not really hard, for it would be an honour
to him to attend in the next world on so great a
chieftainess as the chief's dead mother, and to the
latter to have such an attendant. The chief's family
pride and filial affection were in this way successfully
appealed to, and the fate of the poor wretch was
sealed.

This case serves to show much of the Maori
character. Superstitious and sensitive to a degree,
they have shown themselves nevertheless fearless and
in the main honourable as a race. With few excep-

tions they proved as foes to be worthy of the highest admiration, while as allies they were warm and true friends. Possessed of great intelligence and adaptability, they lost no time in turning to account the lessons in civilisation which were to be learnt from their white visitors. Hongi and Waikato, the former, perhaps, the greatest of their chiefs, having been taken to England by one of the missionaries as early as 1820, were made much of, and loaded with handsome gifts ; but before their return to New Zealand they converted all the presents which had been showered upon them into muskets, and at once on landing in their native country started on the war path against neighbouring tribes, with the result that their enemies fell easy victims to their superior weapons.

The extreme fertility of the islands had in 1825 inspired persons in England with a desire to colonise them, and towards the close of 1826 a vessel carrying sixty settlers arrived under the command of Captain Herd, who purchased two islands in the Hauraki Gulf. But fears of the attacks of the natives discouraged the immigrants, and many of them left the country at the first opportunity. Their apprehensions were not groundless, for in the following year Hongi turned his newly acquired weapons against those from whom they had been obtained, and destroyed the mission station at Whangaroa. A sort of guerilla warfare had long existed, but matters now reached such a stage that peaceful occupation of the country became impossible. There were faults on both sides, and in 1831 thirteen chiefs appealed to the English Government for protection from the

MILFORD SOUND.

(*Painted by Eugène von Ghérard.*)

traders and settlers, while at the same time the Governor of New South Wales—under whose nominal protection New Zealand at that time was—suggested that it would be desirable that a Government resident should be appointed without delay to look after the affairs both of white men and Maoris, and maintain some semblance of authority. Accordingly, two years later, Mr. James Busby was appointed Resident at the Bay of Islands, and shortly afterwards Lieutenant McDonell, R.N., was sent in a similar capacity to the settlement at Hokianga.

As yet the Imperial Government had not formally annexed the islands, although Cook had hoisted the British flag when he visited the country in 1770, and an enterprising foreigner, known as Baron Hyppolitus de Thierry, issued a declaration in 1835 from the Marquesas Islands, one of which (Nuhuneva) he had purchased, asserting that he was " Sovereign Chief .of New Zealand and King of Nuhuneva." On receipt of this rather remarkable news, Mr. Busby at once issued a counter address, in which he directed the attention of the native chiefs to this bold attempt to seize their country, and urged them to offer a combined front to the usurper. A meeting of all the principal chiefs was hastily convened, and a declaration announcing the independence of the Maoris, under the title of the " United Tribes of New Zealand," was issued. A copy of this proclamation was forwarded to the Secretary of State, who in answer announced that England would always guard New Zealand from foreign aggression.

But here the responsibility of England ceased, and

although anarchy still in a large measure prevailed in
New Zealand, no attempt was made to establish any
settled form of government. In spite of their readiness to combine with Mr. Busby in protesting against
the claims of Baron de Thierry, the natives continued
to show hostility to the European missionaries and
traders ; and at last, in 1837, the Governor of New
South Wales despatched Captain Hobson in the
Rattlesnake to the Bay of Islands to examine into the
lawless occurrences which were alarmingly frequent
at Kororareka, the main settlement. At this spot a
considerable village had arisen, and there were already
about a thousand white inhabitants, while the bay was
crowded with whalers of all nationalities. Captain
Hobson fully confirmed the reports of the unsatisfactory position of affairs, but remedial action was
still delayed, until in 1838 the inhabitants of Kororareka could wait no longer, and determined to take
the law into their own hands, and form a sort of
vigilance association for the punishment of crime and
the protection of life and property. This brought
matters to a crisis, for the Imperial Government saw
that the time had come when it must either take some
steps to create a proper administrative authority, or
must entirely abandon all pretence of protecting or
managing the settlement.

But further difficulties were ahead. Schemes for
colonisation were about this time extraordinarily
popular, and a company known as the New Zealand
Company, which afterwards became a great factor in
the affairs of the colony, was formed in London by
Lord Durham to undertake the systematic settlement

of the unclaimed territory. Final arrangements were completed by 1839, and the *Tory* with Colonel William Wakefield and other officers of the New Zealand Company on board, sailed from London, after a quick passage reached its destination and brought up in Queen Charlotte's Sound. The situation did not seem suitable, so weighing anchor the pioneers sailed round to Port Nicholson, where Wakefield took possession of the country in the name of the company, a royal salute was fired, and the New Zealand flag hoisted to commemorate the event. The natives apparently welcomed the new-comers, and all joined in a feast at which the utmost goodwill prevailed. Colonel Wakefield, ignorant of Maori customs, and particularly of their laws relating to the possession of the land, at once proceeded to acquire large tracts of country in the name of the company, for the use of intending settlers. Sailing along the coast, he speedily procured an area of about twenty million acres extending on the west to Taranaki, and along the east coast to Hawke's Bay, at the same time he bought from a chief named Rauparaha the valley of the Wairau in the south island.

In these transactions was laid the foundation of much future trouble. In the honest belief that the land belonged to the chiefs and others who treated with him, Wakefield had paid the price agreed upon, but he was unaware of the fact that each tribe had its own traditional boundaries, that the customs with regard to ownership were most intricate, and that the natives regarded the possession of the soil as of the highest importance. Few Europeans at that time and for many years afterwards understood the position. The land was held by the natives upon a communistic basis, and though there were rights of occupation belonging to individuals, the soil belonged to the tribes, and could not be parted with except upon the authority of the whole. The question of the acquisition of land was the cause of nearly all the subsequent difficulties with the Maoris, and their tribal customs on the subject were most difficult to overcome.

Shortly after the despatch of the *Tory,* four other ships followed with a large number of intending settlers. By the following year no less than twelve hundred colonists had arrived at the port; the town of Wellington was subsequently founded, and a second independent provisional government established. When news of the steps which had been taken by the New Zealand Company became public in London, there was great consternation at the Colonial Office, and it was at last realised that it would be impossible for the Government to elude any longer its responsibility with regard to the colony. Hastily letters-patent were prepared, extending the boundaries of New South Wales so as to include the two islands, and Captain Hobson was despatched to hoist the Union Jack and take charge of the settlement as Lieutenant-Governor. As soon as he had landed he issued a proclamation inviting both British subjects and native chiefs to meet him in conference at an early date, and when they had assembled he read his commission and two proclamations issued by the Governor of New South Wales, asserting the

Queen's authority in the colony, and the illegality of any transactions in land which had not received the confirmation of the Government. Soon afterwards another meeting was arranged with the chiefs of the north island, at Waitangi, Mr. Busby's station, and a draft treaty was presented to the natives for signature, by which the sovereignty of New Zealand was ceded to Great Britain, while in return their proprietary interests in the soil were fully preserved, and all transfers of property to British subjects would have to be sanctioned by the Lieutenant-Governor. It was also arranged that the pre-emption of Maori lands—*i.e.*, the first right of purchase—should be vested in the Crown. The treaty was largely signed by those present ; and then in order to obtain the names of as many chiefs as possible in ratification, it was handed to missionaries and agents to be carried through the country and submitted to all who had not attended the meeting. The Lieutenant-Governor himself visited Hokianga and other places for the same purpose ; and on May 21st in the same year the sovereignty of the Queen was proclaimed over the islands, and Major Bunbury and Captain Nias, R.N., hoisted the English flag at Cloudy Bay.

The Secretary of State had been hastened in his action by fears of the intention of the French to seize New Zealand—fears which proved to be well founded, for in October, 1839, two ships, the *Comte de Paris* and the frigate *L'Aube,* had sailed for Akaroa, in the middle island, and rights had been granted to a colonisation company known as the Nanto-Bordelaise. Captain Stanley was hastily sent round to

Akaroa to unfurl the English flag and take possession before the ships could reach the place, and he had only just accomplished his mission when the Frenchmen hove in sight.

During the next few years new settlements were founded all over the islands, more especially at Wanganui, New Plymouth, and Nelson, and in 1841 New Zealand was proclaimed an independent colony, and Hobson was raised to the rank of Governor. He survived his promotion however but a short time, and Captain Fitzroy was appointed in his stead. Shortly before Fitzroy's arrival an affray occurred with the natives at Wairau, arising out of the purchase of land previously referred to. Some surveyors were engaged in laying out farms in the Wairau Valley when suddenly the chief Te Rauparaha, who claimed the land, protested against the progress of the work, and threatened violence should they attempt to proceed. Colonel Wakefield, persuaded that the company's claim was good, appealed to the authorities, and the police magistrate with a force of police, special constables, and others, made an attempt to arrest the chief. The natives resisted, and the constables were put to rout, seventeen of the surveyors and police being massacred, although they offered to surrender unconditionally. Amongst those slain was Captain Arthur Wakefield, R.N., the leader of the Nelson settlement.

A general panic ensued amongst all the inhabitants of the district. This sudden outbreak on the part of the Maoris had, moreover, a very serious effect on the prospects of the colony indirectly, for the tide of immigration which had been steadily increasing previous to the occurrence, suddenly ceased, and no one could be induced to come to settle in a country where there was no security for life or property, and where at any moment they might be attacked by what they regarded as a barbarous race of savages. The public finances consequently fell into sore straits, and when the new Governor arrived in December, 1843, he found the treasury empty and already liabilities incurred equal in amount to twelve months' probable revenue. But before anything could be done to alleviate the general distress, it was necessary to take some steps to reassure the settlers; so the Governor visited Wellington and Nelson, where he made personal inquiries into the Wairau conflict, and to conciliate the natives, issued a proclamation consenting not to enforce the pre-emptive right, granted to the Government by the treaty of Waitangi, to purchase lands in certain portions of the country. At the same time he sought to appease the settlers by issuing permission for private individuals to complete bargains with the natives on a minimum payment of ten shillings an acre to the Crown; and when this concession did not appear sufficient, a further reduction to one penny per acre was made in the royalty demanded. Several transactions were completed on these terms, but as this was directly contrary to existing laws, the Imperial Government despatched a Special Commissioner, Mr. Spain, to inquire into the whole land question, and to open courts in the colony to decide claims and disputes with regard to land purchases.

The success of the Wairau adventure roused the temper of the native tribes, and though they still, as a rule, outwardly appeared friendly, and contented with the treaty of Waitangi, their respect for the power of the white man had vanished, and there were evidences that it required very little to cause a repetition of the outbreak. Before long the unsettled feeling culminated in the north in open war. Hone Heke—a son-in-law of the great chief Hongi, who was now dead—had become impressed with the significance of the flagstaff and standard at Kororareka, as an emblem of the authority of the foreigner, and was urgent in his efforts to stir up his followers and allies to destroy the token, which he assured them would in its downfall carry with it the supremacy of the invader. Having collected a small force, he came down to Kororareka, and after waiting a couple of days in the neighbourhood, stole up to the flagstaff and cut it down. The matter was at first looked upon rather as a freak than a direct menace ; but the Governor, without delay, sought reinforcements from New South Wales, and a small detachment was sent from Auckland to strengthen the garrison at the scene of the disturbance. Again the flagstaff was erected, and this time guarded day and night by soldiers.

But Hone Heke was determined not to be deterred, and coming suddenly upon the guard with two hundred warriors, he defeated the soldiers, and in triumph carried off the flag. Further reinforcements were at once sent up, as the position appeared to be becoming serious. The Governor himself visited the

district, and endeavoured to explain to the natives
that the intention of the Imperial Government was
entirely peaceful ; but nevertheless, as a sign of his
displeasure at their action, he demanded the surrender of their weapons. A few complied, but Hone
Heke scorned to take any part in the proceedings
and made no secret of the fact that he would continue
his hostility, and would never rest as long as the
obnoxious flag waved in the breeze. While these
events were occurring, a war-party visited Wanganui
and made hostile demonstrations, and a warship was
ordered round to overawe the natives.

The Governor meantime having done all he could,
retired from Kororareka to Auckland, but no sooner
was his back turned than Hone Heke again set to
work to accomplish the downfall of the flagstaff. He
sent a message to the officer in command that on a
particular night he would at once proceed to the hill
and repeat his outrage to the symbol of British
authority. But the warning was disregarded and
made light of, and although the ordinary watch was
kept, no special preparations were made to meet
a sudden attack. When, therefore, in the dead of
night, Hone Heke's natives once more climbed the
hill, no effective resistance could be offered, and the
obnoxious flagstaff fell under the warrior's axe. But
on this occasion Hone Heke did not confine his
attack to the flagstaff. The efforts of the guard to
defend their charge was met by a furious onslaught,
and the whole of the garrison having been utterly
routed by the Maoris, the victors descended upon the
town, which was set on fire. The greatest confusion

followed ; but the natives offered every assistance to the settlers in saving their property from the burning buildings, after which the colonists retreated to the ships in the harbour.

Application had been made by the Governor for reinforcements from Sydney, and as the vessels from Kororareka entered Auckland harbour, it was believed that they were the looked-for troops. The result, when the truth became known, was a panic amongst the residents, who believed that Heke would at once march on the capital. But Waka Hene, with a friendly band of natives kept the insurgents in check, and shortly afterwards the expected reinforcements arrived. The Governor determined to prosecute at once a campaign against Heke, and the necessary forces were despatched to the Bay of Islands. After several small skirmishes Heke's strongly fortified *pah* at Ohaewai, was evacuated, and he and his followers fled. This ended Heke's war for the time being, and the Governor was able to turn his attention to the south, which was now the scene of great unrest.

The natives had welcomed the new settlers at Port Nicholson ; but, as soon as the latter proceeded to take possession of the land purchased by Colonel Wakefield, trouble arose, and in many cases the Maoris refused to give up possession. The attitude of the natives was indeed such that the settlers were prepared for almost any emergency, and took every possible precaution against an outbreak. What had originally been a peaceful agricultural settlement was now surrounded by earthworks, while the settlers were drilled and formed into militia. But the

Governor feared that these preparations might have an irritating effect upon the natives and forbade the assembling of settlers in large bodies, except under the direction of some responsible Government officer. This step, combined with the general state of apprehension and financial stringency, caused great discontent, and Fitzroy speedily became unpopular. A petition was sent to the Imperial Government by the Port Nicholson settlers, praying for his recall, and the Secretary of State for the Colonies, being impressed with the necessity for a change, despatched Captain George Grey, who has already been mentioned in connection with South Australia, as his successor.

XXIX.

EVENTS FROM 1846 TO 1861.

THE outlook when Grey arrived was not promising, but he immediately applied himself with characteristic energy to the task of bringing order out of confusion. He informed the Secretary of State of his intention to keep on friendly terms with the principal chiefs, who would, where possible, be pensioned and made magistrates in their own districts. He had about six hundred and fifty soldiers at his disposal and authority to draw on the Imperial treasury if necessary, so that he was able to speedily bring about an improvement in the colony's affairs. Direct purchase of lands from the Maoris by private individuals was stopped, and sixty natives were enrolled under European officers as a police force. The friendly tribes under Waka Hene were granted rations, and the Executive Council passed an ordinance prohibiting the sale of firearms to natives. This measure having been adopted, Grey issued a proclamation to the natives to the effect that all who failed, when it was in their power, to render active aid to the Government, would be regarded as enemies, and that neutrality would be construed as hostility.

A few days later active operations against Heke, and another chief Kawiti (who had joined him), were commenced, with a force of nearly twelve hundred men, including artillery. Heke was at Kaikohe and Kawiti held a strong *pah*, known as Ruapekapeka, which it was necessary to capture at all hazards as it was of strategical importance. Some friendly tribes, therefore, kept Heke in check while operations were directed against Kawiti, and, after several unsuccessful attempts, one Sunday morning while the natives within Ruapekapeka were engaged in worship, the soldiers made an attack, and after three hours' desperate fighting carried the fortifications. There were serious losses on both sides, but Heke, who had arrived just prior to the attack with sixty men, escaped. The engagement, however, was decisive, and he and his followers were scattered far and wide. A garrison of two hundred soldiers was left at the Bay of Islands, and Grey with the remainder of his force returned to Auckland. This ended Heke's war, which was the only serious trouble with the powerful tribes north of Auckland; as the terms of peace were generous Heke settled at Kaikohe, and afterwards proved himself a warm friend of the Europeans.

Hardly had Grey arrived in Auckland when news was received of fresh disturbances, this time with the natives of the Hutt Valley. He at once hastened south with five hundred soldiers in the hope that the disorder might be nipped in the bud by a display of force. The soldiers were therefore promptly marched up the valley; but the rebels under Rangihaeta, on the approach of the troops, retreated to an inaccessible *pah*, where it was useless to attack them. Grey withdrew; but a strong garrison remained to guard the settlers. The natives quietly awaited a favourable opportunity for attack, and shortly surprised and routed some fifty soldiers who were stationed under Lieutenant Page at a farm in the valley. Emboldened by their success, a month later they fell upon a detachment of the 99th Regiment which was reconnoitring their position, and then began a series of murders. A general panic spread amongst the colonists in the Wellington district, and some fled to the town while others erected stockades and fortified their dwellings. Meanwhile Rangihaeta never gave the troops a chance of a decisive engagement, and always fell back when they appeared in strength.

Amongst the friendly natives was the chief Rauparaha, previously referred to, who was ostensibly a warm ally of the Europeans ; but Grey had reason to believe that he and other chiefs were secretly aiding the insurgents, and so captured him and his companions in perfidy at Porirua and detained them as prisoners on H.M.S. *Calliope*. This, as was expected, had a disheartening effect on Rangihaeta, who left his *pah* at Pahautanui and moved to the head of the Horokiwi Valley, a position from which he was easily dislodged. Pursued from place to place, his band was finally dispersed, and the campaign brought to a close.

Grey was now able to devote his attention to matters of internal reform. In almost every department of Government, affairs were in great disorder, in fact one of the first steps necessary was the repudiation of many of the acts of his predecessor. He declared void any land purchases in which he considered the natives had been unfairly treated, and decided also to cancel the Crown grants of several blocks issued by Fitzroy, in excess of 2,560 acres, the area prescribed by law as the maximum amount to be held by one grantee. Acts such as these necessarily brought him into collision with many of the settlers, and more particularly with the missionaries who had acquired extensive estates and were consequently the principal sufferers. In a despatch to the Colonial Office he expressed the opinion that the Imperial Government might rest assured that these individuals could not be put in possession of their land without a large expenditure of British blood and money, a statement which caused great excitement throughout the colony. The missionaries, who by this time had become a powerful class on account of their influence with the natives, were indignant. A long and bitter controversy followed; but a test case, which was brought before the Supreme Court, resulted in a victory for the Crown, the grants in excess of the legal limit were declared void, and much of the land in the neighbourhood of Auckland consequently reverted to the State.

Grey now became practically all powerful in the country, and his autocratic acts brought him into conflict with many of the most influential settlers. The colony was filled with discontent; but under his rule New Zealand made rapid progress, and appeared to be in a condition of prosperity and peace. With the improved order of things, speedily came a rapid increase of population. But this happy state of affairs was not to last long and trouble was once more experienced with the natives. This time the seat of disturbance was the Wanganui district, where Mrs. Gilfillan and four of her children were murdered by the Maoris. The town of Wanganui was also attacked, but the natives were repulsed with little loss on the European side. Grey hastened to the scene. A few miles above the town six hundred natives had entrenched themselves ; but the tribes of the lower Wanganui readily came to his assistance and offered to march against the insurgents. The rebels retreated before the Government forces up the river, to a point beyond which it was not considered advisable to pursue them, and shortly afterwards they naïvely informed Colonel McCleverty, who was in command of the forces at Wanganui, that they could not face his artillery, and as there was no use in continuing the war, they had decided to give it up.

The threatened trouble thus passed, and Grey, with the intention of once for all settling the native difficulty, visited Taranaki, where he found the Maoris extortionate and insolent. He was firm, though reasonable, in his demands ; he informed them that he should take for the Queen all the land which he considered was not required for their use, and appoint a commission to fix the value. For the time being matters were smoothed over, but it was only for a time. Wiremi Kingi, a native chief of great influence, who had assisted to quell the dis-

turbances in the Wellington district, claimed ances-
tral rights to land at Waitara, in the Taranaki district,
and though stating that it was not his desire to cause
trouble, he expressed his intention of coming to settle
upon it.   Accordingly, in the following year he, with
six hundred of his tribe, migrated to Waitara, a step

A MAORI DWELLING.

which subsequently caused great trouble between the
natives and the Government.   At this time, however,
nothing unpleasant resulted from his action, and
Grey was enabled once more to turn his attention to
matters of internal policy.

A movement had commenced some time previously

in favour of responsible government, and, in 1846, as a result of the agitation, the New Zealand Government Bill was passed through the Imperial Parliament. By this measure a Charter was issued dividing the colony into two provinces, and making provision for the establishment of representative institutions. These divisions were named New Ulster and New Munster; the former comprising almost the whole of the northern island, and the latter the country near Cook's Straits, together with the middle and southern islands. Each province was to have a separate Executive Council, and a Lieutenant-Governor to command under the Governor-in-chief, while a General Legislative Council was to make laws for the whole colony. On the recommendation of Grey, the operation of the Act was suspended for five years, though, as the Charter was still in force, the General Council was called together. It soon became evident that the new body and the Governor could not work in harmony, and after two years of stormy existence, the Council ceased to exist. There was of course much disappointment at the loss of autonomy, when it seemed so nearly in the grasp of the inhabitants, and the agitation was continued.

The great improvement which was meantime taking place in the aspect of affairs in New Zealand had caused a revival of the schemes for colonisation, and during the next few years numerous settlements were established by associations formed in the United Kingdom. Most of these enterprises had been contemplated sometime previously, but the trying ordeal through which the colony had passed had delayed their execution. At Otago 400,000 acres of land were purchased, under the auspices of the Free Church Association of Scotland; and in 1847 two ships, the *John Wycliffe* and *Philip Lang*, dropped anchor at Port Chalmers. Most of the immigrants who arrived in these vessels were Scotch Presbyterians, and Captain William Cargill, of the 74th Regiment, was their leader. By their efforts the town of Dunedin was founded. The Church of England had its special colonisation scheme, and, with the Governor's sanction, obtained land in what is now the province of Canterbury, and established the town of Christchurch. Colonies were also founded at Onehunga, Tauraki, and other places, under the direct supervision of the Governor, consisting entirely of military pensioners to the number of five hundred, with their wives and families.

Grey used every effort to induce the settlers to make full use of the great natural resources of the colony. *Phormium tenax*, the New Zealand flax, was extensively cultivated, while the changes made by the Governor in the price of Crown lands, whereby it was reduced from £1 to 10s. or 5s. per acre, led to the establishment of small farms, more especially in the Wairarapa district. Commerce increased with great rapidity, and in 1853 the first steam merchantman entered New Zealand waters. But this period of prosperity was interrupted by other and unlooked-for misfortunes. First a severe earthquake in the southern part of the north island frightened the inhabitants, and did considerable damage; and then the gold discoveries in California led to an exodus of some of the best class of settlers, and caused for a time grave apprehension in the minds of those who had the colony's interests at heart. This efflux was increased when gold was found in New South Wales and Victoria, and so serious did the position appear to be, that a reward of £500 was offered to any one who should discover a payable gold-field within New Zealand territory. In 1852 the precious metal had been met with in small quantities at Coromandel, but no payable field was found till five years later.

The great growth of the colony had in the interim made it undesirable that the old charter which had been granted to the New Zealand Company should continue. For some years there had been continuous conflict between the executive authority and the officers of the company, and at last it was determined by the Imperial Government to take over the whole of the interests of the company, and, in spite of Grey's opposition, the colony became responsible for a debt of £268,000, to meet the cost of the transaction, which was made a special provision of the Constitution Act. Never before had their relations with the natives appeared to wear so peaceful an aspect. Both Heke and Rauparaha had died, urging their followers to remain faithful to their compact with the Europeans, and on all hands the relations between the two races were most amicable.

Meanwhile, the movement in favour of the establishment of representative government had steadily advanced, and some progress towards the attainment of this end had been made by the granting of municipal or " borough " government ; the duties assigned to which were very large, and included not only the construction of local public works, and the control of the police, education, hospitals, and charitable institutions, but the establishment of sessional courts of justice with limited jurisdiction, and the power to levy rates on real and personal property in order to obtain the requisite funds. Grey, who had assisted in the formation of this scheme, before long saw the necessity for carrying it further, and in 1851 recommended the Imperial Government to establish an entirely new constitution, to replace that granted previously under the suspended Act.

In 1852 a Bill was passed, which contained several new principles, introduced by members of the House of Commons, who apparently had little knowledge of the circumstances of the colony. By its provisions the colony was divided into five provinces ; each province having its own superintendent and provincial council. There was to be a General Legislature to deal with matters of common concern, consisting of a Legislative Council, composed of members nominated by the Crown for life, and a House of Representatives elected by the people for five years. The Provincial Councils were to be elected by the inhabitants, and were to consist of a minimum of nine members. In 1853 the new constitution was formally proclaimed, and Grey remained just long enough to see it introduced. After eight years' service in New Zealand he was transferred to Cape Colony, and his departure was made the occasion for a warm demonstration of esteem, particularly by the natives. Grey, in his long administration, made many enemies, but he certainly steered the colony through a most trying period. He had found it in the midst of native troubles, with an empty exchequer, and a general feeling of despondency pervading the settlers; he left it in a state of perfect peace and prosperity.

The reins of government during the initiation of the new representative system were by Grey's removal placed in the hands of the officer commanding the troops, Colonel Wynyard, who held office for about fifteen months. The elections were duly held, and Parliament met for the first time on May 24, 1854. It was immediately seen that the new constitution was not to be received with perfect acclaim; the chief objection being that the Act did not provide that members of the Executive Council should be necessarily members of the Legislature. Consequently the existing council continued to hold office, but none of its members held a seat in either House, and there was thus no control over the ministry by Parliament, except by the refusal of supplies. The matter was a subject of stormy debate when Parliament met, but the acting Governor pointed out that, under the Constitution Act, he had no power to supersede the Executive Council, which was in existence before the Act had been passed; but in order to satisfy the Legislature, he added to the executive three members of the House of Representatives. Their position, however, on account of their entire want of power, became intolerable, and after seven weeks they resigned.

At the end of three months nothing had been done

by the new houses, and Wynyard decided to prorogue Parliament for a short time, with a promise to
urge the Imperial Government to pass a Bill enabling the appointment of responsible ministers. With
the message conveying this intimation to the house
came another which it was believed contained the
official notice of prorogation, but the first message
having been read, the house was moved into committee nominally to consider it, but really to prevent
the immediate reading of the second. A hot debate
ensued, and resolutions were passed denouncing any
attempt to rule without the authority of Parliament, and threatening all officers who should dare to
disburse money without parliamentary sanction. The
doors of the chamber were locked to prevent any one
from entering with an open message of prorogation,
and one member who was admitted, but was believed
to hold a copy of the *Gazette* containing the proclamation, was assaulted and declared guilty of contempt.
Eventually a permanent committee having been
appointed to watch the proceedings of the Governor
during the recess, Parliament was formally prorogued
for a fortnight and in the interval four other members
of the house were added to the Executive Council.

When Parliament assembled again, Wynyard intimated that it was proposed to make certain alterations in the Constitution Act, though no change was
suggested in regard to the Executive Council. An
amendment on the address in reply was carried by
twenty-two votes to four declaring that the house
had no confidence in a mixed executive of the kind
of men in office, and the four new ministers after

holding their seats three days resigned. Having thus protested, members set seriously to work, and before the commencement of the following session Wynyard had received authority to accept a responsible ministry, on condition that the old executive were granted pensions, to which they were entitled by Imperial regulations. After a short session, therefore, Parliament was dissolved with a view to enabling the constituencies to express their views on the subject of the appointment of responsible ministers.

Colonel Gore Browne was appointed Governor in 1855; he had only been in New Zealand a very short time when trouble with the Taranaki natives once more arose. A number of the Taranaki Maoris had formed a league, binding themselves not to sell land to Europeans, and consequently quarrels between the two races became common. Things were further complicated by other natives who, being willing to dispose of their land, fell out with the league; these coming into conflict, several intertribal fights occurred. But Wiremi Kingi guaranteed that no European should suffer in consequence, and the Government did not interfere. The neutrality of the Governor in these disputes, however, was regarded by the settlers as evidence of an intention on his part to prevent the colonists from acquiring land, and caused widespread discontent. Browne visited Taranaki, but failed to reconcile the hostile tribes, and reported to the Colonial Office that the Maoris regarded the new Parliament with distrust, and that in the existing state of affairs troops to the number of 1,600 and a man-of-war were necessary, as he foresaw danger.

The result of the constant conflicts between the
natives, and the desire on the part of some of them
to combine for defence against the increasing power
of the *pakeha* led at this time to the initiation of a
new movement amongst them, afterwards known as
Kingism, which commenced without any apparent
disloyalty, but eventually developed into a serious
cause of trouble.   Some of the most important chiefs
saw that the new constitution made no provision for
the representation or internal government of the
Maoris themselves, though power was given to deal
with all matters between natives and Europeans ; and
as they considered that their chiefs were not receiving that deference and appreciation which their *mana*
entitled them to and that the nationality of their
people was being undermined, a meeting was held
in 1856 to discuss proposals for establishing a kingship over the natives.   No immediate action followed,
but soon afterwards while their dignity was still
suffering, Wi Tamihana, one of the greatest and
most intelligent of the chiefs, went to Auckland to
interview the Governor with the object of obtaining
a small loan to put up a flour-mill.   Instead of meeting with a warm personal reception, as his rank would
have commanded from previous Governors, everything was done through the new native department ;
and not only was the loan refused, but he did not see
the Governor at all.   This brought matters to a head.
The dignity of the *rangitira* was offended, and the
natives saw in the action of the Governor a step
towards their disintegration as a nation.

Wi Tamihana sent to the Waikato chiefs, informing

THE WAIKATO RIVER.

(*Painted by Kennett Watkins.*)

them that his tribe had determined to make Te Whero Whero their king, and asking them to join in the movement. The selection was good, for Te Whero Whero, one of the oldest and best friends of the Europeans, was a chief of the highest rank, of large influence, and renowned amongst the Maoris as a man of great wisdom. The movement was taken up readily by Te Heu Heu, Renata, and other friendly leaders, and was regarded by those Europeans best able to form an opinion as implying no disloyalty. But the matter assumed great importance in official eyes, and the Governor went to meet Te Whero Whero at Rangiriri. Here a large native meeting was held shortly afterwards, and the old chief told the Governor frankly that he believed they must have a king or some central authority amongst themselves to uphold the law ; but he also asked for a native magistrate to guide and teach them.

At a subsequent meeting, it was decided, after a great deal of talking, that Te Whero Whero should be appointed king, and Mr. F. D. Fenton, who was present to represent the Governor, was appointed to establish a suitable local government system amongst the Maoris and to act as resident magistrate at Whangaroa. Unfortunately there was a conflict of authority and opinion between Mr. Fenton (as the representative of the Governor) and the native department of the executive, and much was done which rendered that gentleman's work nugatory. For instance, he was sent to the Waikato country but without instructions to consult Te Whero Whero, although obliged to pass near to Te Whero Whero's village

on his way, and the old chief regarded this as a direct
and intentional slight to himself. He therefore,
though then and to the day of his death receiving a
pension from the Government, openly accepted the
kingship under the title of Potatau. He was in-
stalled at Ngaruawahia with much native ceremony,
and many of the tribes sent in their submission.

The news of the appointment of the king came
during the sitting of Parliament, and was variously
received. Amongst those who more clearly com-
prehended the native mind, it was understood to
be, as intended, a movement to build up a greater
national feeling amongst the Maoris, and to establish
a self-governing system under the supreme authority
of the Governor, with a special desire for some
central point to which they might appeal in land
disputes and other matters. But the Governor, who
was an old Indian officer, thought otherwise, and
being badly advised, treated the movement as hostile.
It is, however, a matter of fact that from this time
the tribal disputes and incessant feuds ceased, the
natives acted more as one nation and their aspirations appeared to turn towards a higher civilisation
upon European models. At the same time there
were undoubtedly those amongst the natives who
desired to prohibit entirely the sale of land to
Europeans and to combine the Maoris for aggressive
purposes. Meanwhile the restrictions imposed by
Grey on the sale of firearms to the natives were
removed on the plea that they induced smuggling,
and the Maoris eagerly took advantage of the concession and bought all the arms they could obtain.

Some intertribal disputes occurred about this time between a party headed by one Ihaia, and another under a chief named Katatore—who was aided by Wiremi Kingi—in connection with the Waitara lands in Taranaki. The settlers sided with Ihaia, who was willing to sell his land, and desired the Governor to put an end to the trouble by supporting his claims. But Governor Browne sought a solution of the difficulty by offering to convey Ihaia and his people to the Chatham Islands. Ihaia at first agreed, but afterwards refused, and having made peace with Kingi settled on land some fifteen or twenty miles from the Waitara River. The colonists still pressed the Government to acquire land for settlement, but Browne on the advice of Bishop Selwyn (who was highly respected by the natives), Chief Justice Martin, and other men of special experience, came to the conclusion that much harm would be done by any attempt to take possession by force, and therefore declined to interfere.

After a time, Browne again visited Taranaki, and expressed his willingness to purchase land, and at a meeting of a friendly character with the natives, one Teira came forward and offered to sell certain land on the south bank of Waitara; whereupon Wiremi Kingi rose and, stating that the land was under his authority, declined to agree to the purchase; he then at once withdrew. His action was taken as indicating want of respect to the Governor, although it was simply a Maori method of showing that the matter was at an end, and that further discussion was useless. The Governor was urged to maintain his own authority and assert the Queen's sovereignty, and was influenced by these representations. The right of Wiremi Kingi to prohibit the sale was disallowed, though the Maoris asserted that he had a *mana* over the land, which, however, Teira in accordance with Maori usage, had the right to occupy. Thus a combination of ignorance of native customs and a mistaken sense of dignity once more led to a war, which might easily have been averted by the exercise of a little tact. Investigation a few years later showed that Kingi had acted perfectly within his rights, and that Teira's action was taken out of revenge over a domestic matter.

The Governor directed the survey of the block to be made, but when three months later the surveyors set to work they were driven off the land, not violently, but by a crowd of the ugliest and most objectionable old women of the tribe who kissed and hugged them till they fled, and then destroyed their pegs, and obliterated the boundary lines. Governor Browne, after consulting his ministers, thereupon proclaimed martial law in Taranaki, and possession was taken of the land by the military. The Maoris demanded an inquiry into the circumstances, but the Governor, considering that the question was now one of the Queen's sovereignty, which must be vindicated, declined. Passive resistance was at first offered by Kingi's people, but at last they erected a *pah* on the land, which was bombarded and eventually abandoned. Murders by the natives took place as was usual at the commencement of a war, and the

RANGIRIRI.

(*From the Waikato.*)

military and local volunteers were speedily in the field.

The first engagement occurred at Waireka, where, owing to the assistance of sailors from H.M.S. *Niger*, a *pah* was captured. A great meeting of the Waikatos was meanwhile held at Ngaruawahia, at which sympathy with Kingi was shown, the opinion being generally expressed that the Governor should have held an inquiry before acting as he had done. Sympathy with Kingi spread rapidly, and troops were brought from various quarters in anticipation of an open rebellion. A severe repulse was met with before Puketekauere, and the troops in Taranaki were consequently increased to a strength of nearly two thousand. Owing to the difficulty of transport in a wild country without roads, no active operations were instituted until further reinforcements had arrived from India and China. Anxiety was felt meanwhile, as to the position which would be taken up by the Waikatos, and at the invitation of the Governor a great meeting of the chiefs was called at Kohimarama, near Auckland ; not one half the number invited came, the chiefs holding commanding positions in the Waikato country being absent, while of those present the Ngapuhis alone declared open hostility to Kingi. At this meeting resolutions were nevertheless carried expressing the determination of those tribes which were represented not to join in the Kingi movement, though the war was denounced by many of them as hasty and unjust.

Potatau died just prior to this meeting and his son, Matutaera, who adopted the name of Tawhiao, became king in his stead. Though the supply of arms and ammunition to the Maoris had again been prohibited, they were already pretty well supplied. General Pratt having arrived to take command, hostilities were resumed at Taranaki. A strong *pah*, erected by the natives at Mahoetahi, was stormed by a force of about one thousand five hundred troops and volunteers, and a complete defeat inflicted upon the natives. *Pahs* at Matarikoriko and Huirangi were then attacked, and as usual abandoned when untenable, and General Pratt seeing that with the force at his disposal it would be impossible to completely stamp out the insurrection, which was increasing in its proportions, declined to move further south unless provision were made to secure him from attack on the Waikato side. For this purpose he asked for five thousand men, irrespective of garrisons. During the lull which followed, the Maoris again occupied Waireka and other old *pahs*, and operations on a large scale were carried out to dislodge them.

Some of the fortifications they had erected were of very great strength, and chosen with a keen appreciation of their strategical value, notably those at Paketekauere and Pukirangiora. But only that at Pukirangiora, which was defended by a strong force under the chief Hapurona, offered any lengthened resistance. A sap seven miles in length was constructed as being the only means by which the fortifications could be approached on account of the inaccessible character of the country, and several encounters took place before the *pah*. Eventually Hapurona hoisted a flag of truce, with a view if

STRONGHOLD OF THE MAORIS, RANGIRIRI.

possible to bringing about peace, and accepted the conditions offered him by the Governor. These included
a promise to investigate the title of the Waitara
land—as to which the decision of the Governor was
to be final—while all plunder was to be restored and
the natives were to submit to the authority of the
Queen. Kingi did not decline the terms offered to
Hapurona but held aloof, and went with his people
to the Waikato. General Cameron had meanwhile
come to relieve General Pratt, and for the time being
the Taranaki war was at an end.

XXX.

THE END OF THE MAORI WARS.

(1861–1871.)

GENERAL BROWNE opened up negotiations with the Waikato chiefs, but they insisted as a first condition that the Waitara question should be settled by law, and this the Governor, regarding the matter as one affecting the Queen's sovereignty, refused. He stated, moreover, that Kingi and those who obeyed him, were rebels who had forfeited all rights, and he would not listen to any of the terms proposed. An increase of troops was asked for, so that there might be in the colony five thousand men in addition to all garrisons; and in May, 1861, a new proclamation to the Waikatos was issued in which the Governor charged them with breaking the treaty of Waitangi, by setting up a king, and required from them unconditional submission to the Queen, restitution of all plunder, and compensation to the settlers for their losses. The Waikatos, through Wi Tamihana, deprecated forcible and hasty action, and deplored the manner in which the Governor had commenced operations at Taranaki. A petition, signed by 175 chiefs, was presented to the Governor, denying their disloyalty, and asking for a judge to inquire into the cause of the disagreements. Strong representations were also made to the Governor by Europeans averse to hastening into a war with the Waikatos, but his answer was clear and unmistakable. He informed the settlers that they must do as the Taranaki settlers had done, and remove their goods and families from danger.

These troubles came in the midst of disputes with the Imperial Government, as to the conditions upon which troops should be provided, and before any settlement was arrived at news was received of the recall of Governor Browne and the re-appointment of Sir George Grey. Grey found on his return that a great change had taken place in the circumstances of the colony since his departure, and that consequent upon the influx of population, a new order had arisen who did not understand the Maoris—who indeed themselves were also changed—and that the south island, which was unaffected by the wars, was most densely peopled. He went resolutely to work ; the Imperial Government placed six thousand soldiers at his disposal, and these he employed in making roads through the Hunua forest which lay between Auckland and the Waikato country, where, in the event of war, operations must be carried on. The road, though regarded with suspicion by the Maoris whose confidence the Governor made strenuous efforts to regain, was deemed indispensable. Browne's manifesto was quietly set aside, and the chiefs were given to understand that military operations would only be adopted as a last resource.

The north island was divided into twenty native districts, and these again into hundreds, while native assessors and magistrates were appointed, with a civil commissioner to preside over each district. Twelve persons were to be nominated for approval by the Governor as a Maori district council, and native owners, after the boundaries had been duly settled, were to have power to dispose of their land to Europeans, but for the time being only to the extent of one farm in each of the hundreds. The purchaser was also to be recommended by the natives, and approved by the Governor.

The new institutions were successfully started north of Auckland, but in the Waikato district the reforms were coldly received by the Maoris. Wi Tamihana suggested that a better course would be to have the laws made by the Runanga (native council) confirmed by the king, and then submitted to the Governor for approval. Grey, somewhat surprised, visited the Maoris, and found among them an utter distrust in the Government. He now was confronted by the difficulty arising from divided authority, for although under the Constitution he was still supreme in all matters affecting native affairs, he could not proceed without funds; these had to be obtained from his ministers, who disagreed with his policy, and were disinclined to help him.

In the meantime Grey's efforts at conciliation were bearing fruit, and it is probable that if he had been able to proceed the king's authority would soon have disappeared. But to add to his embarrassment the Imperial Government complained of the inactivity of the troops, who were still employed in making a military road to the stream Maungatawhiri, which was the boundary of the King country, and beyond which they could not go without entering native lands. Peremptory instructions were also received from the War Office that no further sums were to be paid from the military chest on any pretext whatever, so that the expense of the war, if it was carried on, must fall upon the shoulders of the colonists themselves. Grey made a last attempt to meet the natives personally, and entered their country to interview the king. He met a number of influential chiefs, including Tamihana, and during the discussion he informed them that he would not fight the king with the sword, but would dig round him till he fell of his own accord. This statement the Maoris construed as showing hostility, and, when added to the intention expressed by Grey of putting a steamer on the Waikato river, it increased their distrust. Differences, which afterwards became almost an open rupture, also arose between General Cameron and the Governor. At length the series of cross purposes and misunderstandings reached a climax. The Governor, pending the settlement of the dispute about the Waitara block in the Taranaki district, had given the Maoris temporary possession of the Tataraimaka block, and when, after full investigation, he was assured of the genuineness of Kingi's statements regarding the Waitara block, he decided to restore the latter to the owners. At the same time, as an indication of his authority, he took possession of Tataraimaka, with one hundred men, intending to hand over the other block immediately.

As ill-luck would have it, his ministers chose this moment to assert themselves, and consequently some delay occurred in regard to the latter step, a delay which proved fatal to the peace of the colony. The natives, misinterpreting Grey's action in regard to Tataraimaka, took it as a declaration of war, and, gathering in the Taranaki district, suddenly attacked a small party of soldiers who were passing from one block to the other, and killed all but one of them. This of course brought matters to a head. The Governor demanded either that the ministry should take full control of native affairs, or that he should be granted the power and funds to carry out a campaign. While the Governor and his advisers were thus squabbling war began. The first blows were struck in Taranaki, and the insurgents were defeated with heavy loss at Katikara. Operations were then transferred to the Waikato district, and all Maoris not willing to declare their allegiance were forced behind the Maungatawhiri stream, action which induced many to enter the King country rather than desert their countrymen. The natives generally were in a wild state of excitement, though some of the chiefs, and notably Wi Tamihana, did all in their power to prevent war.

At length, on July 12, 1863, General Cameron crossed the Maungatawhiri, and on the 17th there was fighting at Koheroa, from which the Maoris were driven with considerable loss. War was now openly declared, and Tamihana, no longer able to resist the course of events, threw in his lot with his own people. In anticipation of the crisis, every possible means had been adopted to increase the European forces. Recruiting officers were sent to Australia, troops came from India, and twenty thousand men of all arms and services were speedily available. Several steamers were placed on the Waikato river, and the colony was fairly launched upon its greatest and most momentous struggle with the native races. The Maoris were no mean foes, and with great bravery prosecuted a guerilla warfare both in the Auckland and Taranaki districts. Galloway, a redoubt twenty miles from Auckland, and to the rear of the base of operations, was attacked, but the natives were gradually driven back, and the campaign was confined almost exclusively to the Waikato district.

Parliament met and considered the position, and a vigorous war policy was agreed upon. It was decided —in opposition to Grey's advice—that two and three-quarter million acres of land in the disturbed districts should be confiscated, and that a loan of £4,000,000 should be raised to defray the charges of the war. Several minor skirmishes followed Koheroa, and on the 30th of October General Cameron took his first important step. An attack both from the river and the shore was planned on the *pah* at Rangiriri, a strongly entrenched position; and—although a brilliant defence was offered by the natives, and no less than 124 Europeans were killed or wounded— during the night the Maoris retreated. A large number of prisoners, taken by Cameron, were placed on the island of Kawan, but they subsequently escaped to the mainland. A strong line of redoubts was now thrown across the country, and General Cameron hemmed in the natives. The Governor, now seeing the victory in his hands, desired to make a generous peace, but his ministers objected, considering that a decisive blow should be struck while the opportunity was there.

A long and acrimonious controversy followed, but nothing came of Grey's proposals, and operations were resumed with vigour. The natives were driven from one position to another, until the crowning conflict of the Waikato war took place at Orakau, where three hundred ill-armed and ill-fed Maoris made an heroic defence against a force of over fifteen hundred British soldiers. After a desperate sortie, the greater part of them were destroyed, and the wretched remnant, with Rewi and the king, escaped to the hilly country, where it was impossible to follow them.

A move was then made by Cameron to the Tauranga district on the eastern coast, where a strong force of Maoris was entrenched at the Gate-pah, a fortification in the vicinity of the Tauranga harbour. No great defence was offered until about three hundred men were inside the *pah*, when fire was opened at close range by the Maoris in concealment, and before a retreat could be made twenty-four soldiers were killed and eighty wounded. The natives then abandoned the *pah*, and retired to rifle-pits near the Wairoa, from which they were dislodged; but they declined the terms of peace which were offered, and put up a new *pah* at Te Ranga, which was stormed and taken after a splendid defence, the loss by the Maoris amounting to a hundred and twenty killed and wounded, while the attacking force had thirteen killed and thirty-nine wounded. The Tauranga tribes, after this reverse, submitted unconditionally, and the troubles in the Waikato and eastern districts closed. The war was now practically at an end, the confiscated land was taken possession of by military settlers, and Wi Tamihana and other chiefs tendered their submission.

But a fresh outbreak had in the meantime taken place in the Taranaki district, which was to result in a series of horrible scenes and much bloodshed. A number of the Maoris, casting off the religion of the pakeha, had embraced what was commonly known as Hauhauism, a strange compound of Judaism, Maori mythology with its attendant barbarous atrocities, and other superstitions. Most of the great chiefs held aloof from the new creed, but sufficient numbers embraced it to be dangerous enemies, and the first effects were seen at Ahuahu, where a reconnoitring party fell into an ambuscade. It was afterwards found that the bodies of those killed had been decapitated, and much mutilated; the heads were dried in the Maori fashion, and carried about on long poles. The new sect, however, gained but small support, for few of the leading chiefs embraced its tenets, and many others came forward in open opposition. At length the friendly tribes on the Wanganui river, under Mete Kingi and other chiefs, challenged the Hauhaus to prove the power of their new gods by a conflict on the island of Moutoa, up the river. A desperate fight took place, resulting in the total defeat of the Hauhaus, who had over forty killed. The fanatics then commenced operations all over the country; at Taranaki and the Wanganui district on the west coast, at Hawke's Bay and Poverty Bay on the east coast, there was a considerable uprising. On the 30th of April the insurgents made a daring attack on the redoubt at Sentry Hill, close to New Plymouth, but were beaten off with much loss; and the remainder of the war in the Taranaki district took the form of skirmishes and bush fights, which were conducted with great bravery and skill on both sides.

Peace was declared by the Governor on October 24, 1864, and a pardon to all excepting a few concerned in specified murders was offered. As a result of the policy of the Governor, the ministry, who disapproved, resigned. The King natives, though holding aloof from the Hauhaus, were implacable, and at the close of the Waikato campaign they sullenly retired into their own country, and drew a boundary line called the *Aukati*, to pass which without permission meant instant death. For many years this frontier was respected, and the King country remained unknown to Europeans; but the restrictions have been gradually broken down, causing an inevitable loss of the king's influence. This was the last serious conflict with the King natives, but a comparatively small number of Maoris in other parts of the colony who adopted Hauhauism continued to fight with singular bravery and skill, frequently against overwhelming odds. Horrible and brutal murders of settlers often occurred, and on both sides

27

in the campaign but little mercy was henceforth shown. On the west coast the Hauhaus caused great uneasiness, and General Cameron again took the field. On the east coast the friendly chiefs, Ropata and Mokena, carried on the war with the fanatics, whom they described as the " mad dogs."

Numerous engagements took place, and in November, 1865, a strong *pah* at Waerenga - a - hika, in Poverty Bay, was captured with seventy prisoners and a loss of 123 Hauhaus. The ill feeling which had arisen between the Governor and General Cameron now became more pronounced than ever; there were constant conflicts between the General and the War Office on one side, and Grey and his ministers on the other, and when the Governor, in the absence of General Cameron in Sydney, took the Wereroa *pah*—which was being attacked by the Imperial troops with the Colonial forces—things reached a climax. General Cameron resigned, and his place was filled by Major-General Chute. Constant skirmishes followed in the neighbourhood of Mount Egmont, and the Patea district, until the campaign was closed by a brilliant forced march of Chute's army through the disturbed districts, the display of force causing a cessation of hostilities on the part of the Maoris and the Imperial troops were mostly withdrawn from New Zealand.

But Grey's conflicts with the Imperial authorities rendered his position untenable, and after a vigorous correspondence, full of recriminations, he was recalled. To prevent a recurrence of misunderstandings, Native Land Courts were created and a Native Rights

Act, confirming the Maori tenure according to their ancient customs and usages, was passed. More generous legislation, including an Act providing four seats for Maori representatives in Parliament followed, and Wi Tamihana visited Wellington and gave evidence before a Select Committee appointed to inquire into the causes of the Maori war. Correspondence with the Imperial Government about the payment of the troops continued, and eventually it was decided at the instigation of Mr. Weld, the Premier, that for the future the colony should carry on its own wars, with its own men, and at its own cost. Only one Imperial regiment remained, and the British troops henceforth played but a very small part in the affairs of the colony.

The Hauhaus were still active in the interior and occasionally made visits to the west coast ; but they were pursued by Major McDonnell with a force of Colonial militia and natives and did but little damage ; meanwhile the confiscated lands were surveyed and prepared for settlement. Open hostilities were re-commenced on the west coast in May, 1868, when Titokowaru, a chief who had hitherto been friendly, tried to prevent the arrest of some Maoris for horse-stealing. Several murders followed, and almost at the same time Te Kooti, a young chief who had been banished to the Chatham Islands, escaped with about seventy followers in the schooner *Rifleman*, which they captured upon its visiting the islands, and landed on the east coast. He was at once pursued by the settlers, but offered a bold resistance, and the militia were called out under Colonel Whitmore.

Then began a long and costly guerilla campaign, in which Te Kooti proved himself a leader of great capacity and courage, and being also an orator of considerable power, he gathered about him a strong band of followers with whom he wrought much havoc in the east coast settlements. There was once more war on both the east and west coasts; but the fighting was carried on principally in the bush.

TE KOOTI.

Colonel McDonnell, in charge of the west coast forces, attacked Titokowaru's *pah* at Te-ngutu-o-te-manu and destroyed it, and an unsuccessful attempt was made to take a new *pah* erected by him at Ruaruru. The Maoris on this occasion lay in ambush, pouring a deadly fire on the attacking force, and inflicting severe loss. A month or two later Colonel McDonnell had again to retire from Okutuku, and the command subsequently was entrusted to

Colonel Whitmore. Another *pah* at Tauranga-ika was taken, but Titokowaru escaped by an underground passage, and continued to attack and harass Whitmore's forces. Some friendly natives under Keepa eventually drove Titokowaru up the Patea River for some distance and quite broke up his band. One of the most distressing events connected with the war on this side of the island was the massacre at the White Cliffs, north of Waitara, of the Rev. John Whitely, an old and highly respected Wesleyan missionary, and several other Europeans, including women and children. The news of this atrocity caused a thrill of horror to run throughout the colony, but the murderers were never punished, although the scene of the outrage was afterwards occupied by armed constabulary for many years.

This ended the Taranaki war, but while there was peace in the west coast, Te Kooti kept his enemies hard at work in the east, and in the interior. With consummate skill and audacity, he carried on the campaign for some time longer, managing always to elude his pursuers even when apparently hopelessly hemmed in. Finally, the pursuit was left to the native chiefs, Ropata, Keepa, and Topia, and a reward of £5,000 was offered by the Government for Te Kooti's capture. Eventually he escaped into the King country, where his *mana* as a fighting chief and priest was sufficient to gain him much sympathy and he was allowed by the Waikatos to remain amongst them, though he received no actual support at their hands. For political reasons the pursuit was then relaxed and he was allowed by the Government to remain ; but on account of the atrocities said to have been committed by his direction, his name was long referred to by the settlers with expressions of opprobrium and execration. With the flight of Te Kooti, the Maori wars closed, and since 1871 there have been no further disturbances. Occasional alarm has been felt in the frontier districts, but confidence has been gradually restored, and peaceful European settlements have sprung up in spots which formerly were the scene of bloodshed and disorder. In 1872, Wiremi Kingi accepted the offer of Mr. Donald McLean to return to his old place at Waitara where he was gladly received by the European population.

Some ten years later a chief known as Te Whiti brought great crowds of natives to his *pah* at Parihaka to discuss what he considered a breach of a promise to the friendly natives, and much uneasiness was felt by the settlers on the west coast. Eventually the minister for the native affairs, Mr. Bryce, with a strong force of armed constabulary and volunteers, effected peaceably Te Whiti's arrest ; and though the legality of the step was much questioned by his opponents, the result was good. A commission was appointed to inquire into the matters complained of, and large areas of land were given to those who had legitimate claims. With the exception of the Hauhaus and a few other individual cases, the Maoris generally proved themselves to be brave and generous foes. They were remarkable fighters, and were led by men with wonderful strategical capacity and military instinct. But the old fighting days are now over, it is hoped, for ever, and the two races are intermingling and living harmoniously side by side. The Maoris are moreover meeting the fate of all savage people who come in contact with a higher civilisation, and are rapidly vanishing from the land of their fathers.

XXXI.

UNDER THE CONSTITUTION.

(1854–1893.)

THE story of the native wars occupies so large a place in New Zealand history that other matters are liable to be lost sight of. While the events already recorded were taking place, however, much solid progress was made in industrial development. In 1860, the first railway in the colony was constructed between Christchurch and Lyttelton, and from this period date many important constitutional and other changes. The colony had now overcome its earlier troubles, and the inhabitants, with a self-reliance bred by the struggles that had so severely tested their courage and endurance, acted decisively in questions which in other colonies were as yet scarcely raised. New Zealand is perhaps in its legislation the most democratic of the Australasian provinces. Notwithstanding the exodus which had taken place during the gold rush to California and Australia, the population had steadily increased, and more especially in the south island rapid progress was being made, while the Maori troubles were retarding the development of the north.

In 1861 very rich deposits of gold were found at Tuapeka, Clutha, and elsewhere, in Otago and later on on the west coast of the south island. Speedily diggers who had worked out the best patches then known in Australia flocked to the colony, and the growth of the population added to the importance of the pastoral and agricultural interests. After constitutional government had been granted, the chief political parties were the advocates of centralisation on one side, and the supporters of the provincial system then prevailing on the other. Many changes were made in the electoral system, and in 1860 the population standard laid down by the Constitution Act as the basis of representation was abandoned, and the wealth and other circumstances of a district were made factors in its claims. A natural result was that inequalities arose which were the cause of much contention. The Provincial Councils were largely dependent for their revenue on the customs duties remaining after the cost of the central government had been met, and the increasing amount required by the central executive on account of the war alarmed those who supported the provincial system.

So strong was the aversion of some to centralisation, that there was a serious danger at one time of a proposal to divide the colony into two separate states being carried into effect ; but fortunately no such error was actually made. In 1864 the seat of government was removed to Wellington which was more generally convenient than Auckland, and the

" Centralists," as the advocates of one administrative authority were called, gradually increased their influence. In 1867 the consolidation of all loans and debentures to the extent of seven millions was effected, and in the following year the ballot was substituted for open voting at elections. The colony was at this time in a very depressed condition owing to the falling off in the yield of gold and the shrinkage in the price of colonial produce in England ; but the settlers gradually adapted themselves to the new conditions, and in 1870 were sufficiently sanguine to support the policy initiated by Sir Julius Vogel, which provided for the borrowing by the Central Government of large sums of money on the English market, for the purposes of public works and immigration, matters which hitherto had been entrusted to the Provincial Councils.

New departments of the Central Government were created to carry on the scheme under which loans to the extent of ten millions were floated, and two and a half million acres of land were sold. It was intended to open up by railways, &c., the land for settlement, and at the same time introduce immigrants, while £1,000,000 was to be devoted to defence during the next five years in maintaining the armed constabulary, as the colonial permanent forces were now termed. The expectations of the framer of the scheme were to a great extent fulfilled, for during the next few years population and the outward signs of prosperity increased by leaps and bounds. The Provincials Councils still remained in force, but they were shorn of much of their influence, and the

principal effect of the new system was a scramble
between the provinces for the loan money which was
being spent with such lavish prodigality.

The effect on the public life of the colony, as may
readily be imagined, was not good. The large expenditure of borrowed money created a corresponding
mania for private speculation, and an unreasonable
inflation of values. One inevitable result of the
centralisation of the public works administration, and
the increased patronage thus given to the General
Government was the collapse of the Provincial
Councils. In 1876 Sir Julius Vogel, who had previously been a warm supporter of the provincial
system, came boldly down with a Bill for their
abolition. A great popular outcry followed this step,
and Sir George Grey, who had for some years lived
in retirement on the island of Kawan, entered political
life. Sir Julius Vogel's Bill was, nevertheless, carried,
though it was stipulated that it should not come into
force until the new parliament was elected. The Act
created sixty-three counties to take the place of the
provinces, and borough councils were provided for the
towns, as well as other machinery for local government. Sir George Grey was a member of the new
Parliament, and became the first premier under the
new order of things, though he had a very small
majority at his back.

The history of the colony has since been a record
of steady progress, and characteristic measures have
found their way on to the statute book. The duration
of Parliament has been reduced from five to three
years ; the provision for payment of members of

AUCKLAND HARBOUR—THE WHARF.

Parliament has been made statutory instead of being by annual vote ; and free and compulsory education by the State of all children to a certain standard has been established. The "one man one vote" principle found favour when in 1889 all persons were prohibited from voting in more than one constituency at any election of members to the House of Representatives. These and many other important measures were carried by different ministries, which have not unfrequently been coalitions.

The policy of lavish borrowing, which was begun in 1870, was followed by an inevitable reaction between the years 1880 and 1890. Severe depression of all industries afflicted the colony, and the value of real property fell to an absurd figure, trade decreased and many of the inhabitants left for Australia and elsewhere. But the situation was boldly faced, and by severe economy in the public expenditure, and a cessation of the construction of unproductive public works, the finances were placed once more upon a sound basis. Confidence was gradually restored, and the position of New Zealand is now as good as that of any of its neighbours. The development of its grand resources is steadily going forward, and much enterprise has been shown in the inauguration of an extensive export of meat by which New Zealand sends annually vast quantities of frozen mutton to London, where it commands a ready sale and high price. Almost simultaneously with the introduction of this trade lines of direct steamers with England were started, and the coastal and intercolonial steam service was greatly improved.

Telegraphic communication is established throughout the colony, which was connected with the mainland of Australia by cable in 1876. A vigorous policy of railway construction has been adopted, and several private lines have been made on the land grant principle. Formed amidst the gravest difficulties, which have only been overcome by the indomitable resolution and courage of the settlers, New Zealand is to-day one of the most prosperous members of the Australian group. Its beautiful scenery and climate make it the playground of pleasure-seekers from all parts of Australia, and the conditions of life are singularly like those prevailing in the most favoured positions of the mother country.

XXXII.

WORK AND WAGES.

(1788–1892.)

FOR many years after Captain Phillip landed at Sydney Cove there were practically no free labourers in Australia. All work was performed by the convicts, under the direction of the Governor, or by servants assigned to private employers. Even when free artisans and other workers began to arrive, the competition in most trades with the assigned convicts caused wages to be meagre, and the standard of living extremely low. The most degrading immorality permeated almost every grade of society, and the working classes were not backward in following the example of their masters. Wages, both of bond and free, were the subject of general orders by the Governor. Thus at one time it was directed that, in addition to the rations according to, and equal with, the Government allowance, the sum of £10 sterling per annum to a man convict, and £7 sterling to a woman convict, as including the value of the slops allowed, and the sum of £7, or £5 10s. exclusive of slops, should be paid to duly-assigned servants; and a schedule of remuneration for free labour much on the same scale was issued in regard to the principal agricultural employments. As yet the number of artificers and mechanics was so small that it was not considered worth while to include them in the regulations. The Government works occupied all the best of the carpenters, stonemasons, and sawyers, so that the few free men who followed these trades were always in demand.

Of course there was evasion of this sort of order, and in a proclamation issued in 1810, after fixing wages at 5s. for an eleven-hour day, it was provided that "persons taking or demanding more, or refusing to work at the above rates to be set in the stocks for two days and one night for the first offence, and for a second or continual refusal three months hard labour. Masters paying more to be imprisoned for ten days without bail, to pay a fine of £5, and to remain in prison until paid." When food and clothing were fairly cheap, employers generally paid a portion of their workman's wages by rations or in kind, a system which had become recognised owing to the hand-to-mouth manner in which most business was conducted. Agriculture was by far the most important industry of the settlement, but the extraordinary fluctuations to which it was liable caused much hardship to those engaged. One year they would be nearly ruined by the abundance of the season ; in the next their whole crop, and frequently the homesteads too, would be swept away by a flood, for as yet cultivation was confined to the banks of the Hawkesbury and Nepean rivers. For instance, in

1804 there was a most disastrously good harvest. The yield of grain was so heavy and so much in excess of the requirements of the population, that its price fell below the actual cost of reaping, threshing, and carting. Much of the grain was quite unmarketable, and the unfortunate farmers were consequently nearly ruined. Next season the whole colony was reduced to the verge of famine, and wheat and maize, which a few months previously had been worthless, ran up to £5 to £6 per bushel, on account of a great flood which came suddenly down the rivers and swept away in a few hours, not only all the old grain which still remained on hand from the previous season, but the whole of the new harvest as well.

The variations in the price of the necessaries of life, due to inundations, or drought, or abnormally good crops, seriously affected the labouring poor. There was little to choose between evils of abundance and famine, for the wage-earner suffered as much from loss of employment on account of excessive production as from the risk of starvation by the scarcity of food. Fortunately meat was plentiful and comparatively cheap—about sixpence per lb.—and not subject to the same influences as grain, so that a dearth of one article of food could be to some extent met by an increase in the consumption of another. Under these conditions agriculture became unpopular, and there was a disproportionate growth in other branches of industry; but it is curious, in view of the extraordinary efforts that have since been made by some colonies to increase manufacturing enterprise, to read that persons at this time regarded with apprehension the rapid development of manufactures. Woollen cloth, hats, earthenware, pipes, salt, candles, soap, beer, leather, and almost all the articles in common demand were made locally, and Wentworth, writing in 1819, considered that the time was close at hand when the necessity of importing manufactured articles from Great Britain would have been entirely removed.

Previous to 1836 the average daily wage of mechanics in building trades was almost 6s. 6d., and farm and other labourers, taking one year with another, were paid at the rate of about £18 per annum, with food and lodging. During the years following 1836, larger numbers of free immigrants came to Australia, bringing with them a higher standard of living, and consequently a desire for better wage than that previously paid. Competition with convict labour had hitherto so degraded the free workers that as a rule they were willing to live upon a wage so small as compared with the current prices of commodities as to render it impossible for them to maintain even a semblance of decency, to say nothing of comfort, and even after the class of assigned servants had been largely diluted by free immigration, the convicts, emancipated or bond, comprised one-third of the total population, and had a proportionate influence on the labour market. But as the colony grew, and the demands of the settlers for assigned servants became far in excess of the supply, the influence of the convict element was to a great extent removed. Wages rapidly rose, and about four years after the arrival of the first assisted settlers the prospects of the working classes greatly improved.

TYPES OF COLOURED LABOURERS.

The advance made was, however, lost in the severe depression which followed the commercial crisis in 1843. All the provinces were more or less influenced, but in New South Wales the effects were most severely felt. Wages, which in the building trades had reached 8s. 9d. per day, fell rapidly to 6s., and then to 4s.—a lower figure than had ever previously been reached. Farm and other labourers who, in 1842, were getting £22 per annum with their board and lodging, were paid £15 in 1843, and were thankful if they could obtain work at these rates. As the panic subsided, there was a slight recovery in both wages and prices, but Australia could not escape long punishment for the extravagant speculation which had been prevalent. Although wages were improved, and in the building trades stood at an average of 5s. 6d. per day in 1847 as compared with 4s. in 1845, there was nothing to sustain the rise, and the average fell during the next three years to 4s. 6d. per day. This state of things continued until the whole of the colonies were thrown into a ferment by the gold discoveries, and the general stampede from the towns made it necessary for employers to pay almost any sum demanded by their men. The state of Melbourne is thus described in a letter written in June, 1852. A carter, it is stated, made £12 per week, his expenses not amounting to more than £4, while a cab or carriage driver obtained fares at the rate of something like £1,400 per annum. Masons and carpenters received £1 a day, but were not inclined to work even for this, and domestic servants could not be got for love or money.

DIAGRAM SHOWING VARIATIONS IN PRICES AND WAGES SINCE 1841.

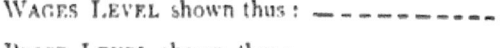

WAGES LEVEL shown thus : — — — — — — — — —

PRICE LEVEL shown thus : ——————————

A load of water cost 18s. ; a load of wood £4 ; boots £4, and a pair of shoes £2. The dangers of the road, according to the writer, caused a great demand for firearms, and a consignment of pistols invoiced at £60 sold in a week for nearly £700.

Probably the condition of things is somewhat exaggerated, but there can be no doubt that the gold discoveries completely changed the status of the working man. Instead of accepting what he could get, for some years he was enabled to dictate his own terms, and the spirit of independence called into life has never yet died out. The labour market was more or less unsettled until about 1857, when things began to slowly slip back into their normal condition. The year 1854 was the highest point reached in money wages. In 1855 the average daily remuneration in the building trades fell to about five shillings, but the annual wages of farm labourers, who were still very scarce, advanced £5.

The wages of building trades mechanics continued to decline until in 1869, when about 8s. 6d. per diem was the ruling figure, but during the next three years there was a slight recovery. Since 1871 the variations in the rates paid to mechanics have been very slight, the range amounting to only about 1s. per diem ; but the progressive increase which was visible in the years immediately following 1851 has been maintained in the case of agricultural and unskilled labour, and about £46 per annum with rations and lodgings is now the average for farm and station hands as compared with £37 10s. in 1881, and £28 at the commencement of the previous decade.

The mechanical trades did not submit quietly to the reductions which took place between 1855 and 1860, and from this period dates the movement in favour of the "eight-hours' day," and the systematic organisation of the labour forces. Of course, prior to 1855, there were some trade unions, but they were insignificant and powerless to materially control matters affecting the hours of labour or wages of their members. The eight-hour agitation first commenced in New Zealand, and was then taken up by the stonemasons of Sydney, and a little later by various classes of operatives in Melbourne. The main plea urged in support of shortening the hours of labour was that by this means employment could be provided for more men. The question of indirectly increasing the earnings of workers by creating more "overtime" does not at first seem to have been a consideration, for the promoters of the movement expressed themselves perfectly willing to accept a corresponding reduction in wages should their request as to the hours be granted. Many of the large employers met the men in a very fair spirit, and with the exception of a few strikes there was wonderfully little friction. Gradually the eight-hour day spread from one trade to another, until now it is the recognised working period in most occupations, and the annual commemoration of its inauguration is made the occasion of a general public holiday.

The power of the Labour Unions has been principally exercised in the endeavour to maintain the standard of wages, and hitherto their efforts in this direction have met with a considerable measure of

success. Naturally any competition which threatens
to undermine the status of labour is regarded with
extreme hostility, and the plodding Chinamen, who
came to Australia in some numbers in the years
following the gold discoveries, became the objects
of popular aversion. At first this feeling was demonstrated by isolated acts of violence perpetrated
on the Chinese at the diggings, but generally a
systematic agitation in favour of the imposition of
some legal restraint on Chinese immigration gained
support, and in 1880 Acts were passed by all the
colonies, with the exception of Western Australia and
South Australia (so far as the Northern Territory is
concerned), imposing a poll tax of £10 on all Chinese
arriving in Australia, and a high fine on all captains
of vessels who allowed more than a specified number
to land from their ships. These precautions did not,
however, have the desired effect, and in 1888 the
various governments were compelled by the force of
public feeling to introduce new legislation of a drastic
character. Masters of vessels are now forbidden
under a heavy penalty to bring more than one
Chinese to every 300 tons of their ships, and a poll
tax of £100 is charged each Chinaman on landing.
In Western Australia the old £10 tax has been
adopted, and in the Northern Territory no tax at all
is as yet imposed. By these means the desired end
was gained, and the immigration of Chinese has
almost entirely ceased. Nevertheless the expressions
of hostility towards the few thousand Chinese who
were already in Australia before the passing of this
law continue, and the Government is constantly being

urged to compel the manufactures of the Chinese cabinetmakers, &c., to be especially branded.

It is difficult to foresee what will be the future of the labour organisations in Australia, but it is not improbable that the limit of their power has been nearly reached. So long as there was a lavish expenditure of borrowed money by the Government on public works, and a consequent inflation of all values, the demand for mechanics was in excess of the supply, and the unions were able with comparative ease to prevent their members from accepting work at prices below the authorised rates. But all this is changed. For many years most of the colonies will have to exercise severe economy in the construction of public works and buildings, and already the decrease thus caused in employment is having its effect. Although the nominal rates of remuneration are maintained in all trades where it is possible, there is considerable increase in the proportion of work done by the piece, and jobs are frequently taken at a figure which cannot possibly yield to the labourer wages equivalent to the union standard. In addition to these considerations the labour bodies are not now prepared for a struggle. The proportion of their members to the total adult wage-earning population is small; their funds, which were at one time considerable, have been exhausted by recent protracted but abortive strikes; and, lastly, the masters have been taught a lesson by their men, and have proved apt pupils. Instead of the whole force of combined labour being directed against one unsupported employer, the unions in any future struggle will have to face an equally if not more perfect organisation than their own, and in a contest under such conditions the victory could only go one way.

The attempt to meet this development by the creation of a " labour party" in Parliament has failed, for it has been found to be the easiest thing in the world for any fairly astute politician to split its ranks whenever he may deem such a course expedient, while the labouring classes themselves hold such very mixed opinions on most questions of importance, that a delegate, such as most labour members really are, finds it impossible to escape the censure of his constituents. The case has been stated as briefly and clearly as possible, but there are other influences at work which there is not space to trace here. It will be a deplorable event, if the labour unions collapse under the great strain to which they must before long be subjected. Although mingled with many foolish and ignorant demands, the main aspirations of the working classes in Australia are entirely good, and the trade societies are the only agencies through which those aspirations can be made known ; while the very fact of the power to organise implies a training in the highest qualities of citizenship. From a labour party in Parliament but little is to be hoped, and it is doubtful if the legislature with the best intentions can do much towards the settlement of matters between employers and employed. The relations between the two classes have been aptly described by a large employer of labour in Australia as similar to those existing between husband and wife. They are utterly dependent one upon the other, and, as they have to pass their life together somehow, this can best be done by the exercise of mutual respect and moderation. Outside intervention is, in one case as in the other, more likely to do harm than good, and the interference of the law, except in the restraint of violence or the punishment of dishonesty, will have no better result.

XXXIII.

FEDERATION.

(1847–1893.)

THE creation of an Assembly, in which all the colonies of Australasia should be represented, to deal with matters affecting the provinces generally, was seriously suggested by Earl Grey when, in 1847, he announced the intentions of the Imperial Government with regard to the proposed alterations in the colonial constitutions. "Some method," wrote the Secretary of State, "would be devised for enabling the various legislatures of the several Australian colonies to co-operate with each other in the enactment of such laws as may be necessary for regulating the interests common to those possessions collectively ; such, for example, are the imposition of duties of import and export, the conveyance of letters, and the formation of roads, railways, or other internal communications traversing any two or more of such colonies." The storm of opposition which greeted the rest of Earl Grey's proposals on this occasion has been described elsewhere, and no steps were consequently taken to give effect to his recommendations with regard to a federal assembly. The importance of the subject was not, however, forgotten, and it was referred to at some length in the Report of the Committee of the Privy Council on Trade and Plantations concerning Australian affairs which was brought up early in 1849. The words of the report are peculiarly significant, in view of the policy which was before long adopted by the colony of Victoria, for the committee saw the "obstruction to the intercolonial trade," and "the check to the development of the resources" which must inevitably follow tariff restrictions preventing goods from being carried from one colony to another "with the same absolute freedom as between any two adjacent counties in England." For this reason it was recommended that an authority should be created "to act for all the colonies conjointly," and it was suggested that the Governor of New South Wales should be made Governor-general, and be empowered to call together a "General Assembly of Australia," comprising himself and a single House of Delegates elected by the legislatures of the various colonies.

The General Assembly was to deal with customs duties, postal arrangements, roads, canals, railways, beacons and lighthouses, shipping, weights and measures, and such other matters as from time to time might be referred to it. The expenses of the administration were to be met by "an equal percentage from the revenue received in all the colonies." In addition a Supreme Court of Appeal was to be established. Although included in the Bill which Earl Grey introduced in 1850, the federal provisions never came into operation, and the question of the creation of a General Assembly remained in abeyance until Wentworth attached to the memorable report of the Select Committee of the New South Wales Council on the Constitution the opinion that "the establishment at once of a General Assembly to make laws in relation to intercolonial questions" was a matter of the highest importance. It was considered inexpedient to embody the provisions for carrying out this scheme in the Constitution Bill of New South Wales, but a wish was expressed that the Imperial Parliament would pass a special Act to attain the desired end. When Wentworth was shortly afterwards in England, he made still further efforts to bring about the establishment of a General Assembly, and took an active part in the proceedings of the "General Association for the Australian Colonies," which in 1857 presented a petition to the Secretary of State urging the necessity of immediate legislation to sanction the formation of a federal body. A Bill was even drafted by Wentworth and sent along with the petition, but the Secretary of State declined to take action in the matter.

In the colonies themselves the subject was also receiving some attention, in both New South Wales in 1856 and in Victoria in 1857 Select Committees were appointed to consider the best means of legislating on matters of common interest. The report of the Victorian Committee, which recommended the holding of an Intercolonial Conference, was passed by both houses; but in New South Wales the necessary resolutions were delayed in the

Assembly, and although the report urged that the matter "could not be longer postponed without the danger of creating serious grounds of antagonism and jealousy, which would tend greatly to embarrass, if not entirely to prevent, its future settlement upon a satisfactory basis," Parliament was prorogued without anything having been done. Many years passed before another attempt to effect federal government was made ; but meanwhile three colonies—New South Wales, South Australia, and Victoria—entered into an agreement to suspend the collection of customs duties on the border for three years, thus making the overland trade between the colonies practically unrestricted. This might have led to a more complete scheme for joint action had not Victoria abrogated the agreement before the three years had expired.

In 1881 a conference was held in Sydney at which a Bill was framed, under the guidance of Sir Henry Parkes, creating a partly legislative and partly administrative body ; but it was only intended " to pave the way to a complete federal organisation hereafter." For the next two years no steps were taken to bring the measure into operation, but in 1883 another conference met in Sydney, at which representatives from all the colonies were present, and the old Bill of 1881 was slightly altered, and forwarded to England, where it was passed by the Imperial Parliament in 1885. Under the Federal Council Act, as this law was called, the function of the Council was simply to give advice, and it possessed no executive authority whatever. The necessary enabling Acts were passed, at first by four colonies and later by South Australia, but New South Wales and New Zealand have persistently declined to join. The first session was held in Hobart in 1886, and several meetings have since taken place, but the inherent weakness of the whole scheme has rendered the deliberations of the Council of but small importance.

In 1887 another step was taken in the direction of common action in matters of mutual interest. The progress of Australian commerce had been so great, and the increase in wealth so rapid, that it became necessary to largely augment the naval force in Australian waters. Accordingly the Australasian Naval Force Act was passed. By this measure it is provided that there shall be a force of sea-going ships of war, consisting of five fast cruisers and two torpedo gunboats, having the same status as warships of the same class in the Imperial Navy, and under the sole control of the naval commander-in-chief of the Australian squadron. The ships are to be retained within the limits of the station in times of peace or war, and they may be only sent beyond those limits with the special consent of the Australian Governments. The Imperial Government agreed to provide for the first cost of these vessels, and all other charges previous to their arrival in Australia, but the colonies at the same time undertook to pay 5 per cent. on the first cost, but such payment not to exceed the sum of £35,000 per annum, and in addition to bear the expense, up to £91,000, of maintaining three fast cruisers with one gunboat in commission and the other in reserve. The annual contribution of the several colonies is calculated in proportion to their population, the agreement is for ten years, terminable only by two years' notice.

The most important step towards the federation of the Australasian colonies was, however, taken in February, 1890, when a conference of the representatives of the seven colonies met in Parliament House, Melbourne, on February 6th. Two representatives attended from each of the colonies except Western Australia, which sent only one, and at seven meetings the question of federation was discussed at length. Finally, the Conference adopted an address to the Queen, expressing loyalty, and enclosing resolutions which affirmed the expediency of an immediate union under the Crown of the Australasian colonies. It was also recommended that steps should be taken for the appointment of delegates to a national Australasian Convention, to frame a scheme for a Federal Constitution. Delegates were subsequently duly appointed by the different Australasian Parliaments, and on March 2, 1891, the Convention met in Sydney. There were forty-five members, the most notable public men in the colonies, each state sending seven delegates, with the exception of New Zealand, which only sent three. Sir Henry Parkes, who was practically the author of this latest federation movement, was unanimously elected President of the Convention, and Sir Samuel Griffiths, Premier of Queensland, Vice-President. The public were admitted to the debates, and an official record of the proceedings was published. A series of resolutions, moved by Sir Henry Parkes, were, after full discussion, adopted

with slight amendment. **The resolutions as carried**
were :—

" That in order to establish and secure an enduring
foundation for the **structure of a Federal** Government,
the principles embodied **in the Resolutions** following
be **agreed to :—**

" (1) That the powers **and** privileges and territorial
rights of the several **existing** colonies shall **remain
intact**, except in respect **to such** surrenders **as may be**
agreed upon as necessary and incidental to the **power
and authority of** the National **Federal Government.**

" (2) No State shall **be formed by separation from**
another State, **nor shall any State be formed by the**
junction of **two or more** States **or parts of States,**
without the consent of the legislatures **of the States**
concerned, as well as of the Federal Parliament.

" (3) That the trade and intercourse **between the**
Federated Colonies, whether by **means of land** carriage
or coastal navigation, shall be absolutely **free.**

" (4) **That the** power **and authority to** impose
Customs duties, and duties **of Excise upon** goods the
subject of Customs duties, **and** to offer bounties, shall
be exclusively lodged in the Federal Government **and
Parliament, subject to such disposal of** the revenues
thence **derived as shall be agreed upon.**

" (5) That **the military and naval** defence of
Australia shall be **entrusted to federal** forces under
one command.

" (6) That **provision should be made** in the Federal
Constitution which **will enable each** State to make
such **amendments** in its constitution as may be necessary for **the** purposes of the Federation.

"Subject to these and other necessary conditions, this Convention approves of the framing of a Federal Constitution which shall establish—

"(1) A Parliament, to consist of a Senate and a House of Representatives, the former consisting of an equal number of members from each colony, to be elected by a system which shall provide for the periodical retirement of one-third of the members, so securing to the body itself a perpetual existence, combined with definite responsibility to the electors, the latter to be elected by districts formed on a population basis, and to possess the sole power of originating all bills appropriating revenue or imposing taxation.

"(2) A Judiciary, consisting of a Federal Supreme Court, which shall constitute a High Court of Appeal for Australia.

"(3) An Executive, consisting of a Governor-General, and such persons as may from time to time be appointed as his advisers."

Three committees were appointed—one to consider and report upon matters relating to Finance, Taxation, and Trade ; another to make recommendations concerning the establishment of a Federal Judiciary ; and a third to frame a Bill for the establishment of a Federal Constitution. On the 31st of March Sir Samuel Griffiths, the chairman of the Committee on Constitutional Machinery, brought up a draft "Bill to constitute the Commonwealth of Australia." After consideration the Bill was adopted on the 9th of April, and it was resolved by the convention that the Parliament of each colony should submit it to the people of the several States.　It was also agreed that so soon as the constitution should be adopted by three of the colonies the Imperial Parliament should be urged to establish the Federal Government forthwith.

So far, although the question has been debated in the Parliaments of some of the colonies, nothing definite has been done, and the whole question has been regarded by the great bulk of the population with singular apathy.　That some such federal organisation must be brought into existence no one can doubt, for the anomalies of hostile tariffs, variations in the gauge of railways, appeal to the Privy Council, and numerous other matters demand attention and reform which can only be effected by joint action on the part of the whole of the provinces. It is difficult to foretell how or when the desired consummation will be reached, but the sooner a Federal Government is established the sooner will the colonies of Australasia take their proper place amongst the nations of the world.

APPENDIX.

STATISTICS OF THE COMMONWEALTH OF AUSTRALIA, 1890-91.

Colony.	Horses.	Horned Cattle.	Sheep.	Wool Exported.	Area under Crop.
	No.	No.	No.	£	Acres.
New South Wales	444,163	1,909,009	55,986,431	9,232,672	852,704
Victoria	436,459	1,782,978	12,736,143	5,933,603	2,031,955
Queensland	365,812	5,558,264	18,007,234	2,524,742	224,993
South Australia ..	199,605	574,032	7,050,544	1,876,240	2,093,515
Western Australia	44,384	130,970	2,524,913	261,352	69,676
Tasmania........	31,165	162,440	1,619,256	419,173	157,376
New Zealand	211,040	831,831	18,117,186	4,150,599	1,636,179
Australasia ..	1,732,628	10,949,524	116,041,707	24,398,381	7,066,398

Colony.	Population.	Shipping Inwards and Outwards.	Total Trade.	Exports of Domestic Produce.	Length of Telegraph Line.	Railways. Length of Line.
	No.	Tons.	£	£	Miles.	Miles.
New South Wales.	1,165,300	4,761,872	44,660,941	17,232,725	11,231	2,263
Victoria	1,157,804	4,363,341	36,220,237	10,291,821	6,958	2,763
Queensland	410,345	910,779	13,621,212	8,412,244	9,830	2,195
South Australia ..	325,766	2,337,674	17,295,765	4,550,139	5,623	1,829
Western Australia .	53,285	904,861	1,546,260	659,661	2,892	585
Tasmania	152,619	951,247	3,384,504	1,430,806	2,004	399
New Zealand	634,058	1,312,474	16,072,245	9,428,761	5,060	1,956
Australasia ..	3,899,177	15,542,248	132,801,164	52,006,157	43,598	11,990

STATISTICS OF THE COMMONWEALTH OF AUSTRALIA, 1890–91.

Colony.	Gold Produce.	Deposits in Banks.	Public Revenue.	Public Debt.
	Oz.	£	£	£
New South Wales	127,761	40,390,159	10,047,152	51,010,433
Victoria	588,560	45,261,932	8,343,588	43,610,265
Queensland	610,587	11,720,112	3,350,223	29,434,734
South Australia	26,086	9,933,135	2,732,222	21,637,300
Western Australia	22,256	1,398,417	497,670	1,617,445
Tasmania	23,451	4,378,448	758,100	6,432,800
New Zealand	193,193	15,806,847	4,193,942	38,802,350
Australasia	1,591,894	128,889,050	29,922,897	192,565,327

OCCUPATION OF LANDS AT THE COMMENCEMENT OF 1891.

Colony.	Area of Colony.	Area Alienated or in process of Alienation.	Area Leased.	Area neither Alienated nor Leased.
	Acres.	Acres.	Acres.	Acres.
New South Wales	198,848,000	44,758,151	148,122,194	5,967,655
Victoria	56,245,760	22,359,054	21,589,767	12,296,939
Queensland	427,838,080	17,819,982	285,703,680	124,314,418
South Australia	578,361,600	11,908,168	235,980,400	330,473,032
Western Australia	678,400,000	5,154,673	104,921,357	568,323,970
Tasmania	16,778,000	4,695,022	666,193	11,416,785
New Zealand	66,710,320	20,182,239	13,425,303	33,102,778
Australasia	2,023,181,760	126,877,289	810,408,894	1,085,895,577

ALIENATION OF LANDS AT THE COMMENCEMENT OF 1891.

Colony.	Area Alienated in Fee Simple.	Area in process of Alienation.	Area Alienated or in process of Alienation.	Area neither Alienated nor in process of Alienation.
	Acres.	Acres.	Acres.	Acres.
New South Wales	26,278,033	18,480,118	44,758,151	154,089,849
Victoria	16,091,880	6,267,174	22,359,054	33,886,706
Queensland	10,258,657	7,561,325	17,819,982	410,018,098
South Australia	7,002,339	4,905,829	11,908,168	566,453,432
Western Australia	5,154,673	†—	5,154,673	673,245,327
Tasmania	4,695,022	—	4,695,022	12,082,978
New Zealand	*19,666,916	515,323	20,182,239	46,528,081
Australasia	89,147,520	37,729,769	126,877,289	1,896,304,471

* Includes 841,621 acres held under perpetual lease.　　† Return not available.

INDEX.

439